Collected
Black Women's
Narratives

THE SCHOMBURG LIBRARY OF
NINETEENTH-CENTURY BLACK WOMEN WRITERS

General Editor, Henry Louis Gates, Jr.

Titles are listed chronologically; collections that include works published over a span of years are listed according to the publication date of their initial work.

Collected
Black Women's
Narratives

With an Introduction by
ANTHONY G. BARTHELEMY

New York   Oxford
OXFORD UNIVERSITY PRESS
1988

Oxford University Press

Oxford   New York   Toronto
Delhi   Bombay   Calcutta   Madras   Karachi
Petaling Jaya   Singapore   Hong Kong   Tokyo
Nairobi   Dar es Salaam   Cape Town
Melbourne   Auckland

and associated companies in
Beirut   Berlin   Ibadan   Nicosia

Published by Oxford University Press, Inc.,
200 Madison Avenue, New York, New York 10016

Oxford is a registered trademark of Oxford University Press

Library of Congress Cataloging-in-Publication Data

Collected black women's narratives.
(The Schomburg library of nineteenth-century
black women writers)
1. Afro-American women—Biography.   2. Afro-American
women—History—19th century.   I. Series.
E185.96.C64   1988   920.72′08996073   87-22130
ISBN 0-19-505260-9
ISBN 0-19-505267-6 (set)

2 4 6 8 10 9 7 5 3
Printed in the United States of America
on acid-free paper

The
Schomburg Library
of
Nineteenth-Century
Black Women Writers
is
Dedicated
in Memory
of
PAULINE AUGUSTA COLEMAN GATES

1916–1987

PUBLISHER'S NOTE

FOREWORD
In Her Own Write

Henry Louis Gates, Jr.

One muffled strain in the Silent South, a jarring chord and a
vague and uncomprehended cadenza has been and still is the
Negro. And of that muffled chord, the one mute and voiceless note has been the sadly expectant Black Woman, ...

The "other side" has not been represented by one who "lives
there." And not many can more sensibly realize and more
accurately tell the weight and the fret of the "long dull pain"
than the open-eyed but hitherto voiceless Black Woman of
America.

. . . as our Caucasian barristers are not to blame if they
cannot *quite* put themselves in the dark man's place, neither
should the dark man be wholly expected fully and adequately
to reproduce the exact Voice of the Black Woman.

—ANNA JULIA COOPER, *A Voice From the South* (1892)

The birth of the Afro-American literary tradition occurred
in 1773, when Phillis Wheatley published a book of poetry.
Despite the fact that her book garnered for her a remarkable
amount of attention, Wheatley's journey to the printer had
been a most arduous one. Sometime in 1772, a young African girl walked demurely into a room in Boston to undergo
an oral examination, the results of which would determine
the direction of her life and work. Perhaps she was shocked
upon entering the appointed room. For there, perhaps gath-

ered in a semicircle, sat eighteen of Boston's most notable
citizens. Among them were John Erving, a prominent Boston merchant; the Reverend Charles Chauncy, pastor of the
Tenth Congregational Church; and John Hancock, who would
later gain fame for his signature on the Declaration of Independence. At the center of this group was His Excellency,
Thomas Hutchinson, governor of Massachusetts, with Andrew Oliver, his lieutenant governor, close by his side.

Why had this august group been assembled? Why had it
seen fit to summon this young African girl, scarcely eighteen
years old, before it? This group of "the most respectable
Characters in *Boston*," as it would later define itself, had assembled to question closely the African adolescent on the
slender sheaf of poems that she claimed to have "written by
herself." We can only speculate on the nature of the questions
posed to the fledgling poet. Perhaps they asked her to iden-
tify and explain—for all to hear—exactly who were the Greek
and Latin gods and poets alluded to so frequently in her
work. Perhaps they asked her to conjugate a verb in Latin
or even to translate randomly selected passages from the Latin,
which she and her master, John Wheatley, claimed that she
"had made some Progress in." Or perhaps they asked her to
recite from memory key passages from the texts of John Milton and Alexander Pope, the two poets by whom the African
claimed to be most directly influenced. We do not know.

We do know, however, that the African poet's responses
were more than sufficient to prompt the eighteen august
gentlemen to compose, sign, and publish a two-paragraph
"Attestation," an open letter "To the Publick" that prefaces
Phillis Wheatley's book and that reads in part:

> We whose Names are under-written, do assure the World,
> that the Poems specified in the following Page, were (as we

verily believe) written by Phillis, a young Negro Girl, who was but a few Years since, brought an uncultivated Barbarian from *Africa*, and has ever since been, and now is, under the Disadvantage of serving as a Slave in a Family in this Town. She has been examined by some of the best Judges, and is thought qualified to write them.

So important was this document in securing a publisher for Wheatley's poems that it forms the signal element in the prefatory matter preceding her *Poems on Various Subjects, Religious and Moral*, published in London in 1773.

Without the published "Attestation," Wheatley's publisher claimed, few would believe that an African could possibly have written poetry all by herself. As the eighteen put the matter clearly in their letter, "Numbers would be ready to suspect they were not really the Writings of Phillis." Wheatley and her master, John Wheatley, had attempted to publish a similar volume in 1772 in Boston, but Boston publishers had been incredulous. One year later, "Attestation" in hand, Phillis Wheatley and her master's son, Nathaniel Wheatley, sailed for England, where they completed arrangements for the publication of a volume of her poems with the aid of the Countess of Huntington and the Earl of Dartmouth.

This curious anecdote, surely one of the oddest oral examinations on record, is only a tiny part of a larger, and even more curious, episode in the Enlightenment. Since the beginning of the sixteenth century, Europeans had wondered aloud whether or not the African "species of men," as they were most commonly called, *could* ever create formal literature, could ever master "the arts and sciences." If they could, the argument ran, then the African variety of humanity was fundamentally related to the European variety. If not, then it seemed clear that the African was destined by nature

to be a slave. This was the burden shouldered by Phillis
Wheatley when she successfully defended herself and the au-
thorship of her book against counterclaims and doubts.

Indeed, with her successful defense, Wheatley launched
two traditions at once—the black American literary tradition
and the black woman's literary tradition. If it is extraordinary
that not just one but both of these traditions were founded
simultaneously by a black woman—certainly an event unique
in the history of literature—it is also ironic that this important fact of common, coterminous literary origins seems to
have escaped most scholars.

That the progenitor of the black literary tradition was a
woman means, in the most strictly literal sense, that all subsequent black writers have evolved in a matrilinear line of
descent, and that each, consciously or unconsciously, has extended and revised a canon whose foundation was the poetry
of a black woman. Early black writers seem to have been
keenly aware of Wheatley's founding role, even if most of
her white reviewers were more concerned with the implica-
tions of her race than her gender. Jupiter Hammon, for example, whose 1760 broadside "An Evening Thought. Salvation by Christ, With Penitential Cries" was the first
individual poem published by a black American, acknowledged Wheatley's influence by selecting her as the subject of
his second broadside, "An Address to Miss Phillis Wheatly
[*sic*], Ethiopian Poetess, in Boston," which was published at
Hartford in 1778. And George Moses Horton, the second
Afro-American to publish a book of poetry in English (1829),
brought out in 1838 an edition of his *Poems By A Slave*
bound together with Wheatley's work. Indeed, for fifty-six
years, between 1773 and 1829, when Horton published *The
Hope of Liberty*, Wheatley was the *only* black person to have
published a book of imaginative literature in English. So

central was this black woman's role in the shaping of the
Afro-American literary tradition that, as one historian has
maintained, the history of the reception of Phillis Wheatley's
poetry *is* the history of Afro-American literary criticism. Well
into the nineteenth century, Wheatley and the black literary
tradition were the same entity.

But Wheatley is not the only black woman writer who
stands as a pioneering figure in Afro-American literature.
Just as Wheatley gave birth to the genre of black poetry, Ann
Plato was the first Afro-American to publish a book of essays
(1841) and Harriet E. Wilson was the first black person to
publish a novel in the United States (1859).

Despite this pioneering role of black women in the tradition, however, many of their contributions before this century have been all but lost or unrecognized. As Hortense
Spillers observed as recently as 1983,

> With the exception of a handful of autobiographical narratives
> from the nineteenth century, the black woman's realities are
> virtually suppressed until the period of the Harlem Renais-
> sance and later. Essentially the black woman as artist, as
> intellectual spokesperson for her own cultural apprenticeship,
> has not existed before, for anyone. At the source of [their]
> own symbol-making task, [the community of black women
> writers] confronts, therefore, a tradition of work that is quite
> recent, its continuities, broken and sporadic.

Until now, it has been extraordinarily difficult to establish
the formal connections between early black women's writing
and that of the present, precisely because our knowledge of
their work has been broken and sporadic. Phillis Wheatley,
for example, while certainly the most reprinted and discussed
poet in the tradition, is also one of the least understood. Ann
Plato's seminal work, *Essays* (which includes biographies and
poems), has not been reprinted since it was published a cen-

tury and a half ago. And Harriet Wilson's *Our Nig,* her
compelling novel of a black woman's expanding consciousness in a racist Northern antebellum environment, never received even *one* review or comment at a time when virtually
all works written by black people were heralded by abolitionists as salient arguments against the existence of human slavery. Many of the books reprinted in this set experienced a
similar fate, the most dreadful fate for an author: that of
being ignored then relegated to the obscurity of the rare book
section of a university library. We can only wonder how
many other texts in the black woman's tradition have been
lost to this generation of readers or remain unclassified or
uncatalogued and, hence, unread.

This was not always so, however. Black women writers
dominated the final decade of the nineteenth century, perhaps
spurred to publish by an 1886 essay entitled "The Coming
American Novelist," which was published in *Lippincott's
Monthly Magazine* and written by "A Lady From Philadelphia." This pseudonymous essay argued that the "Great
American Novel" would be written by a black person. Her
argument is so curious that it deserves to be repeated:

> When we come to formulate our demands of the Coming
> American Novelist, we will agree that he must be native-
> born. His ancestors may come from where they will, but we
> must give him a birthplace and have the raising of him. Still,
> the longer his family has been here the better he will represent
> us. Suppose he should have no country but ours, no traditions
> but those he has learned here, no longings apart from us, no
> future except in our future—the orphan of the world, he
> finds with us his home. And with all this, suppose he refuses
> to be fused into that grand conglomerate we call the "Amer-
> ican type." With us, he is not of us. He is original, he has
> humor, he is tender, he is passive and fiery, he has been

taught what we call justice, and he has his own opinion about it. He has suffered everything a poet, a dramatist, a novelist need suffer before he comes to have his lips anointed. And with it all he is in one sense a spectator, a little out of the race. How would these conditions go towards forming an original development? In a word, suppose the coming novelist is of African origin? When one comes to consider the subject, there is no improbability in it. One thing is certain,—our great novel will not be written by the typical American.

An atypical American, indeed. Not only would the great American novel be written by an African-American, it would be written by an African-American *woman:*

Yet farther: I have used the generic masculine pronoun because it is convenient; but Fate keeps revenge in store. It was a woman who, taking the wrongs of the African as her theme, wrote the novel that awakened the world to their reality, and why should not the coming novelist be a woman as well as an African? She—the woman of that race—has some claims on Fate which are not yet paid up.

It is these claims on fate that we seek to pay by publishing The Schomburg Library of Nineteenth-Century Black Women Writers.

This theme would be repeated by several black women authors, most notably by Anna Julia Cooper, a prototypical black feminist whose 1892 *A Voice From the South* can be considered to be one of the original texts of the black feminist movement. It was Cooper who first analyzed the fallacy of referring to "the Black man" when speaking of black people and who argued that just as white men cannot speak through the consciousness of black men, neither can black *men* "fully and adequately . . . reproduce the exact Voice of the Black Woman." Gender and race, she argues, cannot be conflated, except in the instance of a black woman's voice, and it is this voice which must be uttered and to which we must listen. As Cooper puts the matter so compellingly:

> It is not the intelligent woman vs. the ignorant woman; nor the white woman vs. the black, the brown, and the red,—it is not even the cause of woman vs. man. Nay, 'tis woman's strongest vindication for speaking that *the world needs to hear her voice*. It would be subversive of every human interest that the cry of one-half the human family be stifled. Woman in stepping from the pedestal of statue-like inactivity in the domestic shrine, and daring to think and move and speak,— to undertake to help shape, mold, and direct the thought of her age, is merely completing the circle of the world's vision. Hers is every interest that has lacked an interpreter and a defender. Her cause is linked with that of every agony that has been dumb—every wrong that needs a voice.
>
> It is no fault of man's that he has not been able to see truth from her standpoint. It does credit both to his head and heart that no greater mistakes have been committed or even wrongs perpetrated while she sat making tatting and snipping paper flowers. Man's own innate chivalry and the mutual interdependence of their interests have insured his treating her cause, in the main at least, as his own. And he is pardonably surprised and even a little chagrined, perhaps, to find his legislation not considered "perfectly lovely" in every respect. But in any case his work is only impoverished by her remaining dumb. The world has had to limp along with the wobbling gait and one-sided hesitancy of a man with one eye. Suddenly the bandage is removed from the other eye and the whole body is filled with light. It sees a circle where before it saw a segment. The darkened eye restored, every member rejoices with it.

The myopic sight of the darkened eye can only be restored when the full range of the black woman's voice, with its own special timbres and shadings, remains mute no longer.

Similarly, Victoria Earle Matthews, an author of short stories and essays, and a cofounder in 1896 of the National Association of Colored Women, wrote in her stunning essay, "The Value of Race Literature" (1895), that "when the literature of our race is developed, it will of necessity be different in all essential points of greatness, true heroism and real Christianity from what we may at the present time, for convenience, call American literature." Matthews argued that this great tradition of Afro-American literature would be the textual outlet "for the unnaturally suppressed inner lives which our people have been compelled to lead." Once these "unnaturally suppressed inner lives" of black people are unveiled, no "grander diffusion of mental light" will shine more brightly, she concludes, than that of the articulate Afro-American woman:

> And now comes the question, What part shall we women play in the Race Literature of the future? . . . within the compass of one small journal ["Woman's Era"] we have struck out a new line of departure—a journal, a record of Race interests gathered from all parts of the United States, carefully selected, moistened, winnowed and garnered by the ablest intellects of educated colored women, shrinking at no lofty theme, shirking no serious duty, aiming at every possible excellence, and determined to do their part in the future uplifting of the race.
>
> If twenty women, by their concentrated efforts in one literary movement, can meet with such success as has engendered, planned out, and so successfully consummated this convention, what much more glorious results, what wider spread success, what grander diffusion of mental light will not come forth at the bidding of the enlarged hosts of women writers, already called into being by the stimulus of your efforts?
>
> And here let me speak one word for my journalistic sisters

who have already entered the broad arena of journalism. Before the "Woman's Era" had come into existence, no one except themselves can appreciate the bitter experience and sore disappointments under which they have at all times been compelled to pursue their chosen vocations.

If their brothers of the press have had their difficulties to contend with, I am here as a sister journalist to state, from the fullness of knowledge, that their task has been an easy one compared with that of the colored woman in journalism.

Woman's part in Race Literature, as in Race building, is the most important part and has been so in all ages. . . . All through the most remote epochs she has done her share in literature. . . .

One of the most important aspects of this set is the republication of the salient texts from 1890 to 1910, which literary historians could well call "The Black Woman's Era." In addition to Mary Helen Washington's definitive edition of Cooper's *A Voice From the South,* we have reprinted two novels by Amelia Johnson, Frances Harper's *Iola Leroy,* two novels by Emma Dunham Kelley, Alice Dunbar-Nelson's two impressive collections of short stories, and Pauline Hopkins's three serialized novels as well as her monumental novel, *Contending Forces*—all published between 1890 and 1910. Indeed, black women published more works of fiction in these two decades than black men had published in the previous half century. Nevertheless, this great achievement has been ignored.

Moreover, the writings of nineteenth-century Afro-American women in general have remained buried in obscurity, accessible only in research libraries or in overpriced and poorly edited reprints. Many of these books have never been reprinted at all; in some instances only one or two copies are extant. In these works of fiction, poetry, autobiography, biography, essays, and journalism resides the mind of the nineteenth-century Afro-American woman. Until these works are made readily available to teachers and their students, a significant segment of the black tradition will remain silent.

Oxford University Press, in collaboration with the Schomburg Center for Research in Black Culture, is publishing thirty volumes of these compelling works, each of which contains an introduction by an expert in the field. The set includes such rare texts as Johnson's *The Hazeley Family* and *Clarence and Corinne*, Plato's *Essays*, the most complete edition of Phillis Wheatley's poems and letters, Emma Dunham Kelley's pioneering novel *Megda*, several previously unpublished stories and a novel by Alice Dunbar-Nelson, and the first collected volumes of Pauline Hopkins's three serialized novels and Frances Harper's poetry. We also present four volumes of poetry by such women as Mary Eliza Tucker Lambert, Adah Menken, Josephine Heard, and Maggie Johnson. Numerous slave and spiritual narratives, a newly discovered novel—*Four Girls at Cottage City*—by Emma Dunham Kelley (-Hawkins), and the first American edition of *Wonderful Adventures of Mrs. Seacole in Many Lands* are also among the texts included.

In addition to resurrecting the works of black women authors, it is our hope that this set will facilitate the resurrection of the Afro-American woman's literary tradition itself by unearthing its nineteenth-century roots. In the works of Nella Larsen and Jessie Fauset, Zora Neale Hurston and Ann Petry, Lorraine Hansberry and Gwendolyn Brooks, Paule Marshall and Toni Cade Bambara, Audre Lorde and Rita Dove, Toni Morrison and Alice Walker, Gloria Naylor and Jamaica Kincaid, these roots have branched luxuriantly. The eighteenth- and nineteenth-century authors whose works are presented in this set founded and nurtured the black women's literary tradition, which must be revived, explicated, analyzed, and debated before we can understand more completely the formal shaping of this tradition within a tradition, a coded literary universe through which, regrettably, we are only just beginning to navigate our way. As Anna Cooper said nearly one hundred years ago, we have been blinded by the loss of sight in one eye and have therefore been unable to detect the full *shape* of the Afro-American literary tradition.

Literary works configure into a tradition not because of some mystical collective unconscious determined by the biology of race or gender, but because writers read other writers and *ground* their representations of experience in models of language provided largely by other writers to whom they feel akin. It is through this mode of literary revision, amply evident in the *texts* themselves—in formal echoes, recast metaphors, even in parody—that a "tradition" emerges and defines itself.

This is formal bonding, and it is only through formal bonding that we can know a literary tradition. The collective publication of these works by black women now, for the first time, makes it possible for scholars and critics, male and female, black and white, to *demonstrate* that black women writers read, and revised, other black women writers. To demonstrate this set of formal literary relations is to demonstrate that sexuality, race, and gender are both the condition and the basis of *tradition*—but tradition as found in discrete acts of language use.

A word is in order about the history of this set. For the past decade, I have taught a course, first at Yale and then at Cornell, entitled "Black Women and Their Fictions," a course that I inherited from Toni Morrison, who developed it in the mid-1970s for Yale's Program in Afro-American Studies. Although the course was inspired by the remarkable accomplishments of black women novelists since 1970, I gradually extended its beginning date to the late nineteenth century, studying Frances Harper's *Iola Leroy* and Anna Julia Cooper's *A Voice From the South,* both published in 1892. With the discovery of Harriet E. Wilson's seminal novel, *Our Nig* (1859), and Jean Yellin's authentication of Harriet Jacobs's brilliant slave narrative, *Incidents in the Life of a Slave Girl* (1861), a survey course spanning over a century and a quarter emerged.

But the discovery of *Our Nig,* as well as the interest in nineteenth-century black women's writing that this discovery generated, convinced me that even the most curious and diligent scholars knew very little of the extensive history of the creative writings of Afro-American women before 1900. Indeed, most scholars of Afro-American literature had never even read most of the books published by black women, simply because these books—of poetry, novels, short stories, essays, and autobiography—were mostly accessible only in rare book sections of university libraries. For reasons unclear to me even today, few of these marvelous renderings of the Afro-American woman's consciousness were reprinted in the late 1960s and early 1970s, when so many other texts of the Afro-American literary tradition were resurrected from the dark and silent graveyard of the out-of-print and were reissued in facsimile editions aimed at the hungry readership for canonical texts in the nascent field of black studies.

So, with the help of several superb research assistants—including David Curtis, Nicola Shilliam, Wendy Jones, Sam Otter, Janadas Devan, Suvir Kaul, Cynthia Bond, Elizabeth Alexander, and Adele Alexander—and with the expert advice of scholars such as William Robinson, William Andrews, Mary Helen Washington, Maryemma Graham, Jean Yellin, Houston A. Baker, Jr., Richard Yarborough, Hazel Carby, Joan R. Sherman, Frances Foster, and William French, dozens of bibliographies were used to compile a list of books written or narrated by black women mostly before 1910. Without the assistance provided through this shared experience of scholarship, the scholar's true legacy, this project could not have been conceived. As the list grew, I was struck by how very many of these titles that I, for example, had never even heard of, let alone read, such as Ann Plato's *Essays,* Louisa Picquet's slave narrative, or Amelia Johnson's two novels, *Clarence and Corinne* and *The Hazeley Family.* Through our research with the Black Periodical Fiction and Poetry Project (funded by NEH and the Ford Foundation), I also realized that several novels by black women, including three works of fiction by Pauline Hopkins, had been serialized in black periodicals, but had never been collected and published as books. Nor had the several books of poetry published by black women, such as the prolific Frances E. W. Harper, been collected and edited. When I discovered still another "lost" novel by an Afro-American woman (*Four Girls at Cottage City,* published in 1898 by Emma Dunham Kelley-Hawkins), I decided to attempt to edit a collection of reprints of these works and to publish them as a "library" of black women's writings, in part so that I could read them myself.

Convincing university and trade publishers to undertake this project proved to be a difficult task. Despite the commercial success of *Our Nig* and of the several reprint series of women's works (such as Virago, the Beacon Black Women Writers Series, and Rutgers' American Women Writers Series), several presses rejected the project as "too large," "too limited," or as "commercially unviable." Only two publishers recognized the viability and the import of the project and, of these, Oxford's commitment to publish the titles simultaneously as a set made the press's offer irresistible.

While attempting to locate original copies of these exceedingly rare books, I discovered that most of the texts were housed at the Schomburg Center for Research in Black Culture, a branch of The New York Public Library, under the direction of Howard Dodson. Dodson's infectious enthusiasm for the project and his generous collaboration, as well as that of his stellar staff (especially Diana Lachatanere, Sharon Howard, Ellis Haizip, Richard Newman, and Betty Gubert), led to a joint publishing initiative that produced this set as part of the Schomburg's major fund-raising campaign. Without Dodson's foresight and generosity of spirit, the set would not have materialized. Without William P. Sisler's masterful editorship at Oxford and his staff's careful attention to detail, the set would have remained just another grand idea that tends to languish in a scholar's file cabinet.

I would also like to thank Dr. Michael Winston and Dr. Thomas C. Battle, Vice-President of Academic Affairs and the Director of the Moorland-Spingarn Research Center (respectively) at Howard University, for their unending encouragement, support, and collaboration in this project, and Esme E. Bhan at Howard for her meticulous research and bibliographical skills. In addition, I would like to acknowledge the aid of the staff at the libraries of Duke University, Cornell University (especially Tom Weissinger and Donald Eddy), the Boston Public Library, the Western Reserve Historical Society, the Library of Congress, and Yale University. Linda Robbins, Marion Osmun, Sarah Flanagan, and Gerard Case, all members of the staff at Oxford, were extraordinarily effective at coordinating, editing, and producing the various segments of each text in the set. Candy Ruck, Nina de Tar, and Phillis Molock expertly typed reams of correspondence and manuscripts connected to the project.

I would also like to express my gratitude to my colleagues who edited and introduced the individual titles in the set. Without their attention to detail, their willingness to meet strict deadlines, and their sheer enthusiasm for this project, the set could not have been published. But finally and ultimately, I would hope that the publication of the set would help to generate even more scholarly interest in the black women authors whose work is presented here. Struggling against the seemingly insurmountable barriers of racism *and* sexism, while often raising families and fulfilling full-time professional obligations, these women managed nevertheless to record their thoughts and feelings and to *testify* to all who dare read them that the will to harness the power of collective endurance and survival is the will to write.

The Schomburg Library of Nineteenth-Century Black Women Writers is dedicated in memory of Pauline Augusta Coleman Gates, who died in the spring of 1987. It was she who inspired in me the love of learning and the love of literature. I have encountered in the books of this set no will more determined, no courage more noble, no mind more sublime, no self more celebratory of the achievements of all Afro-American women, and indeed of life itself, than her own.

A NOTE FROM
THE SCHOMBURG CENTER

Howard Dodson

The Schomburg Center for Research in Black Culture, The New York Public Library, is pleased to join with Dr. Henry Louis Gates and Oxford University Press in presenting The Schomburg Library of Nineteenth-Century Black Women Writers. This thirty-volume set includes the work of a generation of black women whose writing has only been available previously in rare book collections. The materials reprinted in twenty-four of the thirty volumes are drawn from the unique holdings of the Schomburg Center.

A research unit of The New York Public Library, the Schomburg Center has been in the forefront of those institutions dedicated to collecting, preserving, and providing access to the records of the black past. In the course of its two generations of acquisition and conservation activity, the Center has amassed collections totaling more than 5 million items. They include over 100,000 bound volumes, 85,000 reels and sets of microforms, 300 manuscript collections containing some 3.5 million items, 300,000 photographs and extensive holdings of prints, sound recordings, film and videotape, newspapers, artworks, artifacts, and other book and nonbook materials. Together they vividly document the history and cultural heritages of people of African descent worldwide.

Though established some sixty-two years ago, the Center's book collections date from the sixteenth century. Its oldest item, an Ethiopian Coptic Tunic, dates from the eighth or ninth century. Rare materials, however, are most available for the nineteenth-century African-American experience. It is from these holdings that the majority of the titles selected for inclusion in this set are drawn.

The nineteenth century was a formative period in African-American literary and cultural history. Prior to the Civil War, the majority of black Americans living in the United States were held in bondage. Law and practice forbade teaching them to read or write. Even after the war, many of the impediments to learning and literary productivity remained. Nevertheless, black men and women of the nineteenth century persevered in both areas. Moreover, more African-Americans than we yet realize turned their observations, feelings, social viewpoints, and creative impulses into published works. In time, this nineteenth-century printed record included poetry, short stories, histories, novels, autobiographies, social criticism, and theology, as well as economic and philosophical treatises. Unfortunately, much of this body of literature remained, until very recently, relatively inaccessible to twentieth-century scholars, teachers, creative artists, and others interested in black life. Prior to the late 1960s, most Americans (black as well as white) had never heard of these nineteenth-century authors, much less read their works.

The civil rights and black power movements created unprecedented interest in the thought, behavior, and achievements of black people. Publishers responded by revising traditional texts, introducing the American public to a new generation of African-American writers, publishing a variety of thematic anthologies, and reprinting a plethora of "classic texts" in African-American history, literature, and art. The reprints usually appeared as individual titles or in a series of bound volumes or microform formats.

The Schomburg Center, which has a long history of supporting publishing that deals with the history and culture of Africans in diaspora, became an active participant in many of the reprint revivals of the 1960s. Since hard copies of original printed works are the preferred formats for producing facsimile reproductions, publishers frequently turned to the Schomburg Center for copies of these original titles. In addition to providing such material, Schomburg Center staff members offered advice and consultation, wrote introductions, and occasionally entered into formal copublishing arrangements in some projects.

Most of the nineteenth-century titles reprinted during the 1960s, however, were by and about black men. A few black women were included in the longer series, but works by lesser known black women were generally overlooked. The Schomburg Library of Nineteenth-Century Black Women Writers is both a corrective to these previous omissions and an important contribution to Afro-American literary history in its own right. Through this collection of volumes, the thoughts, perspectives, and creative abilities of nineteenth-century African-American women, as captured in books and pamphlets published in large part before 1910, are again being made available to the general public. The Schomburg Center is pleased to be a part of this historic endeavor.

I would like to thank Professor Gates for initiating this project. Thanks are due both to him and Mr. William P. Sisler of Oxford University Press for giving the Schomburg Center an opportunity to play such a prominent role in the set. Thanks are also due to my colleagues at The New York Public Library and the Schomburg Center, especially Dr. Vartan Gregorian, Richard De Gennaro, Paul Fasana, Betsy

Pinover, Richard Newman, Diana Lachatanere, Glenderlyn Johnson, and Harold Anderson for their assistance and support. I can think of no better way of demonstrating than in this set the role the Schomburg Center plays in assuring that the black heritage will be available for future generations.

CONTENTS

INTRODUCTION

Anthony G. Barthelemy

Do these Confederate Daughters ever send petitions to prohibit the atrocious lynchings and wholesale murder and torture
of the negro? Do you ever hear of them fearing this would
have a bad effect on the children?

SUSIE KING TAYLOR, *Reminiscences of My Life in Camp*

The four autobiographical narratives published in this volume span a volatile fifty-year period of American history,
from 1853 when Nancy Prince published the enlarged second edition of *A Narrative of the Life and Travels of Mrs.
Nancy Prince* to 1902 when Susie King Taylor published
Reminiscences of My Life in Camp. The women who lived and
wrote during those fifty years witnessed and recorded mo-
mentous events in the history of their oppressed people in
this country. The notorious Fugitive Slave Act passed by
Congress in 1850 threatened the safety and freedom of every
legally free black person in the United States and forced
hundreds of runaway slaves to run even farther to safety in
Canada or Europe. Four years later, the Supreme Court, as
if following the lead of Congress, proclaimed in its Dred
Scott Decision that blacks "had no rights which the white
man was bound to respect." Although the Thirteenth (1865),
Fourteenth (1868), and Fifteenth (1870) Amendments to the
Constitution gave blacks citizenship and rights that white men

were supposed to respect, by the turn of the century the rule
of law regarding blacks once again surrendered to lawlessness
and boastful inhumanity and cruelty. The new citizens suffered legal and illegal attacks on their rights and persons,
attacks that went unchallenged by the federal government.
Lynching became common. The formerly rebellious states,
in virtually unopposed defiance of the Reconstruction
Amendments, passed laws disenfranchising blacks. The spirit
of the Dred Scott Decision continued to inspire Dixie and
most of the nation. Thus in spite of constitutional guarantees,
blacks in America enjoyed neither real protection nor real
security. Their common struggle for security links the narratives of Louisa Picquet, Nancy Prince, Susie King Taylor,
and Bethany Veney. Each woman strove to maintain her dignity and independence in an increasingly violent and consis-
tently racist America.

In a capitalist society, security requires more than protection from bodily attack or from legislative disenfranchisement. Security includes the ability to provide for one's self
financially. And it was this overpowering need for financial
security that prompted each of these women to expose herself
to the public. Nancy Prince writes: "My object [in publishing my narrative] is not a vain desire to appear before the
public; but, by the sale, I hope to obtain the means to supply
my necessities. There are many benevolent societies for the
support of Widows, but I am desirous not to avail myself of
them, so long as I can support myself by my own endeavors." A letter from Colonel C. T. Trowbridge authenticating
Susie King Taylor's *Reminiscences* concludes: "I most sincerely regret that through a technicality you [Taylor] are
debarred from having your name placed on the roll of pensioners, as an Army Nurse; for among all the number of

heroic women whom the government is now rewarding, I know of no one more deserving than yourself." We may infer from this letter that Taylor, unable to secure what was justly hers from the government, attempted to support herself by her own endeavors. We know from Harriet Wilson's *Our Nig* (1859) and Linda Brent's/Harriet Jacobs's *Incidents in the Life of a Slave Girl* (1861) that black women often wrote autobiographies to bring themselves some relief from financial distress. According to William L. Andrews, "More than a few slave autobiographies were published as fund-raisers for their narrators, and most were labeled so."[1] Perhaps if we consider the four relatively obscure narratives in this volume in light of their authors' extraliterary goals and needs, we may come to appreciate them in their own right and recognize their literary merit and success.

Beyond their common struggle and, of course, the shared heritage of racial oppression, the individual circumstances of these women's lives vary greatly. Nancy Prince was born free in Massachusetts in 1799. Her *Narrative* focuses primarily on her travels to Europe, Russia, and Jamaica. Susie King Taylor gained her freedom by escaping behind Union lines with her family in 1862. *Reminiscences* records Taylor's experiences as teacher, laundress, and nurse with the Union army and her later experiences during Reconstruction. Taylor's *Reminiscences* and Prince's *Narrative* are both true autobiographies since neither employed an amanuensis or other collaborator. *The Narrative of Bethany Veney*, published in 1889, documents Veney's experiences in slavery and in freedom and her spiritual growth throughout her life. Veney was emancipated in 1858 by a man who bought her specifically to free her. He then took her North where she worked for him for a few years as his employee, not as his slave. Her

Narrative was almost certainly written by an amanuensis,
presumably the M.W.G. who wrote the preface.[2] Louisa
Picquet was given her freedom in the late 1840s by the man
who held her as slave and concubine. Her autobiography
Louisa Picquet, The Octoroon: A Tale of Southern Slave Life,
published in 1861, is not, strictly speaking, a narrative. Instead, we have Picquet's first-person replies to questions posed
by the Reverend Hiram Mattison who, it appears, transcribed her responses. Because of Mattison's moralistic design, *Louisa Picquet* focuses on Picquet's life as sexual victim
and concubine and on her efforts to buy her mother out of
slavery. Whether writing exclusively by themselves or with
the assistance of someone else, these autobiographers confronted the common challenges encountered by all who try to
recreate and represent their lives in and through language.
They also confronted the special difficulties imposed on black
autobiographers—whether free, freed, or fugitive slaves—by
a frequently doubtful and sometimes hostile white American
reading public.

William L. Andrews, in *To Tell a Free Story*, explores many
of the complexities faced by the black and especially ex-slave
autobiographer. In their efforts to reconstruct themselves
rhetorically, former slaves had to select carefully which events
from their lives they would commit to paper. They also had
to find a suitable style and lexicon with which to record those
lives. As Andrews observes:

> Many slave narrators were aware of the racist and nationalistic
> biases that made the average northern reader suspect any black
> person who characterized southern whites as barbarous and
> inhuman. This caused some slave narrators to declare openly
> the paradoxical preparatory condition of much antebellum
> slave autobiography: white acceptance of a slave narrative as

truth depended on how judiciously the slave had censored the facts of his life into something other than the whole truth. (p. 26)

For the ex-slave attempting to construct rhetorically a free self, or for the committed antislavery activist promulgating abolitionist ideology, the tension of selling one's self and one's story to white America required self-censorship at best and mendacity at worst. But in order to proclaim a discrete self and one's personal emancipation, or to proclaim all African-Americans to be members of the human race and Americans by inclination and acculturation, the autobiographer accepted and accommodated the compromises, ironies, and paradoxes required to achieve this goal.

In addition to these more common constraints and demands, Picquet, Prince, Taylor, Veney, and many other black women had other forces binding and motivating them and their narratives. The individual circumstances by which they attained their freedom do not negate the significance or similarities of their previous conditions of servitude or legal disenfranchisement. Each knew the dangers of being a black woman in antebellum America. Each lived under the shadow of capture and sale. Can we expect, therefore, a female writer who had recently escaped some white man's claim of property in her person, including her sexuality and reproductive capabilities, to meet the structural and rhetorical challenges and compromises of self-exposition in the same way as the triumphant fugitive (and male) slave, especially when the effort is motivated by the need for financial security in a culture that knew her price but not her name? Of Frederick Douglass, Houston Baker writes: "The nineteenth-century slave, in effect, *publicly* sells his voice in order to secure *private* ownership of his voice-person." However, Baker continues: "An analysis of an account by a nineteenth-century black woman [Harriet Jacobs] demonstrates that gender produces striking modifications in the Afro-American discursive subtext. This gender difference does not eradicate the primacy of such governing statements as 'commercial deportation' and the 'economics of slavery,' but it does alter and expand their scope."[3] A new variable constrained the telling of these stories, for these women had to sell their intimate memories and to sort out the property rights to their own lives. The act of recording their lives, ironically, recorded their financial distress. These stories are free of neither anxiety nor exigency. Duress returned these women to the marketplace, and the marketplace often exposed them to humiliation, examination, and sale. Moreover, their female biology itself had once been valued and sold. Was there not a correspondence in valuing and selling their lives as women? Ways to resist this literary return to the auction block had to be found.

The lacunae of which Henry Louis Gates writes in his introduction to *Our Nig* were Harriet Wilson's way of refusing to put everything of hers on the auction block and of maintaining her privacy. Having made available for purchase her humiliation as a child, perhaps she could not bear to trade the personal tragedy of her marriage—that is, her personal life as a woman—just for financial security, for fleeting material comfort. Wilson tells us she will not "divulge every transaction in my own life, which the unprejudiced would declare unfavorable in comparison with treatment of legal bondmen."[4] But many greater and more personal omissions exist in Wilson's story. As Gates observes: "To ask of her [Wilson] even more would be to ask too much. While the scholar wishes for more details of the life to have been named in the novel. . . even he must remain content to grant the author her plea."[5] So it is with Picquet, Prince, Taylor, and Veney. In their narratives, events are reported, but the personal lives are withheld or veiled in a struggle to preserve their already compromised privacy.

When Bethany Veney reports in her narrative, "I rented of John Prince a little house at Dry Run, just at the foot of the mountain, and with my little boy Joe, now about two years old, lived very contentedly," she registers her resistance to the degradation of the marketplace. In this, her first mention of a second child, she reveals nothing of the boy's birth or father. The traditional reading of Veney's laconic under-reporting would suggest that the pious older Veney was ashamed to recall the circumstances of the child's birth, but we ought not read this either as a confession of guilt or as a lack of honesty. Quite the contrary, Veney's secretiveness here is as defiant as the simple sentence that begins Chapter IV: "Year after year rolled on." By the time we reach this coy obfuscation, Veney has already revealed her defiance, ingenuity, fortitude, and independence. In the inhuman grip of chattel slavery, Veney continually demonstrates her humanity, of which maintaining her privacy is merely another manifestation.

Veney reveals how self-consciously she conceals information by frequently emphasizing her uncompromising personal commitment to truth and honesty. In reporting her first marriage to a man who is later sold away from her, Veney says:

> I did not want him [the minister at the wedding] to make us promise that we would always be true to each other, forsaking all others, as the white people do in their marriage service, because I knew that at any time our masters could compel us

to break such a promise; and I had never forgotten the lesson
learned, so many years before [about the importance of telling
the truth].

Her "signifying" here on whites points to the absence of truth
in their dealings with blacks. The missing admonition, "Let
no man put asunder what God has joined together," is nearly
deafening as the reader contemplates the real lesson of Veney's vignette. This omission, unlike her narrative omissions, exposes the hypocrisy of slaveholders. A complete
marriage ritual would have forced Veney to perjure herself;
its abbreviated version, in fact, condemns those who denied
her the right to enter into a true marriage. Veney, unlike her
white masters, will deal honestly with the reader, but truth
does not require exposing herself to the peering eyes of the
public simply to obtain much needed cash. Was it not material greed that dictated the dishonest behavior of whites? Veney refuses to surrender all judgment simply for economic
security, and she will not endure again the demeaning in-
spection to which she was subjected on the auction block.
Veney demonstrates both her defiance and devotion to the
truth when she signifies on the veracity and Christianity of
whites. For Veney, too much of her personal life has already
been sold. "My life in the North as in the South," she tells
us, "has been full of experiences both sad and joyful." We
must accept the truth of that and whatever elaboration she
cares to make.

In her narrative, Nancy Prince writes rather cryptically:
"The first twenty months after my arrival in the city [Bos-
ton], notwithstanding my often infirmities, I labored with
much success, until I hired with and from those with whom
I mostly sympathized, and shared in common the disadvantages and stigma that is heaped upon us in this our professed

Christian land." This sentence carries us from August 1843 until spring 1845. For the next ten lines or so, Prince then records her financial reversals. She begins a new paragraph, saying only, "In 1848 and '49 the Lord was pleased to lay his hand upon me." Prince's friends, knowing her need for money, were perhaps not surprised to see that she failed to mention 1847 and her central role in expelling from the black Boston neighborhood of Smith Court a slaveholder who hunted down runaways. An eyewitness to the event offered this account in 1894:

> One day between eleven and twelve o'clock A.M., there was a ripple of excitement in the rear of Smith's Court. Some children had reported that a slaveholder was in Mrs. Dorsey's. . . . Mrs. Nancy Prince, a colored woman of prominence in Boston . . . with several others, hurried to the scene. Mrs. Prince had seen the kidnapper before. Only for an instance did [her] fiery eyes rest upon the form of the villain, as if to be fully assured that it was he, for the next moment she had grappled with him, and before he could fully realize his position she, with the assistance of the colored women that had accompanied her, had dragged him to the door and thrust him out of the house. By this time quite a number, mostly women and children had gathered near by, whom Mrs. Prince commanded to come to the rescue, telling them to "pelt him with stones and any thing you can get a hold of," which order they proceeded to obey with alacrity. The slaveholder started to retreat, and with his assailants close upon him ran out of the court.[6]

For modern readers of Prince's life, the omission of this event from her narrative is disappointing; it obscures the remarkable woman who traveled to Russia, knew czars and czarinas, survived deceitful stratagems to trick her into slavery, and could and would turn pugilist to aid a fellow Afro-

American. However, instead of reporting how she attacked
a white man and protected a besieged fugitive from America's "peculiar institution," Prince records her economic reversals, her persecutions and, finally, her faith in God:

> But my lot was like the man that went down from Jerusalem,
> and fell among thieves, which stripped him of his raiment,
> and wounding him, departed, leaving him half dead. What
> I did not lose, when cast away, has been taken from my room
> where I hired. Three times I had been broken up in business,
> embarrassed and obliged to move, when not able to wait on
> myself. This has been my lot. In the midst of my afflictions,
> sometimes I have thought my case like that of Paul's, when
> cast among wild beasts. "Had not the Lord been on my side,
> they would have swallowed me up; but blessed be the Lord
> who hath not given me a prey to their teeth."

The reader can hardly believe that Prince was ashamed of
her behavior in Smith Court, especially since she so sarcas-
tically denounces "this our professed Christian land" in the
sentence immediately preceding this quotation. Prince doubt-
less had to weigh the effect of the story of Smith Court on
the marketplace. In her story of exotic travel and missionary
work, she could expect an audience of the righteous and middle class. For a black woman to beat a white man and incite
other blacks to near riot, however, was too much even for
many of the most outspoken abolitionists of her day. Thus in
her narrative, we learn many details of burial in Russia and
of daring sea voyages. We learn about her struggles on behalf of the freed slaves of Jamaica and about threats to her
freedom. But we are deprived of any real knowledge of her
life. Knowing what she hid of the events in 1847, we long
for the real story behind other experiences—for example, the
story that is absent from these lines: "after seven years of

anxiety and toil, I made up my mind to leave my country. September 1st, 1823, Mr. Prince arrived from Russia. February 15, 1824, we were married."

The tensions in *Louisa Picquet, The Octoroon* reveal the conflicts inherent in an autobiographical enterprise motivated primarily by financial distress. While traveling through Buffalo in 1860 to solicit contributions with which to purchase her mother out of slavery in Texas, Picquet met the Methodist minister, Hiram Mattison. An abolitionist, Mattison wanted to discuss the problem of slavery at a General Conference of the Methodist Church in Buffalo. He used Picquet to further his cause. Responding to Mattison's questions, Picquet tells us something of her life in slavery and freedom. Mattison, however, was interested in the institution of slavery itself and in its attendant moral corruption. The minister failed to recognize Picquet as an individual; rather, she and her experiences served to substantiate his argument and to justify his self-righteousness and moral indignation. Ironically, his self-righteousness imposed a prurient obsessiveness on the interview. His description of the former octoroon concubine betrays the minister's obsession, and perhaps her attractiveness made Mattison a little too interested in her answers to his intrusive questions. Mattison notes Picquet to be "easy and graceful in her manners, of fair complexion and rosy cheeks, with dark eyes, a flowing head of hear with no perceptible inclination to curl, and every appearance, at first view, of an accomplished white lady. No one, not apprised of the fact, would suspect that she had a drop of African blood in her veins; indeed, few will believe it, at first, even when told of it." With his subject thus revealed, Mattison then proceeds to ask Picquet questions about her sexual past and the sexual habits of white men and en-

slaved black women. His questions are designed to lead him
to the following conclusion: "There is not a family mentioned, from first to last, that does not reek with fornication
and adultery. It turns up as naturally, and is mentioned with
as little specialty, as walrus beef in the narrative of the Arctic
Expedition, or macaroni in a tour in Italy."

Picquet, of course, had quite a different agenda. She sub-
mitted to Mattison's prying and often lewd questions ("How
were you dressed—with thin clothes, or how?" "Were your
children mulattoes?") because she needed money to rescue her
mother from whom she had been separated for nearly twenty
years. However, as Mattiston focused on moral corruption,
he lost sight of the contrapuntal tale of filial dedication and
maternal devotion. Picquet's primary interest was subordi-
nated to Mattison's own. To Mattison, the mother's and
daughter's past lives as mistresses and concubines occupied
the foreground and his questions on that subject never slacken.
Picquet, therefore, had to develop strategies to focus attention on her concerns as she protected herself and her mother
from the invasive Reverend Mattison. At one point, she does
so by politely chiding her inquisitor for knowing so little
about slavery. When she tells Mattison that she was taken
from the room where female slaves were examined, he replies: "Where was that? In the street, or in a yard?" "At the
market," Picquet answers, "where the block is[.]"[7] The
conversation continues:

MATTISON: What block?
  PICQUET: My! don't you know? The stand, where we have
            to get up[.]
MATTISON: Did *you* get up on the stand?
  PICQUET: Why, of course; we all have to get up to be
            seen.

Picquet clearly understands her relationship to Mattison. Once again, she is on the block; something is for sale. Only Mattison remains unaware of the traditional role he has assumed. Like the gentleman clients of the Southern slave markets, Mattison examines Picquet with an unrelenting prurient interest. Picquet's strategy here pays off; she deflects the minister's prying questions and maintains some control over the examination.

Similarly, as Mattison pries into blatantly sexual matters, Picquet deflects the questions or simply refuses to answer. When relating an incident in which she has once again avoided her master's persistent sexual advances, she says: "Then he order[ed] me, in a sort of commanding way (I don't want to tell what he said), and told me to shut the door." Another time, Mattison enters in brackets: "Here Mrs. P declines explaining further how he whipped her, though she had told our hostess where this was written; but it is too horrible and indelicate to be read in a civilized country." The irony, of course, is that the subject is not too horrible or indelicate for Mattison to ask about, perhaps even with some persistence. Picquet again refuses to offer the American market events so personal that only another woman—the hostess—can be told.

The fact that Picquet's is not really a narrative does not diminish the importance of her omissions. Picquet had to work within the boundaries established by Mattison, but she did not have to surrender to his will or go naked before his questions. That she had to purchase her mother and that she was once bought as a concubine instructed Picquet all too well on the vile appetites of the American marketplace. In her narrative, she struggles to close the market and to stop the victimization. She resists as best she can from placing herself once again on the block.

Susie King Taylor, like others before her, wrote an auto-biography with the hope that its sale would help solve her financial difficulties. In the preface to *Reminiscences of My Life in Camp,* Taylor writes:

> In 1900 I received a letter from a gentleman, sent from the Executive Mansion at St. Paul, Minn., saying Colonel Trowbridge had told him I was about to write a book, and when it was published he wanted one of the first copies. This, coming from a total stranger, gave me more confidence, so I now present these reminiscences to you, hoping they may prove of some interest, and show how much service and good we can do for each other, and what sacrifices we can make for our liberty and rights, and that there were "loyal women," as well as men, in those days, who did not fear shell or shot, who cared for the sick and dying; women who camped and fared as the boys did, and who are still caring for the comrades in their declining years.

Taylor repeats these sentiments throughout her narrative as she leaves a public record of her service in the Union army. However, as she pleads for greater generosity toward those remaining veterans of the Civil War, she, in fact, silently pleads for herself. After forty years of continual sacrifice to the Union cause and its veterans, after forty years of service as nurse and educator of a newly freed people, Taylor deserves both financial support and gratitude for her contributions.

Taylor regards her service to the Union as a badge of pride and an example of her strength and independence. She proudly reports on her many accomplishments and her ability to survive the hazards and rigors of war. "I learned to handle a musket very well while in the regiment," she states, "and could shoot straight and often hit the target. I assisted in cleaning the guns and used to fire them off, to see if the cartridges were dry, before cleaning and reloading, each day. I thought this great fun." Taylor, of course, knew the horror of war; the fun was in demonstrating her competence and her usefulness. Her greatest responsibility, however, was in aiding the wounded and dying, and though there was no fun in that, there was tremendous pride in service. Soberly she observes:

> It seems strange how our aversion to seeing suffering is overcome in war,—how we are able to see the most sickening sights, such as men with their limbs blown off and mangled by the deadly shells, without a shudder; and instead of turning away, how we hurry to assist in alleviating their pain, bind up their wounds, and press the cool water to their parched lips, with feelings only of sympathy and pity.

Reminiscences makes clear the justice of Taylor's claim for an army pension. She proudly served a nation that abandoned its financial responsibilities to her and that shirked its legal and moral obligation to provide equal protection under the law to its black citizens. In the book's penultimate chapter, "Thoughts on Present Conditions," Taylor laments:

> In this "land of the free" we are burned, tortured, and denied a fair trial, murdered for any imaginary wrong conceived in the brain of the negro-hating white man. There is no redress for us from a government which promised to protect all under its flag. It seems a mystery to me. They say, "One flag, one nation, one country indivisible." Is this true? Can we say this truthfully, when one race is allowed to burn, hang, and inflict the most horrible torture weekly, monthly, on another? No, we cannot sing, "My country, 't is of thee, Sweet land of Liberty"! It is hollow mockery.

Taylor's plea for justice in 1902—Booker T. Washington's more ebullient *Up From Slavery* was published in 1901— was ineffective. Like her plea for recognition, it too fell on deaf ears, but she felt compelled to record her betrayal by the nation she had served.

Yet in spite of all of the details of her service to the Union and her work as an educator of the freed people, we really know little of Susie King Taylor's life. As in the other women's narratives, years slip away unrecorded; provocative statements receive no clarification or elaboration. Taylor passes over years with sentences like this: "In December, 1866, I was obliged to give up teaching, but in April, 1867, I opened a school in Liberty County, Georgia, and taught there one year; but country life did not agree with me, so I returned to the city." The intrepid nurse and kind laundress surrenders little of her private life. She accounts for five years and her second marriage in two sentences: "Soon after I got to Boston [in 1874], I entered the service of Mr. Thomas Smith's family, on Walnut Avenue, Boston Highlands, where I remained until the death of Mrs. Smith. I next lived with Mrs. Gorham Gray, Beacon Street, where I remained until I was married, in 1879, to Russell L. Taylor." Moreover, we learn nothing of Russell L. Taylor other than his name. Taylor's reticence need not imply that she thinks her personal life is boring or that it holds no market value. She certainly does not hesitate to record her unpopular opinions on racial matters. Catering to the marketplace, therefore, does not hold tyrannical sway over her. What is of paramount importance for the outspoken Taylor is the establishment of a public record of her service to the country. Her private life is essentially irrelevant to this. When she reports her trip to Shreveport, Louisiana in order to nurse her dying son, she tells that story only to register her disgust with Jim Crowism. She seeks no sympathy for herself or her son; she seeks justice. Unable to secure a sleeping car in which to transport her son out of the South, the loyal Taylor decries the injustice: "It seemed very hard, when his father fought to protect the Union and our flag, and yet his boy was denied, under this same flag, a berth to carry him home to die, because he was a negro." Hard indeed! What more must she give in order to survive in this country? The story that she tells is all that she will tell. It confirms her dignity and independence; it exposes not her but her country; it pleads for justice in a land of injustice. Why should she expose herself further to correct the gross injustices and negligence of her countrymen? She exposed herself to bullets and more in service to the country. That service ought to be enough.

Many conflicts arise for these women in the telling of their stories, and the necessity of conforming to the marketplace or at least appealing to it compounds those conflicts. Paradoxically, after reading these narratives, one still does not know much about the women who wrote them. They remain obscure and manage to become more mysterious. However, these stories leave us wanting and ignorant not because the authors thought their lives uneventful or unremarkable, but because they chose in some very fundamental ways to absent themselves from their own autobiographies. For these black women to expose themselves in the marketplace would require an amnesia powerful enough to blot out the horrific memory of the block. By obscuring their personal lives, these women protected their personhood, and in that sense produced narratives that enact one of the essential struggles of all autobiography as a discursive art—the struggle to meet one's individual psychic needs. As James Olney has written:

We shall never have the experience in consciousness that the autobiographer had, and consequently we shall never know what in his deepest and inaccessible self, he was. But we might, from autobiography, as from drama and poetry, know what man has been, or what forms have proved possible to humanity, which is a knowledge that one seeks with the intention more particularly of knowing what man is.[8]

The challenge in reading these four narratives lies in seeing through the screens, in surrendering our obsession with facts and details, and in accepting the will of these women to possess their own lives. Of course, there is much to be learned in the narratives, but in order to avail ourselves of the opportunity of learning about their authors, we must learn from them something about the genre and the act of writing autobiography. William L. Andrews suggests ways of approaching autobiography that provide the reader with a useful entrée into the narratives:

Because the ontology of autobiography is so problematic, it seems to me more fruitful to treat the form more as a complex of linguistic acts in a discursive field than as the verbal emblem of an essential self uniquely stamped on a historical narrative. This does not mean that historical or self-referentiality has no place in a discussion of the evolution of black American autobiography. It does mean that the assumptions of referentiality in autobiography that have usually informed our discussions of the genre can no longer claim privileged status. We must be more discerning in our thinking about the dynamics of signification in autobiography.[9]

Reading these four narratives unbiased by traditional notions of literary value, one may discover something about these women and the art of writing. We know that the women knew more about language than the biased critic would admit. We have seen Taylor effectively deconstruct the myths, and language of the myths, of American liberty and freedom. These women, like Frederick Douglass and all black Americans, knew that language could be "perverted" from its "obvious meaning."[10] Yet they had to rely upon that same language to reveal and to hide themselves. They had to reconstruct their lives aware of their economic and psychic needs. We must construe their reconstructions aware of their efforts to obstruct our success.

NOTES

1. William L. Andrews, *To Tell a Free Story* (Urbana: University of Illinois Press, 1986), p. 108.

2. M.W.G. writes in that preface: "It is greatly to be regretted that the language and personal characteristics of Bethany cannot be transcribed. The little particulars that give coloring and point, tone and expression, are largely lost. Only the outline can be given. As it is, possessing only the merit of a 'plain, unvarnished tale,' it asks for generous consideration and extended sale." Whether M.W.G. did more than transcribe and render into standard English Veney's story cannot be determined. From M.W.G.'s comments, however, it seems clear that Veney was a competent storyteller. I certainly have no reason to doubt that Veney had her story set down as she wanted it. The strength of will recounted in the narrative implies that Veney was a woman who had things done her way.

3. Houston A. Baker, Jr., *Blues, Ideology, and Afro-American Literature: A Vernacular Theory* (Chicago: University of Chicago Press, 1984), p. 50.

4. Harriet Wilson, *Our Nig; or, Sketches from the Life of a Free Black* (New York: Random House, 1983), p. 3.

5. Henry Louis Gates, "Introduction," in Harriet Wilson, *Our Nig* (New York: Random House, 1983, p. xxxviii.

6. Thomas B. Hilton, *Women's Era*, August 1894, cited in *We Are Your Sisters,* ed. Dorothy Sterling (New York: W. W. Norton, 1984), p. 222.

7. In this sentence and a later one, the text is punctuated with question marks. It seems clear, however, that these are declarative sentences, so I have inserted periods in brackets.

8. James Olney, *Metaphors of Self: The Meaning of Autobiography* (Princeton, N.J.: Princeton University Press, 1972), p. xi.

9. William L. Andrews, *To Tell a Free Story,* p. 23.

10. Frederick Douglass, *The Life and Times of Frederick Douglass* (New York: Macmillan, 1962), p. 548.

A

NARRATIVE

OF THE

LIFE AND TRAVELS

OF

MRS. NANCY PRINCE.

WRITTEN BY HERSELF.

SECOND EDITION.

BOSTON:
PUBLISHED BY THE AUTHOR.
1853.

WM. A. HALL, PRINTER, 22 SCHOOL ST., BOSTON.

PREFACE.

———

By divine aid, I attempt a second edition of my narrative, with the additions suggested to me by my friends. My object is not a vain desire to appear before the public; but, by the sale, I hope to obtain the means to supply my necessities. There are many benevolent societies for the support of Widows, but I am desirous not to avail myself of them, so long as I can support myself by my own endeavors. Infirmities are coming upon me, which induce me to solicit the patronage of my friends and the public, in the sale of this work. Not wishing to throw myself on them, I take this method to help myself, as health and strength are gone.

CONTENTS.

———

NARRATIVE.

I was born in Newburyport, September the 15th, 1799. My mother was born in Gloucester, Massachusetts — the daughter of Tobias Wornton, or Backus, so called. He was stolen from Africa, when a lad, and was a slave of Captain Winthrop Sargent; but, although a slave, he fought for liberty. He was in the Revolutionary army, and at the battle of Bunker Hill. He often used to tell us, when little children, the evils of Slavery, and how he was stolen from his native land. My grandmother was an Indian of this country; she became a captive to the Engglish, or their descendants. She served as a domestic in the Parsons family. My father, Thomas Gardner, was born in Nantucket; his parents were of African descent. He died in Newburyport, when I was three months old. My mother was thus a second time left a widow, with her two children, and she returned to Gloucester to her father. My mother married her third husband, by whom she had six children. My step-father was stolen from Africa, and while the vessel was at anchor in one of our Eastern ports, he succeeded in making his escape from his captors, by swimming ashore. I have often heard him tell the tale. Having some knowledge of the English language, he found no trouble to pass. There were two of them, and they found, from observation, that they were in a free State. I have heard my father describe the beautiful moon-light night when they two launched their bodies into the deep, for liberty. When they got upon soundings, their feet were pricked with a sea-plant that grew under water, they had to retreat, and, at last they reached the shore. When day began to break, they laid down under a fence, as naked as they were born — soon they heard a rattling sound, and trembling, they looked to see what it meant. In a few minutes, a man with a broad-brimed hat on, looked over the fence and cried out, " Halloo boys ! you are from that ship at anchor?" Trembling, we answered, yes. He kindly took us by the hand, and told us not to fear, for we were safe. " Jump, boys," said he, " into my cart," which we readily did. He turned about, and soon entered a large yard — we were taken to his house and carried to an apartment, where he brought us clothes and food, and cheered us with every kindness. No search was made for us; it was supposed we were drowned, as many had jumped over-board on the voyage, thinking they could get home to Africa again. I have often heard my step-father boast how brave they were, and say they stood like men and saw the ship set sail with less than half they stole from Africa. He was selling his bamboo baskets, when he was seized by white men, and put in a boat, and taken on board the ship that lay off; many such ships there were! He was called "Money Vose," and his name may be found on the Custom House books in Gloucester. His last voyage was with Captain Elias Davis, in the brig Romulus, belonging to Captain Fitz William Sargent, in whose employ he had been twelve years. During the war, the brig was taken by a British privateer, and he was pressed into their service. He was sick with the dropsy a long while, and died oppressed, in the English dominions. My mother was again left a widow, with an infant six weeks old, and seven other children. When she heard of her husband's death, she exclaimed, " I thought it; what shall I do with these children ?" She was young, inexperienced, with no hope in God, and without the knowledge of her Saviour. Her grief, poverty, and responsibilities, were too much for her; she never again was the mother that she had been before. I was, at this time, in Captain F. W. Sargent's family. I shall never forget the feelings I experienced, on hearing of the decease of my father-in-law, although he was not kind to me or my sister; but, by industry a humble home was provided, for my mother and her younger children. Death had twice visited our family, in less than three months. My grandfather died before my father-in-law sailed. I thought I would go home a little while, and try and comfort my mother. The three oldest children were put into families.

My brother and myself stayed at home that Summer. We gathered berries and sold them in Gloucester; strawberries, raspberries, blackberries and whortleberries, were in abundance, in the stony environs, growing spontaneously. With the sale of these fruits, my brother and myself nearly supported my mother and her children, that Summer. My brother George, young as he was, caught fish and sold them, and run of errands, and was always watching for something to do, that he might help his mother. At one time he was missing; we expected he was drowned; a search was made for him in the water; the neighbors were all on the alert. Poor mother returning from a hard day's work, supposing the boy was lost, was like a lunatic. The lad was supposed to have fallen from the wharf, where he was fishing. Our friends had all given up the search — it was then eleven o'clock at night. Mother and I locked up the children and went round to the harbor, to one Captain Warner, who traded to the Eastward. Mrs. Warner informed us that my brother came there in the morning, with his bundle, and they supposed he was sent, as the Captain wished to take him with him. He went on board, and the vessel sailed that afternoon. In three weeks, he came home, to the comfort of his mother and all of us. He brought back, for his pay, four feet of wood and three dollars.

We stayed with our mother until every resource was exhausted; we then heard of a place eight miles out of town, where a boy and girl were wanted. We both went and were engaged. We often went home with our wages, and all the comforts we could get; but we could not approach our mother as we wished. God in mercy took one little boy of seven years, who had been in a consumption one year.

My oldest sister, Silvia, was seventy miles in the country, with the family that brought her up; so we were scattered all about. Soon as the war

1*

was over, I determined to get more for my labor.
I left Essex and went to Salem, in the month of
April, 1814, without a friend, without a guide.
I first went to Gloucester, to bid my mother and
the family adieu. George, my brother, I left
with a promise to send for him when I should be
settled. When I reached the Cove, about five
miles from Gloucester, I stopped at a friend's,
who urged me not to go, holding up obstacles. It
rained and snowed, but I travelled along, following the guide-posts, until I reached Beverly bridge.
I crossed it when the clock struck four, in the
afternoon. I now wished to find a friend in
Becket Street, Salem, but was afraid of the people that I met near the Bridge, they were so
covered with rags and dirt. I kept on until I
reached the Common ; I then asked a woman who
was neatly dressed, for the lady I wished to find.
She did not know. I asked for another person,
that I knew was not very good ; she took me
there, but I soon found my friend that I wished,
and stopped there two weeks, and then went to
live with a respectable colored family. My
mother was not satisfied, and came after me. I
would not go to Gloucester. She left me at a
friend's, and this woman had a daughter, who
came home from service, sick. I took her place,
and thought myself fortunate to be with religious

people, as I had enjoyed the happy privilege of religious instruction. My dear grandfather was a member of a Congregational Church, and a good man ; he always attended meeting in the morning, and took his children with him. In the afternoon he took care of the smaller children, while my mother attended with her little group. He thought it was wrong for us to go to school where the teacher was not devoted to God. Thus I early knew the difference between right and wrong.

There were seven in the family, one sick with a fever, and another in a consumption ; and of course, the work must have been very severe, especially the washings. Sabbath evening I had to prepare for the wash ; soap the clothes and put them into the steamer, set the kettle of water to boiling, and then close in the steam, and let the pipe from the boiler into the steam box that held the clothes. At two o'clock, on the morning of Monday, the bell was rung for me to get up ; but, that was not all, they said I was too slow, and the washing was not done well ; I had to leave the tub to tend the door and wait on the family, and was not spoken kind to, at that.

Hard labor and unkindness was too much for me ; in three months, my health and strength were gone. I often looked at my employers, and thought to myself, is this your religion ? I did

not wonder that the girl who had lived there previous to myself, went home to die. They had
family prayers, morning and evening. Oh! yes,
they were sanctimonious! I was a poor stranger,
but fourteen years of age, imposed upon by these
good people; but I must leave them. In the
year 1814, they sent me to Gloucester in their
chaise. I found my poor mother in bad health,
and I was sick also; but, by the mercy of God,
and the attention and skill of Dr. Dale, and the
kindness of friends, I was restored, so that in a
few months, I was able again to go to work,
although my side afflicted me, which I attributed
to overworking myself.

In the Spring of 1815, I returned to Salem,
accompanied by my eldest sister, and we obtained
good places. She took it into her head to go to
Boston, as a nursery girl, where she lived a few
months and was then deluded away. February
7th, 1816, a friend came to Salem and informed
me of it. To have heard of her death, would
not have been so painful to me, as we loved each
other very much, and more particularly, as our
step-father was not very kind to us. When little
girls, she used to cry about it, and we used to
say, when we were large enough we would go
away.

It was very cold; but notwithstanding, I was so

distressed about my sister that I started the next morning for Boston, on foot. A friend was with me. At Lynn Hotel we refreshed ourselves, and all seemed much interested about me; two women took me aside, and inquired how it was that I was with that woman. I told my reason; she was well known all about; she lived as a cook in Boston, she came after her son, a little child whom she held in her arms. By the time we were seven miles from Salem, cold and fatigued, I could walk no farther, and we hired a horse and sleigh, and a man to drive us to Boston, where we arrived at seven o'clock in the evening. The house where we stopped was in Green street, the lady kindly invited me to stop; I refused; I was suspicious the house was not good; the woman I came with took me to Belknap street, where I found an old friend; I would not stop, they went with me to Bedford street, where I intended to put up. The inmates received me very kindly; my feet, hands and ears were all frostbitten. I needed all the hospitality that was extended to me. I was young and inexperienced, but God knew that my object was good. "In wisdom he chooses the weak things of the earth." Without his aid, how could I ever have rescued my lost sister? Mr. Brown, when he learned my errand, kindly offered to assist me. He found where my sister resided, and taking with him a

large cane, he accompanied me to the house, on
Sabbath evening. My sister I found seated with
a number of others round a fire, the mother of
harlots at the head. My sister did not see me
until I clasped her round the neck. The old
woman flew at me, and bid me take my hands
off of her; she opened a door that led down
into a cellar kitchen, and told me to come
down, she attempted to take my hands off of
my sister. Mr. Brown defended me with his
cane; there were many men and girls there,
and all was confusion. When my sister came to
herself, she looked upon me and said: "Nancy,
O Nancy, I am ruined!" I said, "Silvia, my
dear sister, what are you here for? Will you
not go with me?" She seemed thankful to get
away; the enraged old woman cried out, "she
owes me, she cannot go." Silvia replied, "I will
go." The old woman seized her to drag her
down into the kitchen; I held on to her, while
Mr. Brown at my side, used his great cane; he
threatened her so that she was obliged to let my
sister go, who, after collecting her things, accompanied Mr. Brown and myself.

Now while I write, I am near the spot that
that was then the hold of all foul and unclean things·
"The lips of a strange woman drop as an honey
comb, and her mouth is smoother than oil; there
she has slain her thousands; her end is bitter as

wormwood, sharp as a two-edged sword, and lieth in wait at every corner, with an impudent face, saying, I have peace offerings, I have payed my vows. With her much fair speeeh, she flattereth: she hath cast down many wounded, yea, many strong have been slain by her; her house is the way to hell going down to the chambers of death." Even now, I cannot refrain my feelings, although death has long separated us; but her soul is precious; she was very dear to me; she was five years older than myself, and often protected me from the blows of an unkind step-father. She often said she was not fit to live, nor fit to die.

The next day, after breakfast, one of Mrs. Brown's daughters accompanied us to the stage office; we expected Mr. Low, the driver of the Gloucester stage, who knew us as his towns-people, would let us take passage with him without any difficulty; but he refused unless we would ride upon the top. It was very cold; I had sent my mother my wages the week before, and what money I had, I had taken in advance, of my employers. We were greatly embarrassed, when a colored man, unknown to us, penetrated our difficulty, and asked us if we had two dollars; we told him we had; he very kindly took us to the stage office, and we bargained for a horse and sleigh to carry us to Salem, where we arrived

safely in about two hours and a half; and we
gave up our conveyance to the same owners, with
ten thousand thanks to our colored friend, and to
our Heavenly Father ; had we attempted to walk,
we must have frozen by the way. The horse
and sleigh belonged to the stage-office, so we had
no more care for that. The man who let it to
us was very humane, although a stranger. The
price was two dollars, of which he not only gave
us back fifty cents to pay our toll, but went with
us as far as to Charlestown bridge.

I often thought of the contrast between our
townsman, Mr. Low, and the stranger who was
so kind to us. The lady I lived with, Mrs. John
Deland, received us very kindly, and permitted
my sister to remain with me awhile ; then she
returned to Gloucester, to the family who brought
her up, and I thought we had gained a great victory.

My brother George and myself were very desirous to make our mother comfortable: he went
to sea for that purpose ; the next April, I came
to Boston to get a higher price for my labor ; for
we had agreed to support my mother, and hoped
she would take home our little brother and take
care of him, who was supported by the town.
George came home, and sailed again in the same
employ, leaving mother a draw bill for half his
wages. My sister returned to Boston to find me,

and wished to procure a place to work out. I had just changed my place for one more retired, and engaged my sister with me as a chamber maid; she tried me much. I thought it a needy time, for I had not yielded my heart to the will of God, though I had many impressions, and formed many resolutions; but the situations that I had been placed in, (having left my mother's house at the age of eight,) had not permitted me to do as I wished, although the kind counsels of my dear grandfather and pious teachers followed me wherever I went. Care after care oppressed me — my mother wandered about like a Jew — the young children who were in families were dissatisfied; all hope but in God was lost. I resolved, in my mind, to seek an interest in my Savior, and put my trust in Him; and never shall I forget the place or time when God spake to my troubled conscience. Justified by faith I found peace with God, the forgiveness of sin through Jesus Christ my Lord. After living sixteen years without hope, and without a guide, May 6th, 1819, the Rev. Thomas Paul, baptized myself, and seven others, in obedience to the great command.

> We, on him our anchor cast—
> Poor and needy, lean on him,
> He will bring us through at last.

The same day, we received the right hand of

fellowship from our then beloved pastor. After
the absence of nine years, I had the happy privilege of meeting with two of the number, who were
unshaken in the faith; they have since gone to
join the spirits in glory. I had the happy privilege of attending them in sickness.

I now turn to the scenes of youth. George
again returned home, and we again provided a
home for mother and the little ones. He shipped
in the same vessel again, and affairs now seemed
to promise comfort and respectability; but mother chose to marry again; this was like death to
us all. George returned home, but was so disappointed that he shipped again to return no
more. Although a boy of sixteen, he was as
steady as most men at twenty. My cares were
consequently increased, having no one to share
them with me. My next brother, who lived
in South Essex, came to Salem to his mother's,
but was driven away by her husband, and came
to me; I carried him to Gloucester and left him
in the hands of the town; he stayed but three
weeks, and returned to me again; I then boarded him out for one dollar a week, until I could
procure suitable employment for him. When
winter came, poor mother's health was declining.
Little Samuel could do but little; my father-in-
law was very cross, his disappointment was very

great, for he expected to be supported by my
brother George and myself. I could not see my
mother suffer, therefore I left my place and went
to Salem to watch over her and Samuel, and lived
in the Rev. Dr. Bolle's family. In the Spring, I
returned to Boston, and took my brother Samuel
with me ; soon after, my sister Lucy left her
place and went to her mother, but was not
permitted to stay ; my mother wrote to me, re-
questing me to take care of her. I then determined, in my mind, to bring her to Boston, and
if possible, procure a place for her ; I then had
Samuel and John on my hands ; Lucy was not
nine, and very small of her age, I could not easily get her a place, but fortunately obtained board
for her and Samuel for one dollar a week. My
brother John, whom I had boarded, at last got a
place where he had wages. Soon the Lord opened the way for little Samuel ; Dr. Phelps took
him to bring up : so that I was left with one
only to sustain ; soon my hopes were blasted.
John left his place, and was several months on my
hands again ; finally, he made up his mind to go
to sea ; I was so thankful that he had concluded
to do something, that I took two months' wages
in advance to fit him out for Liverpool, in five
months he returned without a single thing but the
clothes he had on. The ship brought passengers

from Ireland.   As soon as the vessel arrived, he
came to seek me ; I went with him for his things ;
but passengers and all were gone.   His wages
were small, not enough to make him comfortable :
and, had not a friend given him a home, he would
again have been dependent on my exertions ;
another friend took Lucy, with whom she stayed
eleven months.   She lived in different familes
until she was about twelve years old ; I then put
her in the Rev. Mr. Mann's family, at Westmin-
ster, for a certain time, thinking it would be best
for her ; and John I left to fight his own battles.
My sister Silvia, was one of my greatest trials.
Knowing she was in Boston, my mother, in one
of her spells of insanity, got away from her
home and travelled to Boston after her ; she
came where I lived, my employers were very
kind to her, she tarried a few days, when I hired
a horse and chaise and took them both back to
Salem, and returned to my place in 1822, with a
.determination to do something for myself ; I left
my place after three months, and went to learn a
trade ; and after seven years of anxiety and toil,
I made up my mind to leave my country.   September 1st, 1823, Mr. Prince arrived from Russia.   Februrary 15th, 1824, we were married.
April 14th, we embarked on board the Romulus,
captain Epes Sargent commander, bound for

Russia. May 24th, arrived at Elsinore, left the same day for Copenhagen, where we remained twelve days. We visited the king's palace, and several other extensive and beautiful buildings. We attended a number of entertainments, among the Danes and English, who were religious; observed that their manners and customs were similar; they are attentive to strangers; the Sabbath is very strictly observed; the principal religion is Lutheran and Calvinistic, but all persuasions are tolerated. The languages are Dutch, French and English. The Danes are very modest and kind, but like all other nations, they know how to take the advantage. We left Copenhagen the 7th of June, and arrived at Cronstadt on the 19th; left there the 21st for St. Petersburg, and in a few hours, were happy to find ourselves at our place of destination, through the blessing of God, in good health, and soon made welcome from all quarters. We took lodgings with a Mrs. Robinson, a native of our country, who was Patience Mott, of Providence, who left here in the year 1813, in the family of Alexander Gabriel, the man who was taken for Mr. Prince. There I spent six weeks very pleasantly, visiting and receiving friends, in the manner of the country. While there I attended two of their parties; there were various amusements in which I did not par-

2*

take, which caused them much disappointment.
I told them my religion did not allow of dancing
or dice playing, which formed part of the amusements. As they were very strict in their religion, they indulged me in the same privilege. By
the help of God I was ever enabled to preserve
my stand.

Mr. Prince was born in Marlborough, and lived
in families in this city. In 1810 he went to
Gloucester, and sailed with captain Theodore
Stanwood, for Russia. He returned with him,
and remained in his family, and at this time
visited at my mother's. He sailed with captain Stanwood in 1812, for the last time. The
Captain took with him his son Theodore, in order
to place him in School in St. Petersburg. When the
Captain sailed for home, Mr. Prince went to serve
the Princess Purtossof, one of the noble ladies of
the Court. The palace where the imperial family reside is called the court, or the seat of Government. This magnificent building is adorned
with all the ornaments that possibly can be explained ; there are hundreds of people that inhabit
it, besides the soldiers that guard it. There are
several of these splendid edifices in the city and
vicinity. The one that I was presented in, was
in a village, three miles from the city. After
leaving the carriage, we entered the first ward ;

where the usual salutation by the guards was performed. As we passed through the beautiful
hall, a door was opened by two colored men in
official dress. The Emperor Alexander, stood on
his throne, in his royal apparel. The throne is
circular, elevated two steps from the floor, and
covered with scarlet velvet, tasseled with gold;
as I entered, the Emperor stepped forward with
great politeness and condescension, and welcomed me, and asked several questions; he then
accompanied us to the Empress Elizabeth; she
stood in her dignity, and received me in the same
manner the Emperor had. They presented me
with a watch, &c. It was customary in those
days, when any one married, belonging to the
court, to present them with gifts, according to
their standard; there was no prejudice against
color; there were there all casts, and the people
of all nations, each in their place.

The number of colored men that filled this
station was twenty; when one dies, the number
is immediately made up. Mr. Prince filled the
place of one that had died. They serve in turns,
four at a time, except on some great occasions,
when all are employed. Provision is made for
the families within or without the palace. Those
without go to court at 8 o'clock in the morning;
after breakfasting, they take their station in the

halls, for the purpose of opening the doors, at signal given, when the Emperor and Empress pass.

First of August, we visited the burying-ground where the people meet, as they say, to pay respect to their dead. It is a great holiday; they drink and feast on the grave stones, or as near the grave as they can come; some groan and pray, and some have music and dancing. At a funeral no one attends except the invited; after the friends arrive, a dish of rice, boiled hard, with raisins, is handed round; all are to take a spoonful, with the same spoon, and out of the same dish; in the meanwhile the priest, with his clerk, performs the ceremony, perfuming the room with incense. The lid is not put on to the coffin, the corpse being laid out in his or her best dress. The torch-men (who are dressed in black garments, made to slope down to their feet, with broad brimmed hats that cover their shoulders,) form a procession, with lighted torches in their hands, bowing their heads as they pass along very gravely; then comes one more with the lid on his head; then the hearse with the corpse drawn by four horses, covered with black gowns down to their feet; they all move along with great solemnity. Before entering the grave-yard, the procession goes to an adjoining church, where there are many ladies, placed on benches, side by side, according to their ages; the ladies dressed as if they were going to a ball-room, displaying a most dreadful appearance. Each one has her hands crossed, and holding in one of them a pass to give to Peter, that they may enter into Heaven. At this place they light their candles, and receive their rice in the manner before mentioned. The top is then put on to the coffin, and the procession forms and repairs to the grave; the priest sanctifies the grave, then casts in dust, and the coffin is consigned to its narrow-house; then commence the yells; they drink, eat cake, black bread, and finish their rice, when the party return back to dinner, where every thing has been prepared during their absence. This is the Greek mode of burying their dead. On the birth of a child, the babe is not dressed until it is baptized; it is immersed all over in water; a stand with an oval basin, is brought for the purpose by the clerk. The mother is presented with gifts, which are placed under her pillow. Should the babe die before this rite is performed, it is not placed with the others; but should it die having been baptized, although not more than two hours old, it is dressed and placed on the bench at church with the rest. In this manner, the common people bury their dead.

When any of the imperial family dies, they are laid in state forty days, and every thing accordingly. There is a building built expressly for the imperial families, where their remains are deposited. In the front part of it, the criminals that have rebelled against the imperial family are placed in cells, thus combining the prison and the tomb; and in sailing by, these miserable creatures are exposed to the careless gaze of unfeeling observers.

St. Petersburg was inundated October 9th, 1824. The water rose sixteen feet in most parts of the city; many of the inhabitants were drowned. An island between the city and Cronstadt, containing five hundred inhabitants, was inundated, and all were drowned, and great damage was done at Cronstadt. The morning of this day was fair; there was a high wind. Mr. Prince went early to the palace, as it was his turn to serve; our children boarders were gone to school; our servant had gone of an errand. I heard a cry, and to my astonishment, when I looked out to see what was the matter, the waters covered the earth. I had not then learned the language, but I beckoned to the people to come in. The waters continued to rise until 10 o'clock, A. M. The waters were then within two inches of my window, when they ebbed and went out as fast as they had come in, leaving to our view a dreadful sight. The people who came into my house for their safety retired, and I was left alone. At four o'clock in the afternoon, there was darkness that might be felt, such as I had never experienced before. My situation was the more painful, being alone, and not being able to speak. I waited until ten in the evening; I then took a lantern, and started to go to a neighbor's, whose children went to the same school with my boarders. I made my way through a long yard, over the bodies of men and beasts, and when opposite their gate I sunk; I made one grasp, and the earth gave away; I grasped again, and fortunately got hold of the leg of a horse, that had been drowned. I drew myself up, covered with mire, and made my way a little further, when I was knocked down by striking against a boat, that had been washed up and left by the retiring waters; and as I had lost my lantern, I was obliged to grope my way as I could, and feeling along the walk, I at last found the door that I aimed at. My family were safe and they accompanied me home. At 12 o'clock, Mr. Prince came home, as no one was permitted to leave the palace, till his majesty had viewed the city. In the morning the children and the girl returned, and I went to view the pit into which I had sunk.

It was large enough to hold a dozen like myself, where the earth had caved in. Had not the horse been there, I should never again have seen the light of day, and no one would have known my fate. Thus through the providence of God, I escaped from the flood and the pit.

> My helper, God, I bless thy name;
> The same thy power, thy grace the same;
> I 'midst ten thousand dangers stand,
> Supported by thy guardian hand."

Should I attempt to give an account of all the holidays, it would fill volumes. The next to notice is Christmas and New Year. The first day of January a grand masquerade is given by his majesty, at the winter palace; forty thousand tickets are distributed; every thing is done in order; every gentleman wears a mask and cloak, and carries a lady with him. They are formed in a procession, and enter at the west gate; as they pass through, all the golden vessels and ornaments are displayed; these were back of a counter, which extends two hundred feet; there the company receive a cup of hot chocolate, and a paper of comfits, and a bun; a great many are in attendance, as a vast many persons are permitted to pass in and view the palace, and go out at the east gate.

The 6th of January is a still greater day, for then the water is christened; a church is built on the ice, ornamented with gold and evergreens, and a row of spruce trees, extending from the door of the palace to the church. At this time all the nobles, of different nations, make their appearance in their native costume. The Patriarch, Archbishops, and other dignitaries of the court, have a service; then they pass through and christen the water, and make it holy; then there is a great rush of the people for this holy water. On the plain an ice hill is built, eighty feet high, where the emperor and his court exercise themselves.

Februrary 10th is another holiday. Buildings are constructed on the plain for the occasion. All kinds of amusements may be found here, and all kinds of animals seen; much time and money are spent. The buildings are built in rotation. All the children of the different seminaries and institutions of education, are driven round in gilded carriages to witness the performances. After this is the great Fast, previous to the crucifixion of our Saviour. Then Christ is represented as riding into Jerusalem; branches of trees are placed on the ice, and strewed through the streets, and every performance is carried out. The Saviour is made of white marble; he is crucified and buried, and on the third day he rises, according to the Scriptures; then the can-

3

nons are fired.   At the close of this forty day's
Fast, they have a great feast and fair; all business is suspended, and the festivity and frolic
continue for one week.

The first day of May is another great holiday.
The merchant's daughters are arranged on each
side of a long mall, in the beautiful gardens, and
arrayed in their best clothes, under the care of
an old woman known in their families; the gentlemen walk round and observe them, and if they
see one they fancy, they speak to the old woman;
she takes him to the parents and introduces him;
if the parties agree, they prepare for the be-
trothal.   It is their custom to marry one of their
own station.   All these holidays are accounted
sacred.   The first year I noted them all, as I
was accustomed to attend them.

May, 1825. I spent some time visiting the
different towns in the vicinity of St. Petersburg.
In the fall of the same year, the Emperor retired
to a warmer climate for the health of the Empress
Elizabeth.   January, 1826, the corpse of Alexander was brought in state, and was met three
miles from the city by the nobles of the court;
and they formed a procession, and the body was
brought in state into the building where the
imperial family were deposited.   March, of the
same year, the corpse of Elizabeth was brought

in the same manner. Constantine was then king of Poland, he was next heir to the throne, and was, unanimously voted by the people, but refused and resigned the crown in favor of his brother Nicholas. The day appointed the people were ordered to assemble as usual, at the ringing of the bells; they rejected Nicholas; a sign was given by the leaders that was well understood, and the people great and small rushed to the square and cried with one voice for Constantine. The emperor with his prime minister, and city governor, rode into the midst of them, entreating them to retire, without avail; they were obliged to order the cannons fired upon the mob; it was not known when they discharged them that the emperor and his ministers were in the crowd. He was wonderfully preserved, while both his friends and their horses were killed. There was a general seizing of all classes, who were taken into custody. The scene cannot be described; the bodies of the killed and mangled were cast into the river, and the snow and ice were stained with the blood of human victims; as they were obliged to drive the cannon to and fro in the midst of the crowd, the bones of those wounded, who might have been cured, were crushed. The cannon are very large, drawn by eight horses, trained for the purpose. The scene was awful;

all business was stopped. This deep plot originated in 1814, in Germany, with the Russian
nobility and German, under the pretence of a Free
Mason's Lodge. When they returned home they
increased their numbers and presented their chart
to the emperor for permission, which was granted. In the year 1822, the emperor being suspicious that all was not right, took their chart from
them. They carried it on in small parties, rapidly increasing, believing they would soon be
able to destroy all the imperial branches, and
have a republican government. Had not this
taken place, undoubtedly they would at last have
succeeded. So deep was the foundation of this
plot laid, both males and females were engaged
in it. The prison-houses were filled, and thirty
of the leading men were put in solitary confine-
ment, and twenty-six of the number died, four
were burned. A stage was erected and faggots
were placed underneath, each prisoner was secured by iron chains, presenting a most appalling
sight to an eye-witness. A priest was in attendance to cheer their last dying moments, then fire
was set to the faggots, and those brave men were
consumed. Others received the knout, and even
the princesses and ladies of rank were imprisoned
and flogged in their own habitations. Those that
survived their punishment were banished to Sibe-

ria. The mode of banishment is very imposing
and very heart-rending, severing them from all
dear relatives and friends, for they are never permitted to take their children.   When they arrive
at the gate of the city, their first sight is a guard
of soldiers, then wagons with provisions, then the
noblemen in their banished apparel guarded, then
each side, conveyances for the females, then ladies in order, guarded by soldiers.

Preparations were now being made for the
coronation of the new Emperor and Empress.
This took place September, 1826, in Moscow,
555 miles south-east from St. Petersburg. All
persons engaged in the court were sent before-
hand, in order to prepare for the coming event.
After his majesty's laws were read, as usual on
such occasions, those who wished to remain in
his service did so, and those who did not were
discharged.

After the coronation, the Emperor and his
court returned to St. Petersburg. June, 1827, war
was declared between Russia and Turkey. They
had several battles, with varied success. The Russians surrounded and laid siege to Constantinople.
The Sultan of Turkey sued for peace, and a
treaty was at last signed, and peace was proclaimed in 1829. In March, of the same year,
war was declared with Poland.   1831. The chol-
3*

era, that malignant disease, made its appearance
in Austria, from thence to little Russia, making
great ravages, thousands of people falling a prey.
It then began to rage in St. Petersburg, carrying
off 9255.   This disease first appeared in Mada-
gascar, 1814, where most of the inhabitants died.
It is called the plague, that God sent among the
people of Israel and other nations, for centuries
back.   Much might be said of this dreadful disease and others that are but little known in this
country.   God often visits nations, families, and
persons, with judgments as well as mercies.

The present Emperor and Empress are cour-
teous and affable.   The Empress would often
send for the ladies of the court at 8 oclock in the
evening to sup with her : when they arrive at the
court they form a procession and she takes the
lead.   On entering the hall, the band strikes up ;
there are two long tables on each side, and in the
midst circular tables for the Imperial family.   The
tables are spread apparently with every variety
of eatables and desserts, but everything is artificial,
presenting a novel appearance.   When the company are seated, the Emperor and Empress walk
around the tables and shake hands with each individual, as they pass.   The prisoners of war who
are nobles, are seated by themselves with their
faces veiled.   There is a tender or waiter to each

person, with two plates, one with soup and the other with something else. After a variety of courses, in one hour they are dismissed by the band. They then retire to another part of the palace to attend a ball or theatrical amusements. At the Empress' command they are dismissed. She carries power and dignity in her countenance, and is well adapted to her station. And after her late amusements at night, she would be out at an early hour in the morning, visiting the abodes of the distressed, dressed in as common apparel as any one here, either walking, or riding in a common sleigh. At her return she would call for her children, to take them in her arms and talk to them. " She riseth while it is yet night and giveth meat to her household and a portion to her maidens, she stretcheth out her hands to the poor, yea, she reacheth out her hands to the needy ; she is not afraid of the snow, for all her household are clothed in scarlet." Then she would go to the cabinet of his Majesty ; there she would write and advise with him.

The Russian ladies follow the fashions of the French and English. Their religion is after the Greek Church. There are no seats in their churches ; they stand, bow, and kneel, during the service. The principal church is on the Main street. There are the statues of the great com-

manders that have conquered in battle. They
are clad in brass, with flags in their hands, and
all their ancient implements of war are deposited
there. The altar is surrounded by statues of the
Virgin Mary and the twelve apostles. When
Russia is at war, and her armies are about to
engage in battle, it is here that the Emperor and
his family and court, come to pray for victory
over the enemy. The day they engaged in battle against the Poles, the Empress Dowager took
her death; she was embalmed and laid in state
six weeks in the hall of the winter palace. I
went a number of times to see her, and the people pay her homage, and kiss the hands of that
lump of clay. All religion is tolerated, but the
native Russians are subject to the Greek Church.
There are a number of institutions in St. Petersburg where children of all classes have the privilege of instruction. The sailors' and soldiers'
boys enter the corps at the age of seven, and are
educated for that purpose. The girls remain in
the barracks with their parents, or go to some
institution where they are instructed in all the
branches of female education. There are other
establishments, where the higher classes send
their children.

There is another spacious building called the
Market, half a mile square, where all kinds of

articles may be bought. Between the Market and the church there is a block of buildings where silver articles of all kinds are to be purchased. These stores present a very superb appearance and are visited by every foreigner that comes into the place. Besides these buildings, Main Street is lined with elegant buildings with projecting windows, to the extent of twelve miles. Nearly at the termination of the street there is a spacious building of stone which encloses the Taberisey Garden, so called from its having every kind of tree, shrub, flower and fruit, of the known world, which flourish alike in winter as in summer. There is an extensive Frozen Market which forms a square as large as Boston Common. This space of ground is covered with counters, on which may be purchased every variety of eatable, such as frozen fish, fowl, and meats of every description, besides every other article of commerce which will bear the extreme cold of a St. Petersburg winter. This city was founded by Peter the Great, and built upon a bog which was occupied by a few fishermen's huts, and belonged to the Finns. It is situated at the extremity of the Gulf of Finland, and is built partly on the main land and partly on several small islands. The foundation of the city is extremely marshy, which subjects it to frequent inundations. For

this reason there are canals which are cut through
the streets, very beautifully laid out, faced with
granite, railed with iron chains nubbed with brass,
with bridges to cross from one street to the other.
The city houses are built of stone and brick, and
twice the thickness of American houses. They
are heated by Peaches, of similar construction to
our furnaces; the outside of which is faced with
China tiles, presenting a very beautiful appearance. The village houses are built of logs corked
with oakum, where the peasants reside. This
class of people till the land, most of them are
slaves and are very degraded. The rich own the
poor, but they are not suffered to separate families or sell them off the soil. All are subject to
the Emperor, and no nobleman can leave without
his permission. The mode of travelling is prin-
cipally by stages which are built something like
our omnibusses, with settees upon the top railed
and guarded by soldiers, for the purpose of protecting the travellers from the attacks of wild
beasts. The common language is a mixture of
Sclavonian and Polish. The nobility make use
of the modern Greek, French and English. I
learned the languages in six months, so as to be
able to attend to my business, and also made some
proficiency in the French. My time was taken
up in domestic affairs; I took two children to

board, the third week after commencing house-
keeping, and increased their numbers. The
baby linen making and childrens' garments were
in great demand. I started a business in these
articles and took a journeywoman and apprenti-
ces. The present Empress is a very active one,
and inquired of me respecting my business, and
gave me much encouragement by purchasing of
me garments for herself and children, handsome-
ly wrought in French and English styles, and
many of the nobility also followed her example.
It was to me a great blessing that we had the
means of grace afforded us. The Rev. Richard
Kenell, was the Protestant pastor. We had service twice every Sabbath, and evening prayer
meetings, also a female society, so that I was
occupied at all times.

At the time of the inundation, the Bibles and
other books belonging to the society, were injured.
But Mr. Kenell took the liberty to purchase at
full price and sell at an advance. In order that
the poor might have them, we all agreed to labor
for that purpose. I often visited the matron of
the Empress' children, and encouraged by her I
took some to the Palace, and by this means disposed of many at head quarters. Other friends
without the court continued to labor until hundreds and thousands were disposed of. The old

Bishop finding his religion was in danger sent a petition to the Emperor that all who were found distributing Bibles and Tracts should be punished severely. Many were taken and imprisoned, two devoted young men were banished; thus the righteous were punished, while evil practices were not forbidden, for there the sin of licentiousness is very common.

I have mentioned that the climate did not agree with me; in winter my lungs were much affected. It was the advice of the best physicians that I had better not remain in Russia during another cold season. However painful it was to me to return without my husband, yet life seemed desirable, and he flattered me and himself that he should soon follow. It is difficult for any one in the Emperor's employment to leave when they please. Mr. Prince thought it best for me to return to my native country, while he remained two years longer to accumulate a little property, and then return — but death took him away. I left St. Petersburg, August 14th, 1833, having been absent about nine years and six months. On the 17th, I sailed from Cronstadt, for New York. Arrived at Elsinore the 25th. Tuesday, 29, left. September the 2d, laid to in a gale. September 18th, made Plymouth, Old England, 19th sailed. Arrived in New York, Oct. 10th.

Left there Tuesday 18th, arrived in Boston the 23d. Sabbath, Nov. 9th, I had the privilege of attending service in the old place of worship. On this day I also had the pleasure of meeting with an old friend of my grandfather, nearly one hundred years of age. I found things much changed ; my mother and sister Silvia died in 1827, (that I was aware of.) The Rev. T. Paul was dead, and many of my old friends were gone to their long home. The old church and society was in much confusion ; I attempted to worship with them but it was in vain. The voyage was of great benefit to me. By the advice of friends I applied to a Mrs. Mott, a female physician in the city, that helped me much. I am indebted to God for his great goodness in guiding my youthful steps ; my mind was directed to my fellow brethren whose circumstances were similar to my own. I found many a poor little orphan destitute and afflicted, and on account of color shut out from all the asylums for poor children. At this my heart was moved, and I proposed to my friends the necessity of a home for such, where they might be sheltered from the contaminating evils that beset their path. For this purpose I called a meeting of the people and laid before them my plan : as I had had the privilege of assisting in forming an Asylum for

such a purpose in St. Petersburg, I thought it
would be well to establish one on the same princi-
ples, not knowing that any person had had a
thought of anything of the kind. We commenced with eight children. I gave three months of
my time. A board was formed of seven females,
with a committee of twelve gentlemen of standing, to superintend. At the end of three months
the committee was dispensed with, and for want
of funds our society soon fell through.

I passed my time in different occupations and
making arrangements for the return of my husband, but death took him from me. I made my
home at the Rev. J. W. Holman's, a Free Will
Baptist, until I sailed for Jamaica. There had
been an Anti-Slavery Society established by W.
L. Garrison, Knapp, and other philanthropists of
the day. Their design was the amelioration of
the nominally free colored people of these States,
and the emancipation of the slaves in other States.
These meetings I attended with much pleasure,
until a contention broke out among themselves;
there has been a great change in some things,
but much remains to be done; possibly I may
not see so clearly as some, for the weight of
prejudice has again oppressed me, and were it
not for the promises of God, one's heart would
fail, for *He* made man in his own image, in the

image of God, created he him, male and female, that they should have dominion over the fish of the sea, the fowl of the air, and the beast of the field, &c. This power did God give man, that thus far should he go and no farther; but man has disobeyed his Maker, and become vain in his imagination, and their foolish hearts are darkened. We gather from this, that God has in all ages of the world punished every nation and people for their sins. The sins of my beloved country are not hid from his notice; his all seeing eye sees and knows the secrets of all hearts; the angels that kept not their first estate but left their own habitations, he hath reserved in everlasting chains unto the great day.

My mind, after the emancipation in the West Indies, was bent upon going to Jamaica. A field of usefulness seemed spread out before me. While I was thinking about it, the Rev. Mr. Ingraham, who had spent seven years there, arrived in the city. He lectured in the city at the Marlboro' Chapel, on the results arising from the emancipation at the British Islands. He knew much about them, he had a station at a mountain near Kingston, and was very desirous to have persons go there to labor. He wished some one to go with him to his station. He called on me with the Rev. Mr. William Collier, to per-

suade me to go. I told him it was my intention
to go if I could make myself useful, but that I
was sensible that I was very limited in education.
He told me that the moral·condition of the people was very bad, and needed labor aside from
any thing else.

I left America, November 16th, 1840, in the
ship Scion, Captain Mansfield, bound for Jamaica,
freighted with ice and machinery for the silk fac-
tory. There were on board a number of handi-
craftsmen and other passengers. We sailed on
Monday afternoon, from Charlestown, Massachusetts. It rained continually until Saturday. Sunday, the 23d, was a fine day. Mr. De Grass, a
young colored clergyman, was invited to perform
divine service, which he did with much propriety.
He spoke of the dangers we had escaped and the
importance of being prepared to meet our God,
(he died of fever about three weeks after arriving at Jamaica,) some who were able to attend
came on deck, and listened to him with respect,
while others seemed to look on in derision ; these
spent the afternoon and evening in card-playing.
About twelve at night a storm commenced ; on
Monday were in great peril ; the storm continued
until Friday, the 27th. On that day a sail was
seen at some distance making towards us, the
captain judging her to be a piratical vessel, or-

dered the women and children below, and the
men to prepare for action. The pirates were
not inclined to hazard an engagement; when
they saw the deck filled with armed men they
left us. Thus were we preserved from the storm
and from the enemy. Sabbath, 29th, divine service,—our attention was directed to the goodness
of God, in sparing us.

Monday, and we mortals are still alive. Tues-
day, thus far the Lord has led us on. Wednesday, thus far his power prolongs our days.
Thursday, December 3d, to-day made Turks
Island. Friday, this day had a view of Hayti,
its lofty mountains presented a sublime prospect.
Saturday, we had a glance at Cuba. Sunday,
December 6th, at six o'clock in the evening,
dropped anchor at St. Ann Harbor, Jamaica.
We blessed the Lord for his goodness in sparing
us to see the place of our destination; and here
I will mention my object in visiting Jamaica. I
hoped that I might aid, in some small degree, to
raise up and encourage the emancipated inhabitants, and teach the young children to read and
work, to fear God, and put their trust in the
Saviour. Mr. Whitmarsh and his friend came on
board and welcomed us. On Tuesday we went
on shore to see the place and the people; my intention had been to go directly to Kingston, but

4*

the people urged me to stay with them, and I thought it my duty to comply, and wrote to Mr. Ingraham to that effect. I went first to see the minister, Mr. Abbott; I thought as he was out, I had better wait his return. The people promised to pay me for my services, or send me to Kingston. When Mr. Abbott returned he made me an offer, which I readily accepted. As I lodged in the house of one of the class-leaders I attended her class a few times, and when I learned the method, I stopped. She then commenced her authority and gave me to understand if I did not comply I should not have any pay from that society. I spoke to her of the necessity of being born of the spirit of God before we become members of the church of Christ, and told her I was sorry to see the people blinded in such a way.

She was very angry with me and soon accomplished her end by complaining of me to the minister ; and I soon found I was to be dismissed, unless I would yield obedience to this class-leader. I told the minister that I did not come there to be guided by a poor foolish woman. He then told me that I had spoken something about the necessity of moral conduct in church members. I told him I had, and in my opinion, I was sorry to see it so much neglected. He replied, that he hoped I would not express myself so except to

him; they have the gospel, he continued, and
let them into the church. I do not approve of
women societies; they destroy the world's con-
vention; the American women have too many of
them. I talked with him an hour. He paid me
for the time I had been there. I continued with
the same opinion, that something must be done
for the elevation of the children, and it is for that
I labor. I am sorry to say the meeting house is
more like a play house than a place of worship.
The pulpit stands about the middle of the building, behind are about six hundred children that
belong to the society; there they are placed for
Sabbath School, and there they remain until service is over, playing most of the time. The
house is crowded with the aged and the young,
the greater part of them barefooted. Some have
on bonnets, but most of the women wear straw
hats such as our countrymen wear.

I gave several Bibles away, not knowing that
I was hurting the minister's sale, the people buy
them of him at a great advance. I gave up my
school at St. Ann, the 18th of March. I took the
fever and was obliged to remain until the 7th of
April. The people of St. Ann fulfilled their
promise which they made to induce me to stop
with them. On the 11th of April I arrived at
Kingston, and was conducted to the Mico Institu-

tion, where Mr. Ingraham directed me to find him; he had lost his pulpit and his school, but Mr. Venning, the teacher, kindly received me. I remained there longer than I expected; the next morning he kindly sent one of the young men with me to the packet for my baggage. I then called on the American Consul, he told me he was very glad to see me for such a purpose as I had in view in visiting Jamaica, but he said it was a folly for the Americans to come to the island to better their condition; he said they came to him every day praying him to send them home.

He likewise mentioned to me the great mortality among the emigrants. The same day I saw the Rev. J. S. Beadslee, one of our missionaries, who wished me to accompany him forty miles into the interior of the country.

On May the 18th, I attended the Baptist Missionary meeting, in Queen Street Chapel; the house was crowded. Several ministers spoke of the importance of sending the gospel to Africa; they complimented the congregation on their liberality the last year, having given one hundred pounds sterling; they hoped this year they would give five hundred pounds, as there were five thousand members at the present time. There was but one colored minister on the platform. It is generally the policy of these missionaries to have the sanction of colored ministers, to all their assessments and taxes. The colored people give more readily, and are less suspicious of imposition, if one from themselves recommends the measure; this the missionaries understand very well, and know how to take advantage of it. On the 22d and 23d of June, the colored Baptists held their missionary meeting, the number of ministers, colored and mulattoes, was 18, the colored magistrates were present. The resolutions that were offered were unanimously accepted, and every thing was done in love and harmony. After taking up a contribution, they concluded with song and prayer, and returned home saying jocosely, " they would turn macroon hunters."

Mack is the name of a small coin in circulation at Jamaica. I called, on my return, at the market, and counted the different stalls. For vegetables and poultry 196, all numbered and under cover; beside 70 on the ground; these are all attended by colored women. The market is conveniently arranged, as they can close the gates and leave all safe. There are nineteen stalls for fresh fish, eighteen for pork, thirty for beef, eighteen for turtle. These are all regular built markets, and are kept by colored men and

women. These are all in one place. Others
also may be found, as with us, all over the city.
Thus it may be hoped they are not the stupid set
of beings they have been called; here *surely we
see industry;* they are enterprising and quick in
their perceptions, determined to possess themselves, and to possess property besides, and quite
able to take care of themselves. They wished
to know why I was so inquisitive about them. I
told them we had heard in America that you are
lazy, and that emancipation has been of no benefit to you; I wish to inform myself of the truth
respecting you, and give a true account on my
return. Am I right? More than two hundred
people were around me listening to what I said.

They thanked me heartily. I gave them some
tracts, and told them if it so pleased God I would
come back to them and bring them some more
books, and try what could be done with some of
the poor children to make them better. I then
left them, and went to the East Market, where
there are many of all nations. The Jews and
Spanish looked at me very black. The colored
people gathered around me. I gave them little
books and tracts, and told them I hoped to see
them again.

There are in this street upwards of a thousand
young women and children, living in sin of every

kind. From thence I went to the jail, where there were seventeen men, but no women. There were in the House of Correction three hundred culprits; they are taken from there, to work on plantations. I went to the Admiral's house, where the emigrants find a shelter until they can find employment, then they work and pay[1] for their passage. Many leave their homes and come to Jamaica under the impression that they are to have their passage free, and on reaching the island are to be found, until they can provide for themselves.

How the mistake originated, I am not able to say, but on arriving here, strangers poor and un-acclimated, find the debt for passage money hard and unexpected. It is remarkable that whether fresh from Africa, or from other islands, from the South or from New England, they all feel de-ceived on this point. I called on many Ameri-cans and found them poor and discontented,— rueing the day they left their country, where, notwithstanding many obstacles, their parents lived and died,—a country they helped to conquer with their toil and blood; now shall their children stray abroad and starve in foreign lands.

There is in Jamaica an institution, established in 1836, called the Mico Institution. It is named after its founder, Madame Mico, who left a large sum of money to purchase, (or rather to ransom, the one being a Christian act, the other a sin against the Holy Ghost, who expressly forbids such traffic.) Madame Mico left this money to ransom the English who were in bondage to the Algerines; if there was any left, it was to be devoted to the instruction of the colored people in the British Isles.

Beside the Mico establishment, there are in Jamaica twenty-seven church missionary schools, where children are taught gratis. Whole number taught, 952. London Missionary Society Schools, sixteen; the number taught not ascertained. National Schools, thirty-eight. There are also the Wesleyan, Presbyterian and Moravian Schools; it is supposed there are private schools, where three or four thousand are educated in the city of Kingston, and twice the number in the street without the means of instruction. All the children and adults taught in the above named schools, are taxed £1 a year, except the English Church School, this is the most liberal. The Rev. Mr. Horton, a Baptist minister in Kingston, told me he had sent ninety children away from the Baptist school because they did not bring their money. It is sufficient to say they had it not to bring!

Most of the people of Jamaica are emancipated

slaves, many of them are old, worn out and degraded. Those who are able to work, have yet
many obstacles to contend with, and very little to
encourage them; every advantage is taken of
their ignorance; the same spirit of cruelty is opposed to them that held them for centuries in bondage; even religious teaching is bartered for their
hard earnings, while they are allowed but thirty-
three cents a day, and are told if they will not
work for that they shall not work at all; an extraordinary price is asked of them for every thing
they may wish to purchase, even the Bibles are
sold to them at a large advance on the first purchase. Where are their apologists, if they are
found wanting in the strict morals that Christians
ought to practice? Who kindly says, forgive
them when they err. "Forgive them, this is the
bitter fruit of slavery." Who has integrity sufficient to hold the balance when these poor people
are to be weighed? Yet their present state is
blissful, compared with slavery.

Many of the farmers bring their produce twenty or thirty miles. Some have horses or ponys,
but most of them bring their burdens on their
head. As I returned from St. Andrew's Mountain, where I had been sent for by a Mr. Rose, I
was overtaken by a respectable looking man on
horseback; we rode about ten miles in company.

The story he told me of the wrongs he and his
wife had endured while in slavery, are too horrible
to narrate.   My heart sickens when I think of it.
He asked me many questions, such as where I
came from? why I came to that Isle? where
had I lived, &c.   I told him I was sent for by
one of the missionaries to help him in his school.
Indeed, said he, our color need the instruction.
I asked him why the colored people did not hire
for themselves?   We would be very glad to, he
replied, but our money is taken from us so fast
we cannot.   Sometimes they say we must all
bring 1*l.*; to raise this, we have to sell at a loss
or to borrow, so that we have nothing left for
ourselves; the Macroon hunters take all—this is
a nickname they give the missionaries and the
class-leaders—a cutting sarcasm this!

Arrived at a tavern, about a mile from Kingston, I bade the man adieu, and stopped for my
guide.   The inn-keeper kindly invited me in;
he asked me several questions, and I asked him
as many.   How do the people get along, said I,
since the emancipation?   The negroes, he replied, will have the island in spite of the d——.
Do not you see how they live, and how much
they can bear?   We cannot do so.   This man
was an Englishman, with a large family of mulatto children.   I returned with my mind fully

made up what to do. Spent three weeks at the Mico establishment, and three with my colored friends from America. We thought something ought to be done for the poor girls that were destitute; they consulted with their friends, called a meeting, and formed a society of forty ; each agreed to pay three dollars a year and collect, and provide a house, while I came back to Ameriica to raise the money for all needful articles for the school. Here I met Mr. Ingraham for the first time ; he had come from the mountains, and his health had rapidly declined. Wishing to get his family home before the Lord took him away, he embarked for Baltimore in the Orb, and I sailed for Philadelphia, July 20th, 1841, twenty-one days from Jamaica, in good health. I found there, Fitz W. Sargent's family, from Gloucester, who I lived with when a little girl ; they received me very kindly, and gave donations of books and money for that object.

I met the Anti Slavery Society at Mrs. Lucretia Motts, who took great interest in the cause. I visited among the friends, and spent my time very pleasantly. August 5th, I started for New York ; arrived safely, and staid with an old friend ; ascertained that Mr. Ingraham's family were at Newark, at Theodore Wells'. He died four days after his arrival. I was invited to Mrs. Ingraham's, (his cousin's widow) to spend a week. There I met with much encouragement to labor in the cause. Missionaries were coming and going, and all seemed to be interested in my object. Saturday evening I went to the bath room, where I left my neck ribbon: returning after it, I had the misfortune to fall through an open trap door, down fifteen feet, on hard coal. I had no light with me. I dislocated my left shoulder, and was generally very much bruised; my screams brought the girl to my assistance, and by the help of God she brought me out of the cellar; it was some time before a surgeon could be procured; at last Dr. Josselyn came to my relief, and set my shoulder. I was obliged to remain at Mrs. Ingraham's three weeks; as soon as I was able, I left there for Boston. I intended to have gone by the western boat, but by mistake got on board Captain Comstock's, and was exposed on deck all night in a damp east wind, and when I arrived at the landing I could not assist myself; a sailor, who saw and pitied my situation, kindly took care of me and my baggage, and, on my arrival in Boston, procured a carriage for me. If it had not been for his kindness, I know not how I should have got along.

As soon as I was able, I commenced my task of collecting funds for my Free Labor School in

Jamaica. I collected in Boston and vicinity, in New York and Philadelphia, but not sufficient to make up the required sum, and I was obliged to take fifty dollars from my own purse, thinking that when I returned to Jamaica, they would refund the money to me. April 15th, embarked on board the brig Norma, of New York, for Jamaica. I arrived at Kingston May 6th, and found every thing different from what it was when I left; the people were in a state of agitation, several were hanged, and the insurrection was so great that it was found necessary to increase the army to quell it. Several had been hanged. On the very day I arrived a man was hanged for shooting a man as he passed through the street. Such was the state of things that it was not safe to be there.

A few young people met to celebrate their freedom on an open plain, where they hold their market; their former masters and mistresses, envious of their happiness, conspired against them, and thought to put them down by violence. This only served to increase their numbers; but the oppressors were powerful, and succeeded in accomplishing their revenge, although many of them were relations. There was a rule among the slave holders, to take care of the children they have by their slaves; they select them out and place them in asylums. Those who lived with

5*

their white fathers were allowed great power over
their slave mothers and her slave children; my
heart was often grieved to see their conduct to
their poor old grand parents. Those over twenty-
one were freed in 1834, all under twenty-one were
to serve their masters till twenty-one. It is well
known that at that time, the children, alike with
others, received twenty-five dollars a head for
their relatives. Were I to tell all my eyes have
seen among that people, it would not be credited.
It is well known that those that were freed, knowing their children were still in bondage, were not
satisfied. In the year 1838, general freedom
throughout the British Islands gave the death blow
to the power of the master, and mothers received
with joy their emancipated children; they no
longer looked the picture of despair, fearing to
see their mulatto son or daughter beating or abu-
sing their younger brothers and sisters of a darker
skin. On this occasion there was an outrage committed by those who were in power. What little
the poor colored people had gathered during their
four years of freedom, was destroyed by violence;
their fences were broken down, and their horses
and hogs taken from them. Most of the mulattoes and masters are educated, many of them are
very poor, some are very rich; the property is
left to the oldest daughter, she divides it with her

brothers and sisters ; since slavery ended many
of them have married ; those who are poor, and
mean to live in sin, make for New Orleans and
other slave States ; many of the planters left the
island when slavery was abolished. In June, 1841,
a number of people arrived from Sierra Leone at
Jamaica ; these were Maroons who were banished
from the island. They were some of the original
natives who inhabited the mountains, and were
determined to destroy the whites. These Maroons
would secrete themselves in trees, and arrest the
whites as they passed along ; they would pretend
to guide them, when they would beat and abuse
them as the whites did their slaves ; the English,
finding themselves defeated in all their plans to
subdue them, proposed to take them by craft.
They made a feast in a large tavern in Kingston,
and invited them to come. After they had eaten,
they were invited on board three ships of war that
were all ready to set sail for Sierra Leone ; many
of them were infants in their mother's arms,
they were well taken care of by the English and
instructed ; they were removed about the year
1796—they are bright and intelligent; I saw and
conversed with them ; when they heard of the
abolition of slavery, they sent a petition to Queen
Victoria that they might return to Jamaica, which
was granted. Several of them were very old

when they returned ; they were men and women when they left the island, they had not forgot the injuries they had received from the hands of man, nor the mercies of God to them, nor his judgments to their enemies. Their numbers were few, but their power was great ; they say the island, of right, belongs to them. Had there been a vessel in readiness, I should have come back immediately, it seemed useless to attempt to establish a Manual Labor School, as the government was so unsettled that I could not be protected. Some of my former friends were gone as teachers to Africa, and some to other parts of the island. I called on the American Consul to consult with him, he said that although such a school was much wanted, yet every thing seemed so unsettled that I had no courage to proceed. I told him there was so much excitement that I wished to leave the island as soon as he could find me a passage, it seemed useless to spend my time there. As soon as it was known that I intended to return, a movement was made to induce me to remain. I was persuaded to try the experiment for three months, not thinking their motive was bad. Before I left the United States, I got all that was needed, within fifty dollars. The fifty dollars I got from my own purse, expecting they would pay me. It cost me ten dollars for freight, and twenty-five for passage money ; these people that I had hoped to serve, were much taken up with the things I had brought, they thought that I had money, and I was continually surrounded ; the thought of color was no where exhibited, much notice was taken of me. I was invited to breakfast in one place, and to dine in another, &c. A society was organized, made up of men and women of authority. A constitution was drafted by my consent, by those who were appointed to meet at my rooms. Between the time of the adjournment they altered it to suit themselves. At the time appointed we came together with a spirit apparently becoming any body of Christians ; most of them were members of Christian churches. The meeting was opened with reading the Scriptures and prayer. Then said the leader, since our dear sister has left her native land and her friends to come to us, we welcome her with our hearts and hands. She will dwell among us, and we will take care of her— Brethren think of it ! after which he sat down, and the constitution was called for. The Preamble held out all the flattery that a fool could desire ; after which they commenced the articles, supposing that they could do as they thought best. The fourth article unveiled their design. As we have designed to take care of our sister, *we the undersigned will take charge of all she has brought* ;

the vote was called, every person rose in a moment except myself : every eye was upon me ; one asked me why I did not vote, I made no answer—they put the vote again and again, I remained seated. Well, said the President, we can do nothing without her vote ; they remained some time silent, and then broke up the meeting. The next day the deacon called to see what the state of my mind was, and some of the women proposed that we should have another meeting. I told them no, I should do no more for them. As soon as they found they could not get the things in the way they intended, they started to plunder me ; but I detected their design, and was on my guard. I disposed of the articles, and made ready to leave when an opportunity presented. A more skilful plan than this, Satan never designed, but the power of God was above it. It is not surprising that this people are full of deceit and lies, this is the fruits of slavery, it makes master and slaves knaves. It is the rule where slavery exists to swell the churches with numbers, and hold out such doctrines as, *obedience to tyrants*, is a duty to God. I went with a Baptist woman to the house of a minister of the Church of England, to have her grandchild christened before it died ; she told me if she did not have it christened, it would rise up in judgment against her. This poor deluded creature was a class leader in the Baptist Church, and such is the condition of most of the people : they seemed blinded to every thing but money. They are great for trade, and are united in their determination for procuring property, of which they have amassed a vast amount. Notwithstanding I had made over various articles to one of the American missionaries, a Mr. J. S. O. Beadslee, of Clarendon Mountains, I also gave to others, where they were needed, which receipts and letters I have in my possession. Notwithstanding all this, they made another attempt to rob me, and as a passage could not be obtained for me to return home, I was obliged to go to the Mico establishment again for safety, such was the outrage. Houses were broken open and robbed every night. I came very near being shot : there was a certain place where we placed ourselves the first of the evening. A friend came to bring us some refreshments, I had just left the window when a gun was fired through it, by one that often sat with us ; this was common in the time of slavery. Previous to vessels arriving, passages were engaged. I disposed of my articles and furniture at a very small profit. On the 1st of August, Capt. A. Miner arrived, and advertised for passengers. The American Consul procured me a passage, and on the 18th of August, myself and nine other passengers embarked for New York.

Before giving an account of the voyage from Jamaica, it may prove interesting to some readers, to have a brief description of the country. With her liberty secured to her, may she now rise in prosperity, morality, and religion, and become a happy people, whose God is the Lord.

WEST INDIES.

A denomination under which is comprehended a large chain of islands, extending in a curve from the Florida shore on the northern peninsula of America, to the Gulf of Venezuela on the southern. These islands belong to five European powers, viz : Great Britain, Spain, France, Holland, and Denmark. An inhabitant of New England can form no idea of the climate and the productions of these islands. Many of the particulars that are here mentioned, are peculiar to them all.

The climate in all the West India Islands is nearly the same, allowing for those accidental differences which the several situations and qualities of the lands themselves produce ; as they lie within the tropic of Cancer, and the sun is often almost at the meridian over their heads, they are continually subjected to a heat that would be intolerable but for the trade winds, which are so refreshing as to enable the inhabitants to attend to their various occupations, even under a noonday sun ; as the night advances, a breeze begins to be perceived, which blows smartly from the land, as it were from the centre towards the sea, to all points of the compass at once. The rains make the only distinction of seasons on these islands. The trees are green the year round ; they have no cold or frost; our heaviest rains are but dews comparatively ; with them floods of water are poured from the clouds. About May, the periodical rains from the South may be expected. Then the tropical summer, in all its splendor, makes its appearance. The nights are calm and serene, the moon shines more brightly than in New England, as do the planets and the beautiful galaxy. From the middle of August to the end of September the heat is most oppressive, the sea breeze is interrupted, and calms warn the inhabitants of the periodical rains, which fall in torrents about the first of October.

The most considerable and valuable of the British West India Islands, lies between the 75th and the 79th degrees of west longitude from London, and between 17 and 18 north latitude ; it is of an oval figure, 150 miles long from east to west, and sixty miles broad in the middle, containing 4,080,000 acres. An elevated ridge, called the Blue Mountains, runs lengthwise from east to west, whence numerous rivers take their rise on both sides. The year is divided into two seasons, wet and dry. The months of July, August, and September, are called the hurricane months. The best houses are generally built low, on account of the hurricanes and earthquakes. However pleasant the sun may rise, in a moment the scene may be changed ; a violent storm will suddenly arise, attended with thunder and lightning ; the rain falls in torrents, and the seas and rivers rise with terrible destruction. I witnessed this awful scene in June last, at Kingston, the capital of Jamaica ; the foundations of many houses were destroyed ; the waters, as they rushed from the mountains, brought with them the produce of the earth, large branches of trees, together with their fruit ; many persons were drowned, endeavoring to reach their homes ; those who succeeded, were often obliged to travel many miles out of their usual way. Many young children, without a parent's care, were at this time destroyed. A poor old woman, speaking of these calamities to me, thus expressed herself : " Not so bad now as in the time of slavery ; then God spoke very loud to *Bucker*, (the white people,) to let us go. Thank God,

ever since that they give us up, we go pray, and
we have it not so bad like as before." I would
recommend this poor woman's remark to the fair
sons and daughters of America, the land of the
pilgrims. " Then God spoke very loud." May
these words be engraved on the post of every
door in this land of New England. God speaks
very loud, and while his judgments are on the
earth, may the inhabitants learn righteousness !

The mountains that intersect this island, seem
composed of rocks, thrown up by frequent earthquakes or volcanoes. These rocks, though having little soil, are adorned with a great variety
of beautiful trees, growing from the fissues,
which are nourished by frequent rains, and
flourish in perpetual spring. From these mountains flow a vast number of small rivers of pure
water, which sometimes fall in cataracts, from
stupendous heights ; these, with the brilliant ver-
dure of the trees, form a most delightful land-
scape. Ridges of smaller mountains are on each
side of this great chain ; on these, coffee grows
in great abundance ; the valleys or plains between
these ridges, are level beyond what is usually
found in similar situations. The highest land in
the island is Blue Mountain Peak, 7150 feet above
the sea. The most extensive plain is thirty miles
long and five broad. Black River, in the Parish

of St. Elizabeth, is the only one navigable; flat-boats bring down produce from plantations about thirty miles up the river. Along the coast, and on the plains, the weather is very hot; but in the mountains the air is pure and wholesome; the longest days in summer are about thirteen hours, and the shortest in winter about eleven. In the plains are found several salt fountains, and in the mountains, not far from Spanish Town, is a hot bath of great medicinal virtues; this gives relief in the complaint called the dry-bowels malady, which, excepting the bilious and yellow fevers, is one of the most terrible distempers of Jamaica. The general produce of this island is sugar, rum, molasses, ginger, cotton, indigo, pimento, cocoa, coffees, several kinds of woods, and medicinal drugs. Fruits are in great plenty, as oranges, lemons, shaddoks, citrons, pomegranates, pine-apples, melons, pompions, guavas, and many others. Here are trees whose wood, when dry, is incorruptible; here is found the wild cinnamon tree, the mahogany, the cabbage, the palm, yielding an oil much esteemed for food and medicine. Here, too, is the soap tree, whose berries are useful in washing. The plantain is produced in Jamaica in abundance, and is one the most agreeable and nutritious vegetables in the world: it grows about four feet in height,

and the fruit grows in clusters, which is filled
with a luscious sweet pulp. The Banana is very
similar to the plantain, but not so sweet. The
whole island is divided into three counties, Mid-
dlesex, Surry, and Cornwall, and these into six
towns, twenty parishes, and twenty-seven villages.

This island was originally part of the Spanish
Empire in America, but it was taken by the
English in 1656. Cromwell had fitted out a
squadron under Penn and Venables, to reduce
the Spanish Island of Hispaniola; but there this
squadron was unsuccessful, and the commanders,
of their own accord, to atone for this misfortune,
made a descent on Jamaica, and having arrived
at St. Jago, soon compelled the whole island to
surrender.

Ever since, it has been subject to the English;
and the government, next to that of Ireland, is
the richest in the disposal of the crown. Port
Royal was formerly the capital of Jamaica; it
stood upon the point of a narrow neck of land,
which, towards the sea, forms part of the border
of a very fine harbor of its own name. The con-
veniences of this harbor, which was capable
of containing a thousand sail of large ships, and
of such depth as to allow them to load and unload
with the greatest ease, weighed so much with the
inhabitants, that they chose to build their capital

6*

on this spot, although the place was a hot, dry
sand, and produced none of the necessaries of
life, not even fresh water. About the beginning
of the year 1692, no place for its size could be
compared to this town for trade, wealth, and an
entire corruption of manners. In the month of
June in this year, an earthquake which shook
the whole island to the foundation, totally overwhelmed this city, so as to leave, in one quarter,
not even the smallest vestige remaining. In two
minutes the earth opened and swallowed up nine-
tenths of the houses, and two thousand people.
The waters gushed out from the openings of the
earth, and the people lay as it were in heaps : some
of them had the good fortune to catch hold
of beams and rafters of houses, and were afterwards saved by boats. Several ships were cast
away in the harbor, and the Swan Frigate, which
lay in the Dock, was carried over the tops of
sinking houses, and did not overset, but afforded
a retreat to some hundreds of people, who saved
their lives upon her. An officer who was in the
town at that time, says the earth opened and shut
very quick in some places, and he saw several
people sink down to the middle, and others appeared with their heads just above ground, and
were choked to death. At Savannah above a
thousand acres were sunk, with the houses and

people in them, the place appearing, for some time, like a lake; this was afterwards dried up, but no houses were seen. In some parts mountains were split, and at one place a plantation was removed to the distance of a mile. The inhabitants again rebuilt the city, but it was a second time, ten years after, destroyed by a great fire. The extraordinary convenience of the harbor tempted them to build it once more, and in 1722 it was laid in ruins by a hurricane, the most terrible on record.

Such repeated calamities seemed to mark out this spot as a devoted place; the inhabitants, therefore, resolved to forsake it forever, and to reside at the opposite bay, where they built Kingston, which is now the capital of the island. In going up to Kingston, we pass over a part of and between Port Royal, leaving the mountains on the left, and a small town on the right. There are many handsome houses built there, one story high, with particos, and every convenience for those who inhabit them. Not far from Kingston stands Spanish Town, which, though at present far inferior to Kingston, was once the capital of Jamaica, and is still the seat of government.

On the 3d of October, 1780, there was a dreadful hurricane, which overwhelmed the little

seaport town of Savannah, in Jamaica, and part
of the adjacent country ; very few houses were
left standing, and a great number of lives were
lost ; much damage was done also, and many
lives lost, in other parts of the island.

In January, 1823, a society was formed in
London for mitigating and gradually abolishing
slavery, throughout the British dominions, called
the Anti-Slavery Society. His Royal Highness,
the Duke of Gloucester, was President of the
Society ; in the list of Vice Presidents are the
names of many of the most distinguished philanthropists of the day, and among them that
of the never to be forgotton Mr. Wilberforce ; as
a bold champion, we see him going forward,
pleading the cause of our down-trodden brethren.
In the year 1834, it pleased God to break the
chains from 800,000 human beings, that had
been held in a state of personal slavery ; and
this great event was effected through the instru-
mentality of Clarkson, Wilberforce, and other
philanthropists of the day.

The population of Jamaica is nearly 400,000 ;
that of Kingston, the capital, 40,000. There are
many places of worship of various denominations, namely, Church of England, and of Scotland, Wesleyan, the Baptist, and Roman Cath-
olics, besides a Jewish Synagogue. These all

differ from what I have seen in New England, and from those I have seen elsewhere. The Baptist hold what they call class-meetings. They have men and women deacons and deaconesses in these churches; these hold separate class-meetings; some of these can read, and some cannot. Such are the persons who hold the office of judges, and go round and urge the people to come to the class, and after they come in twice or three times, they are considered candidates for baptism. Some pay fifty cents, and some more, for being baptized; they receive a ticket as a passport into the church, paying one mark a quarter, or more, and some less, but nothing short of ten pence, that is, two English shillings a year. They must attend their class once a week, and pay three pence a week, total twelve English shillings a year, besides the sums they pay once a month at communion, after service in the morning. On those occasions the minister retires, and the deacons examine the people, to ascertain if each one has brought a' ticket; if not, they cannot commune; after this the minister returns, and performs the ceremony, then they give their money and depart. The churches are very large, holding from four to six thousand; many bring wood and other presents to their class-leader, as a token of their attachment; where there are so many communicants, these presents, and the money exacted, greatly enrich these establishments. Communicants are so ignorant of the ordinance, that they join the church merely to have a decent burial; for if they are not members, none will follow them to the grave, and no prayers will be said over them; these are borne through the streets by four men, the coffin a rough box; not so if they are church members; as soon as the news is spread that one is dying, all the class, with their leader, will assemble at the place, and join in singing hymns; this, they say, is to help the spirit up to glory; this exercise sometimes continues all night, in so loud a strain, that it is seldom that any of the people in the neighborhood are lost in sleep.

After leaving Jamaica, the vessel was tacked to a south-west course. I asked the Captain what this meant. He said he must take the current as there was no wind. Without any ceremony, I told him it was not the case, and told the passengers that he had deceived us. There were two English men that were born on the island, that had never been on the water. Before the third day passed, they asked the Captain why they had not seen Hayti. He told them they passed when they were asleep. I told them it was not true, he was steering south south-west.

The passengers in the steerage got alarmed, and every one was asking the Captain what this meant. The ninth day we made land. "By ——," said the Captain, "this is Key West; come, passengers, let us have a vote to run over the neck, and I will go ashore and bring aboard fruit and turtle." They all agreed but myself. He soon dropped anchor. The officers from the shore came on board and congratulated him on keeping his appointment, thus proving that my suspicions were well founded. The Captain went ashore with these men, and soon came back, called for the passengers, and asked for their vote for him to remain until the next day, saying that he could by this delay, make five or six hundred dollars, as there had been a vessel wrecked there lately. They all agreed but myself. The vessel was soon at the side of the wharf. In an hour there were twenty slaves at work to unload her; every inducement was made to persuade me to go ashore, or set my feet on the wharf. A law had just been passed there that every free colored person coming there, should be put in custody on their going ashore; there were five colored persons on board; none dared to go ashore, however uncomfortable we might be in the vessel, or however we might desire to refresh ourselves by a change of scene. We remained at Key West four days.

September 3d, we set sail for New York, at 3 o'clock in the afternoon. At 10 o'clock a gale took us, that continued thirty-six hours; my state-room was filled with water, and my baggage all upset; a woman, with her little boy, and myself, were seated on a trunk thirty-six hours, with our feet pressed against a barrel to prevent falling; the water pouring over us at every breaker. Wednesday, the 9th, the sun shone out so that the Captain could take an observation. He found himself in great peril, near the coast of Texas. All hands were employed in pumping and bailing. On the eleventh, the New Orleans steamer came to our assistance; as we passed up the river, I was made to forget my own condition, as I looked with pity on the poor slaves, who were laboring and toiling, on either side, as far as could be seen with a glass. We soon reached the dock, and we were there on the old wreck a spectacle for observation; the whites went on shore and made themselves comfortable, while we poor blacks were obliged to remain on that broken, wet vessel. The people were very busy about me; one man asked me who I belonged to, and many other rude questions; he asked me where I was born; I told him Newburyport. "What were your parents' names?" I told him my father's name was Thomas Gardner; his countenance changed; said he, " I knew him well ; " and he proved friendly to me. He appeared very kind, and offered to arrange my affairs so that I might return to New York through the States. I thought it best to decline his proposal, knowing my spirit would not suffer me to pass on, and see my fellow-creatures suffering without a rebuke. We remained four days on the wreck; the boxes that contained the sugar were taken out ; the two bottom tiers were washed out clean. There were a great many people that came to see the vessel; they were astonished that she did not sink; they watched me very closely. I asked them what they wished. In the mean time, there came along a drove of colored people, fettered together in pairs by the wrist; some had weights, with long chains at their ankles, men and women, young and old. I asked them what that meant. They were all ready to answer. Said they, " these negroes have been impudent, and have stolen ; some of them are free negroes from the northern ships ; " " and what," I asked " are they there for ? " " For being on shore, some of them at night." I asked them who made them Lord over God's inheritance. They told me I was very foolish; they should think I had suffered enough to think of myself. I looked pretty bad, it is true ; I was seated on a box, but poorly dressed; the mate had taken my clothes to a washer-woman; why he took this care, he was afraid to send the cook or steward on shore, as they were colored people. I kept still; but the other woman seemed to be in perfect despair, running up and down the deck, wringing her hands and crying, at the thought of all her clothes being destroyed; then her mind dwelt upon other things, and she seemed as if she were deranged; she took their attention for a few minutes, as she was white. Soon the washer-woman came with my clothes; they spoke to her as if she had been a dog. I looked at them with as much astonishment as if I had never heard of such a thing. I asked them if they believed there was a God. "Of course we do," they replied. "Then why not obey him?" "We do." "You do not; permit me to say there is a God, and a just one, that will bring you all to account." "For what?" "For suffering these men that have just come in to be taken out of these vessels, and that awful sight I see in the streets." "O that is nothing; I should think you would be concerned about yourself." "I am sure," I replied, "the Lord will take care of me; you cannot harm me." "No; we do not wish to; we do not want you here." Every ship that comes in, the colored men are dragged to prison. I found it necessary to be stern with them; they were very rude; if I had not been so, I know not what would have been the consequences. They went off for that day; the next day some of them came again. "Good morning," said they; "we shall watch you like the d—— until you go away; you must not say any thing to these negroes whilst you are here." "Why, then, do you talk to me, if you do not want me to say any thing to you? If you will let me alone, I will you." "Let me see your protection," they replied, "they say it is under the Russian government." I pointed them to the 18th chapter of Revelations and 15th verse: "The merchants of these things which were made rich by her, shall stand afar off, for the fear of her torment, weeping and wailing. For strong is the Lord God who judgeth her." They made no answer, but asked the Captain how soon he should get away.

On the 17th, the Captain put eight of us on board the bark H. W. Tyler, for New York; we had about a mile to walk; the Captain was in honor bound to return us our passage money, which we had paid him at Jamaica; he came without it to see if we were there, and went away saying he would soon return with it; but we saw no more of him or our money! Our bark, and a vessel loaded with slaves, were towed down the

river by the same steamer ; we dropped anchor at
the bottom of the bay, as a storm was rising. The
18th, on Sabbath, it rained all day. Capt. Tyler
knocked at my door, wishing me to come out ; it
rained hard ; the bulwark of the bark was so high
I could not look over it ; he placed something for
me to stand on, that I might see the awful sight,
which was the vessel of slaves laying at the side
of our ship ! the deck was full of young men, girls,
and children, bound to Texas for sale ! Monday,
the 19th, Capt. Tyler demanded of us to pay him
for our passage. I had but ten dollars, and was
determined not to give it ; he was very severe with
all. I told him there were articles enough to pay
him belonging to me. Those who had nothing, were
obliged to go back in the steamer. Tuesday, the
20th, we set sail ; the storm was not over. The
22d the gale took us ; we were dismasted, and to
save sinking, sixty casks of molasses were stove
in, and holes cut in the bulwarks to let it off. All
the fowls, pigs, and fresh provisions were lost.
We were carried seventy-five miles up the bay of
Mexico. The Captain was determined not to pay
the steamer for carrying him back to New Orleans,
and made his way the best he could.

The 3d of October we arrived again at Key
West. The Captain got the bark repaired, and
took on board a number of turtles, and a plenty

of brandy. Friday, the 7th, set sail for New York; the Captain asked me why I did not go ashore when there in the Comet; "had you," said he, "they intended to beat you. John and Lucy Davenport, of Salem, laid down the first ten dollars towards a hundred for that person who should get you there." The Florida laws are about the same as those at New Orelans. He was very talkative: wished to know if I saw anything of the Creole's crew while at Jamaica. I told him they were all safe, a fine set of young men and women; one dear little girl, that was taken from her mother in Virginia, I should have taken with me, if I had had the money. He said his brother owned the Creole, and some of the slaves were his. "I never owned any; I have followed the sea all my life, and can tell every port and town in your State."

October 19th, 1842, arrived at New York, and thankful was I to set my feet on land, almost famished for the want of food; we lost all of our provisions; nothing was left but sailors' beef, and that was tainted before it was salted. I went at once to those who professed to be friends, but found myself mistaken. I hardly knew what was best. I had put up at Mrs. Rawes'; she did all she could to raise the twenty-five dollars that I must pay before I could take my baggage from the vessel. This seemed hard to obtain; I travel-

7*

led from one to another for three days ; at last I
called at the Second Advent office ; Mr. Nath'l
Southard left his business at once, and took me to
Mr. Lewis Tappan, and others; he raised the
money, and went with me to the ship after my
baggage. It was three o'clock on Saturday afternoon when I called on Mr. Southard ; the vessel
and Captain belonged to Virginia, was all ready
for sea, waiting for a wind ; they had ransacked
my things. I took from Jamaica forty dollars'
worth of preserved fruits; part were lost when we
were cast away in the Comet, and some they had
stolen. At 8 o'clock on Saturday evening, I made
out to have my things landed on the wharf; it was
very dark, as it rained hard. My kind friend did
not leave me until they were all safely lodged at
my residence. I boarded there three weeks,
thinking to come home ; but it was thought best
for me to wait, and see if Capt. Miner came or
not, hoping that I might recover my loss through
him. I took a room, and went to sewing, and
found the people very kind.

February, 1843, the colored men that went back
to New Orleans, for the want of passage money,
arrived at New York, wearied out. All the white
people remained there. I waited in New York
until the last of July, when I started for Boston.
August 1st, 1843, arrived, poor in health, and

poor in purse, having sacrificed both, hoping to benefit my fellow creatures. I trust it was acceptable to God, who in his providence preserved me in perils by land, and perils by sea.

> " God moves in a mysterious way
>   His wonders to perform ;
> He plants his footsteps on the sea,
>   And rides upon the storm.

> " Deep in unfathomable mines
>   Of never failing skill,
> He treasures up his bright designs,
>   And works his sovereign will."

Having lost all, I determined, by the help of God, to leave the event ; some of my friends in this city sympathized with me, and others took the advantage to reproach me. But in the hands of the Lord there is a cup ; the Saviour drank it to the dregs. They gather themselves together ; they hide themselves ; they mark my steps ; they waited for my soul, but the Lord is my defence, the Holy one of Israel is my Saviour. I'll trust him for strength and defence. What things were gain to me, I counted loss for Christ, for whom I have suffered all things ; and do count them nothing, that I may win Christ, and be found in him, not having mine own righteousness, which is of the law, but that which is through the faith of Christ, that which is of God by faith, that I may know

him, and the power of his resurrection, and the
fellowship of his sufferings, being made conform-
able unto his death, strengthened with all might,
according to his glorious power, unto all patience
and long-suffering, with joyfulness, thinking it not
strange concerning the fiery trials, as though some
strange thing happened ; for saith the apostle, it is
better if the will of God so be that ye suffer for
well doing, than for evil ; they think it strange
that ye run not with them to the same excess of
riot, speaking evil of you. If they do these things
in a green tree, what shall be done in a dry !

> " I hate to walk, I hate to sit
>   With men of vanity and lies ;
> The scoffer and the hypocrite
>   Are the abhorrence of my eyes.
>
> God knows their impious thoughts are vain,
>   And they shall feel his power ;
> His wrath shall pierce their souls with pain,
>   In some surprising hour."

The first twenty months after my arrival in the
city, notwithstanding my often infirmities, I labored with much success, until I hired with and from
those with whom I mostly sympathized, and shared
in common the disadvantages and stigma that is
heaped upon us, in this our professed Christian
land. But my lot was like the man that went
down from Jerusalem, and fell among thieves,

which stripped him of his raiment, and wounding him, departed, leaving him half dead. What I did not lose, when cast away, has been taken from my room where I hired. Three times I had been broken up in business, embarrassed and obliged to move, when not able to wait on myself. This has been my lot. In the midst of my afflictions, sometimes I have thought my case like that of Paul's, when cast among wild beasts. " Had not the Lord been on my side, they would have swallowed me up ; but blessed be the Lord who hath not given me a prey to their teeth."

In 1848 and '49 the Lord was pleased to lay his hand upon me. Some of my friends came to my relief; but the promises of God were neither few nor small ; he knows them that trust and fear him. No one has greater reason to be grateful than I. God has preserved me through much suffering the past winter. I have passed through another furnace of affliction, and may God's dispensations be sanctified to me. The sufferings of this present life are not worthy to be compared with the glory that shall be revealed hereafter. Who shall separate us from the love of Christ ? Shall tribulation, or distress, or persecution, or famine, or nakedness, or peril, or sword ? Nay, in all these things we are more than conquerors, through him that loved us, and gave himself for us. Soon he will come ; here we live by faith ; if any one draw back, my soul shall have no pleasure in him.

Truly the promises of God are given for our encouragement ; they are yea and amen, in Christ Jesus ; they are a covert from the storm, a shelter from the heat, a sure retreat for the weary and way worn traveller.

Many are the trials and temptations to which we are exposed in this vale of tears, but in heaven we shall be freed from the bondage of sin. Nothing can enter there to annoy or molest the redeemed ones : the Captain of our salvation was made perfect through suffering ; he was despised and rejected of men, a man of sorrows, and acquainted with grief; and that he might sanctify the people with his own blood, suffered without the gate. Let us go forth, therefore, unto him, bearing his reproach. Here we have no continuing city nor abiding place.

I have much to be thankful to God for ; for the comforts of this life, and the kind friends who have so kindly bestowed their favors upon me, and while they in this life have an abundance, may they have the presence of God ; and when the King shall come, may they have their lamps trimmed and burning : then shall he say, " Come ye blessed of my Father, inherit the kingdom prepared for you from the foundation of the world: for I was an hungered, and ye gave me meat, I was thirsty, and ye gave me drink, naked, and ye clothed me, sick, and in prison, and ye visited me. Then shall the righteous answer, saying: when saw we thee an hungered, and fed thee, and thirsty, and gave thee drink, naked, and clothed thee, sick, and in prison, and ministered unto thee, or a stranger, and took thee in?" And the King shall answer and say: "Inasmuch as ye have done it unto one of the least of my disciples, ye have done it unto me. The poorest can do something for the cause of Christ; even a cup of cold water, given with a desire to benefit a fellow creature, will be acceptable to God. May the power of God, and the spirit of Christ rule and reign in all hearts. He knoweth them that love and trust in him.

I am a wonder unto many, but the Lord is my strong refuge, and in him will I trust. I shall fear no evil, for thou, O Lord, art ever near to shield and protect thy dependent children. Underneath him is the everlasting arm of mercy; misfortune is never mournful for the soul that accepts it, for such do always see that every cloud is an angel's face; sorrow connects the soul with the invisible.

O Father, fearful indeed is this world's pilgrimage, when the soul has learned that all its sounds are echoes, all its sights are shadows. But lo! a cloud opens, a face serene and hopeful looks forth and saith, " Be thou as a little child, and thus shalt thou become a seraph, and bow thyself in silent humility and pray, not that afflictions might not visit, but be willing to be purified through fire, and accept it meekly."

THE HIDING PLACE.

Amid this world's tumultuous noise,
For peace my soul to Jesus flies;
If I've an interest in his grace,
I want no other hiding place.

The world with all its charms is vain,
Its wealth and honors I disdain:
All its extensive aims embrace,
Can ne'er afford a hiding place.

A guilty, sinful heart is mine,
Jesus, unbounded love is thine!
When I behold thy smiling face,
Tis then I see my hiding place.

To save, if once my Lord engage,
The world may laugh, and Satan rage:
The powers of hell can ne'er erase
My name from God's own hiding place.

I'm in a wilderness below,
Lord, guide me all my journey through,
Plainly let me thy footsteps trace,
Which lead to heaven, my hiding place.

Should dangers thick impede my course,
O let my soul sustain no loss;
Help me to run the Christian race,
And enter safe my hiding place.

Then with enlarged powers,
I'll triumph in redeeming love,
Eternal ages will I praise
My Lord for such a hiding place.

LOUISA PICQUET,

THE

OCTOROON:

A TALE OF SOUTHERN SLAVE LIFE.

BY REV. H. MATTISON, A.M.,

PASTOR OF UNION CHAPEL, NEW YORK.

NEW YORK:

PUBLISHED BY THE AUTHOR, Nos. 5 & 7 MERCER STREET.

1861.

LOUISA PICQUET,

THE

OCTOROON:

OR

INSIDE VIEWS

OF

SOUTHERN DOMESTIC LIFE.

BY H. MATTISON,

PASTOR OF UNION CHAPEL, NEW YORK.

New York:

PUBLISHED BY THE AUTHOR, Nos. 5 & 7 MERCER ST.

1861.

CONTENTS.

LOUISA PICQUET,

THE OCTOROON SLAVE.

CHAPTER I.

ILLUSTRIOUS BIRTH AND PARENTAGE.

LOUISA PICQUET, the subject of the following narrative, was born in Columbia, South Carolina, and is apparently about thirty-three years of age. She is a little above the medium height, easy and graceful in her manners, of fair complexion and rosy cheeks, with dark eyes, a flowing head of hair with no perceptible inclination to curl, and every appearance, at first view, of an accomplished white lady.* No one, not apprised of the fact, would suspect that she had a drop of African blood in her veins; indeed, few will believe it, at first, even when told of it.

But a few minutes' conversation with her will convince almost any one that she has, at least, spent most of her life in the South. A certain menial-like diffidence, her plantation expression and pronunciation, her inability to read or write, together with her familiarity with and readiness in describing plantation scenes and sorrows, all attest the truthfulness of her declaration that she has been most of her life a slave. Besides, her artless simplicity and sincerity are sufficient to dissipate the last doubt. No candid person can talk with her without becoming fully convinced that she is a truthful, conscientious, and Chris-

---

* The cut on the outside title-page is a tolerable representation of the features of Mrs. P., though by no means a flattering picture.

tian woman. She is now, and has been for the last eight years, a member of the Zion Baptist Church in Cincinnati, Ohio, of which Rev. Wallace Shelton is now (May, 1860) the pastor.

But, notwithstanding the fair complexion and lady-like bearing of Mrs. Picquet, she is of African descent on her mother's side—an octoroon, or eighth blood—and, consequently, one of the four millions in this land of Bibles, and churches, and ministers, and "liberty," who "have *no rights that white men are bound to respect.*"

The story of her wrongs and sorrows will be recited, to a large extent, in her own language, as taken from her lips by the writer, in Buffalo, N. Y., in May, 1860.

CHAPTER II.

LOOKS TOO MUCH LIKE MADAME RANDOLPH'S CHILDREN, AND IS SOLD OUT OF THE FAMILY.

"I was born in Columbia, South Carolina. My mother's name was Elizabeth. She was a slave owned by John Randolph,* and was a seamstress in his family. She was fifteen years old when I was born. Mother's mistress had a child only two weeks older than me. Mother's master, Mr. Randolph, was my father. So mother told me. She was forbid to tell who was my father, but I looked so much like Madame Randolph's baby that she got dissatisfied, and mother had to be sold. Then mother and me was sent to Georgia, and sold. I was a baby —don't remember at all, but suppose I was about two months old, may be older."

---

* What " John Randolph" this was, we know not ; but suppose it was not the celebrated " John Randolph of Roanoke," though it may have been, and probably was, one of the same family. A gentleman in Xenia, Ohio, told Mrs. P. that if she could only make it out that her mother was one of John Randolph's slaves, there was money somewhere, now, of John Randolph's estate, to buy her mother and brother.

CHAPTER III.

THE SECOND MASTER FAILS, AND HIS SLAVES ARE SCATTERED.

"Then I was sold to Georgia, Mr. Cook bought mother and me. When mother first went to Georgia she was a nurse, and suckled Madame Cook's child, with me. Afterward, she was a cook. I was a nurse. I always had plenty to do. Fast as one child would be walkin', then I would have another one to nurse."

Question (by the writer).—"Did your master ever whip you?"

Answer.—"Oh, very often; sometimes he would be drunk, and real funny, and would not whip me then. He had two or three kinds of drunks. Sometimes he would begin to fight at the front door, and fight every thing he come to. At other times he would be real funny."

Q.—"He was a planter, was he?"

A.—"Yes; he had a large cotton plantation, and warehouse where he kept all the cotton in, and stores up the country, in a little town—Monticello—and then he had some in Georgia. He used to give such big parties, and every thing, that he broke up. Then his creditors came, you know, and took all the property; and then he run off with my mother and me, and five other slaves, to Mobile, and hired us all out. He was goin' to have enough to wait on him, for he could not wait on his self. I was hired out to Mr. English. He was a real good man; I wouldn't care if I belonged to him, if I had to belong to any body. I'd like to swap Mr. Cook for him. Mr. English and his wife were very clever to me. They never whipped me. Mother had a little baby sister when we first went to Mobile—a little girl just running round. She died in Alabama. She had one before that, while she was in Georgia; but they all died but me and my brother, the oldest and the youngest."

Q.—"Had she any one she called her husband while she was in Georgia?"

A.—"No."

Q.—"Had she in Mobile?"

A.—"No."

Q.—" Had she any children while she lived in Mobile ?"

A.—" None but my brother, the baby when we were all sold."

Q.—" Who was the father of your brother, the baby you speak of ?"

A.—" I don't know, except Mr. Cook was. Mother had three children while Mr. Cook owned her."

Q.—" Was your mother white ?"

A.—" Yes, she pretty white ; not white enough for white people. She have long hair, but it was kind a wavy

Q.—" Were you hired out in Mobile ?"

A.—" Yes ; with Mr. English."

CHAPTER IV

A WHITE SLAVE LOVE ADVENTURE.

" While I was living in Mobile, a gentleman there owned a colored man that was more white than I am. He was about my age. He had no beard ; just a young man, might have been nineteen or twenty. His master was not married, but had a girl belong to him, a very light girl he bought from Charleston ; he bought her for himself, though he kept her boarding out.

" This colored man I spoke of used to drive out when his master's sisters wanted to go out. They often came to Mr. English's with them, and ring the bell. There I met him often at the door before I knew he was colored, and when he found out I was colored, he was always very polite, and say, ' Good morning, miss,' and ask if the ladies was in. Then, after he got acquainted, he used to come and see me Sundays. He wanted me to marry him, and I liked him very well, and would have had him if he had not run off."

Q.—" How came he to run off ?"

A.—" You see Mr. ——* kept that girl, but never go where she was ; but, whenever he want to see her he send for her to

---

* Mrs. P. dare not have *any* of these names published, as all the parties are still living.

the office. And this young man who wanted me had to go always and tell that girl, and go with her to the office, whenever his master wanted him to.

"Then this man had another waitman, one was perfectly white, and the other jet black; and the black one got jealous of the other one, and thought his master thought more of his other servant, the white one. (He did think more of him.) So the two had a falling out; and, to seek revenge, the dark one told the master he see something which he did not see—that the other one was out walking with this girl. He knew [that is, the black one] that his master would whip him [the light one] for that, when he would not whip him for any thing else. That night his master had not sent for her, and, of course, he thought it might be true.

"Then he ask T—— about it, and he denied it, but the owner believed it. Then he whipped him awfully, soon as he came to the office that morning; and sent for the girl, and whipped her, and sent her off to New Orleans.

"Then the partner of this man, he spoke to T—— afterward, and told him he would go away. He was an Englishman, or Scotchman. He came out that way—was not raised there. He never would own a slave. He felt sorry that T—— was whipped so, and told him he would go away. His first excuse was he had no money, and the next was on account of being acquainted with me. Then the man inquire what kind of looking girl I was, and told him if I was white as he represented there would be no difficulty at all about getting away, and he would let him have money for both of us to go away.

"Then he told me what this gentleman said to him, and that he had the money from this gentleman, and wanted me to go away with him. Well, I knew that he could neither read nor write, and was afraid that we would be caught, and so I dare not go. We had about two hours' talk then, but when he found out I would not go, he said he must go; he had the money, and all his arrangements made. That's the last I saw of him. I suppose T—— left that night. 'Twas not very long after that I went to Mr. Bachelor's to live, and we were all sold."

We shall hear of this fugitive T—— again, further on in our narrative.

CHAPTER V.

INTRIGUES OF A MARRIED "SOUTHERN GENTLEMAN."

Q.—" DID Mr. Cook always treat *you* well, as to any in·
sults ?"

A.—" No. After we went to Mobile, I went to Mr. Bache·
lor's, after I was at Mr. English's, and Mr. Cook was boarding
there. I was a little girl, not fourteen years old. One day
Mr. Cook told me I must come to his room that night, and take
care of him. He said he was sick, and he want me and another
slave girl to come to his room and take care of him. In the
afternoon he went to his room, and said he was sick. I was
afraid to go there that night, and I told Mrs. Bachelor what
Mr. Cook said to me. Then she whispered with her sister, Mrs.
Simpson, and then told me I need not go. She said she would
go up and see Mr. Cook, and have some one else go and take
care of him. Then I went up after Mrs. Bachelor, not to let
him see me, and listen to the door. Mrs. Bachelor went in and
ask him how he done. She said, ' I heard you was sick, and I
thought I would come up and see if there was any thing serious.
He groaned, and seemed to get worse than ever—told how bad
he felt about his head, and one thing an'other. Then her reply
was, that she would have some water put on to bathe his feet
and some mustard, and have one of the boys come up and take
care of him. She went right on in that way, without his ask·
ing, and smooth it off in that way, so as not to let on that she
thought any thing, at the same time clearing me.

" Then he thanked her very kindly. So she went down, and
had the water sent up. Then, pretty soon, he sent down by the
boy, to tell me to bring up some more *mustard*. Then Mrs.
Bachelor, she understood it, and *she* took up the mustard her·
self. Then the boy stay with him all night, and just about day·
light he come down. When he come down he come to the
room (you see, I slept in Mrs. Bachelor's room)—he call me and
says, ' Your massa, Henry, says you must take him up a fresh
pitcher of water ;' and Mrs. Bachelor told him to go and take
it up himself ; that I was busy.

Q.—" Were you hired to Mrs. Bachelor then ?"

A.—" I don't know. I was workin' there ; it might have been in part for his board, for aught I know. Mrs. Bachelor kept boarding-house. She was Scotch ; came from Scotland."

Q.—" Well, what happened next ?"

A.—" I didn't go up till breakfast-time. At breakfast-time I had to take his breakfast up to his room, on a waiter. He had not got up yet—I take the waiter up to the bed. Well, him thinking that all the boarders gone down, talk rather louder than he would if he'd a thought they were there. The door was open wide enough for a person to come in.

" Then he order me, in a sort of commanding way (I don't want to tell what he said), and told me to shut the door. At the same time he was kind a raising up out of the bed ; then I began to cry ; but before I had time to shut the door, a gentleman walk out of another room close by, picking his nails, and looking in the room as he passed on. Then Mr. Cook turned it off very cute. He said, ' What you stand there crying for, you dam' fool ? Go 'long down stairs, and get me some more salt.' Same time he had not taste his breakfast, to see whether he want any salt, or not. That was to blind with that gentleman, because he see me there crying, or heard me, or something. Then I was very glad to get out to get the salt, but still I knew I should have to come back again, and it would not be much better. Then I went down to get the salt, and Mrs. Bachelor caught my looks, and spoke and said, ' Louisa, one of the boys will take that salt up, I want you a minute.' Then I thought she was the best friend I had in the world. She had such a nice way of turning off things. Then I didn't go up till that day, some time. He did not come down, but call out of the window for me to bring him up a pitcher of water. Then I brought the water up, and he want to know why I did not come up with the salt. I told him the reason, that Mrs. Bachelor said she wanted me, and sent it up by one of the boys. Then he said he wanted me to understand that I belong to him, and not to Mrs. Bachelor—that when he called, or wanted me, I was not to consult with Mrs. Bachelor, or any person else.

" Then he told me I must come up in his room that night ; if

I didn't he'd give me hell in the mornin'. Then I promised him I would, for I was afraid to say any thing else. Then he forbid me sayin' any thing to Mrs. Bachelor about what he said to me—you see there where he got me. Then I came to conclusion he could not do any thing but whip me—he could not kill me for it ; an' I made up my mind to take the whippin'. So I didn't go that night.

"Then in the mornin' he want to know why I didn't come up, and I told him I forget it. Then he said, I don't believe you forgot it ; but if you forget that, I won't forget what I told you. So he whip me, so that I won't forget another time.

Q.—" Well, how did he whip you ?"

A.—" With the cowhide."

Q.—" Around your shoulders, or how ?"

A.—" That day he did."

Q.—" How were you dressed—with thin clothes, or how ?"

A.—" Oh, very thin ; with low-neck'd dress. In the summer-time we never wore but two pieces—only the one under, and the blue homespun over. It is a striped cloth they make in Georgia just for the colored people. All the time he was whippin' me I kept sayin' I forgot it, and promisin' I would come another time."

Q.—" Did he whip you hard, so as to raise marks ?"

A.—" Oh yes. He never whip me in his life but what he leave the mark on, I was dressed so thin. He kept asking me, all the time he was whippin' me, if I intended to mind him. Of course I told him I would, because I was gettin' a whippin'. At the same time, I did not mean to go to his room ; but only did it so that he would stop whippin' me. He want to know what I was afraid of—if I could not sleep as well there as any-where else ? Of course I told him, yes, sir ; and that I wan't afraid of any thing. At the same time, I was afraid of him ; but I wouldn't tell him. Then he let me go. Then, as luck would have it, he got playin' cards with some gentlemen after dinner, about two or three o'clock, and never stop all night ; so I thought from appearance of things in the mornin'. They were playin' and drinkin' together all night ; so I did not go to his room till mornin'. I had my excuse all made up—

because he had company, and I was waitin', and got to sleep. At the same time I didn't intend, and expect to take another whippin' in the mornin'.

"Then, in the mornin', I went up to call him to breakfast; and, as I knock at the door to call him, to tell him that breakfast was ready, he told me to come in. He came to the door, and I smelt his breath, and see from the way he spoke to me that he had been drinkin'. He told me to come in, that he had somethin' for me. At the same time, he took hold of my hand, and kind a pull me, and put a whole handful of half-dollars in my hand. Then I knew he was drunk, but it surprise me so that I didn't know what to think. At the same time, he was holdin' on to me, and askin' me if I would come back. I told him, yes. But I thought he was so drunk he would forget, and so I have all that money. I never had any money but copper and five cents before; and, of course, my hand full of half-dollars looked to me like a fortune. I thought he had got it that night playin' cards. I went on, then, down stairs; and in the afternoon, when he got a little sober, he ask me what I done with that money. First I ask him, what money? I thought he would forget it, and didn't let on that I knew any thing about it. Then he said, that money I let you have this mornin'. Then I knew he had not forgot.

"Then, you see, I had seen a flowered muslin dress in the store several times, and I take a fancy to it; I thought it look beautiful. It was perfectly white, with a little pink leaf all over it. So I went to the store, and ask the man what's the price of it. Then he told me, but I could not reckon it, so I lay the money out, and told him to give just as many yards as I had half-dollars. Then he told me that would be too large a pattern for me; but I told him, no, I wanted a nice full dress. That was the largest pattern I ever had afore, or since. Then I told Mr. Cook I put the money away, and could not find it. I had sense enough to know he would not dare tell any one that he gave me the money, and would hardly dare to whip me for it. Then he say no more about it, only he told me to come up there that night. He said he want to see some more about that money; he didn't believe I lost it. Then I told Mrs. Bach-

elor that I guess I'd have to go up stairs that night; and ask
her what I should do. She was the best friend I had; but she
could not interfere no more, because if she did he'd know that
I told her. Then she said she had no patience with him—he
was the meanest man she ever saw. She abused him then a
great deal, before her sister and before me. Then she said
the best plan would be to keep out of his way, and if he called
me, not to answer. I was to keep in her room that evening as
much as possible.

"Well, about tea-time he wanted water. That was sent up.
Then he wanted to know where I was; he wanted a button
sewed on his wristband. Then Mrs. Bachelor sent him word
that, if he could not find me, to send the shirt down, and her
sister, or one of the girls, would put a button on for him, if he
was in a hurry. The shirt came down, and the button was
sewed on. I suppose he just took the button off for an excuse.
Then, when they went up with the shirt, he sent word down
that, when I came, I must come up and get his boots and black
them. He did not care about waitin' so long for them in the
mornin'. He thought I'd give out somewhere. Then, about
bedtime, he call one of the boys to know if they told me about
the boots; and they said they hadn't seen me. I was all the
time in Mrs. Bachelor's room, but none of them knew it. I
sewed the button on, but he didn't know it. Then he pretended to be mad because I was gone out at night, and she excuse
me, and said, perhaps I had gone out with some children, and
got to playin', and didn't know it was so late. He was mad,
and told her his wife never allowed me to go out nights, and
she must not; and allowed he would give me a floggin' for it.
He said I knew better than to go out. He thought I was out,
or, perhaps, he thought it was a trick to keep me from him
and that made him so mad.

"In the mornin' he came down, and want to know where I
was. You see, I'd made up my mind to take the whippin'. I
knew he would not kill me, and I'd get over it the same as I
had before. So I told him I was down stairs asleep.

"Then he came to me in the ironin'-room, down stairs, where
I was, and whip me with the cowhide, naked, so I 'spect I'll

take some of the marks with me to the grave. One of them I know I will." [Here Mrs. P. declines explaining further how he whipped her, though she had told our hostess where this was written ; but it is too horrible and indelicate to be read in a civilized country.] Mrs. P. then proceeds, "He was very mad, and whipped me awfully. That was the worst whippin' I ever had."

Q.—"Did he cut through your skin ?"

A.—"Oh yes ; in a good many places. I don't believe he would whip me much worse, if I struck his wife or children ; and I didn't do any thing. He pretended it was because I was out, but I knew what it was for When he came out of the room, after he had whipped me, he said, to make Mrs. Bachelor believe, 'I'll be bound she won't go out another time without permission.' Then, when he was whippin' me so awfully, I made up my mind 'twas of no use, and I'd go, and not be whipped any more ; and told him so. I saw he was bent on it, and I could not get Mrs. Bachelor to protect me any more. Then he went away, and that was the last I ever saw him. That very day, about noon, we was taken by the sheriff, and was all sold the next mornin'. I tell you I was glad when I heard I was taken off to be sold, because of what I escape ; but I jump out of the fryin'-pan into the fire. Mrs. Bachelor said it was a good thing, when I went away."

Q.—"Where was Mrs. Cook all this time ?"

A—"She was up the country, in Georgia, with a sister of hers. When he failed in Georgia, he sent her up to her sister. I suppose she was willing to do it ; she must have understood it."

Q.—"How many children had she ?"

A.—"I could not tell ; they had a lot of them. I know I been nursin' all my life up to that time."

CHAPTER VI.

Q.—"How did you say you come to be sold?"

A.—"Well, you see, Mr. Cook made great parties, and go off to watering-places, and get in debt, and had to break up [fail], and then he took us to Mobile, and hired the most of us out, so the men he owe should not find us, and sell us for the debt. Then, after a while, the sheriff came from Georgia after Mr. Cook's debts, and found us all, and took us to auction, and sold us. My mother and brother was sold to Texas, and I was sold to New Orleans."

Q.—"How old were you, then?"

A.—"Well, I don't know exactly, but the auctioneer said I wasn't quite fourteen. I didn't know myself."

Q.—"How old was your brother?"

A.—"I suppose he was about two months old. He was little bit of baby."

Q.—"Where were you sold?"

A.—"In the city of Mobile."

Q.—"In a yard? In the city?"

A.—"No. They put all the men in one room, and all the women in another; and then whoever want to buy come and examine, and ask you whole lot of questions. They began to take the clothes off of me, and a gentleman said they needn't do that, and told them to take me out. He said he knew I was a virtuous girl, and he'd buy me, anyhow. He didn't strip me, only just under my shoulders."

Q—"Were there any others there white like you?"

A.—"Oh yes, plenty of them. There was only Lucy of our lot, but others!"

Q.—"Were others stripped and examined?"

A.—"Well, not quite naked, but just same."

Q.—"You say the gentleman told them to 'take you out.' What did he mean by that?"

A.—" W.iy, take me out of the *room* where the women and rls wer. kept ; where they examine them—out where the ctioneer sold us."

Q.—" Where was that ? In the street, or in a yard ?"

A.—" At the market, where the block is ?"

Q.—" What block ?"

A.—" My ! don't you know ? The stand, where we have to get up ?"

Q.—" Did *you* get up on the stand ?"

A.—" Why, of course ; we all have to get up to be seen."

Q.—" What else do you remember about it ?"

A.—" Well, they first begin at upward of six hundred for me, and then some bid fifty more, and some twenty-five more, and that way."

Q.—" Do you remember any thing the auctioneer said about you when he sold you ?"

A.—" Well, he said he could not recommend me for any thing else only that I was a good-lookin' girl, and a good nurse, and kind and affectionate to children ; but I was never used to any hard work. He told them they could see that. My hair was quite short, and the auctioneer spoke about it, but said, ' You see it good quality, and give it a little time, it will grow out again. You see Mr. Cook had my hair cut off. My hair grew fast, and look so much better than Mr. Cook's daughter, and he fancy I had better hair than his daughter, and so he had it cut off to make a difference."

Q.—" Well, how did they sell you and your mother ? that is, which was sold first ?"

A.—" Mother was put up the first of our folks. She was sold for splendid cook, and Mr. Horton, from Texas, bought her and the baby, my brother. Then Henry, the carriage-driver, was put up, and Mr. Horton bought him, and then two field-hands, Jim and Mary. The women there tend mills and drive ox wagons, and plough, just like men. Then I was sold next. Mr. Horton run me up to fourteen hundred dollars. He wanted I should go with my mother. Then some one said ' fifty.' Then Mr. Williams allowed that he did not care what they bid, he was going to have me anyhow. Then he bid fifteen hundred.

Mr. Horton said 'twas no use to bid any more, and I was so to Mr. Williams. I went right to New Orleans then "

Q.—" Who was Mr. Williams ?"

A.—" I didn't know then, only he lived in New Orlea. Him and his wife had parted, some way—he had three childre. boys. When I was going away I heard some one cryin', and prayin' the Lord to go with her only daughter, and protect me. I felt pretty bad then, but hadn't no time only to say good-bye. I wanted to go back and get the dress I bought with the half-dollars, I thought a good deal of that ; but Mr. Williams would not let me go back and get it. He said he'd get me plenty of nice dresses. Then I thought mother could cut it up and make dresses for my brother, the baby. I knew she could not wear it ; and I had a thought, too, that she'd have it to remember me."

Q.—" It seems like a dream, don't it ?"

A.—" No ; it seems fresh in my memory when I think of it— no longer than yesterday. Mother was right on her knees, with her hands up, prayin' to the Lord for me. She didn't care who saw her : the people all lookin' at her. I often thought her prayers followed me, for I never could forget her. Whenever I wanted any thing real bad after that, my mother was always sure to appear to me in a dream that night, and have plenty to give me, always."

Q.—" Have you never seen her since ?"

A.—" No, never since that time. I went to New Orleans, and she went to Texas. So I understood."

Q.—" Well, how was it with you after Mr. Williams bought you ?"

A.—" Well, he took me right away to New Orleans."

Q.—" How did you go ?"

A.—" In a boat, down the river. Mr. Williams told me what he bought me for, soon as we started for New Orleans. He said he was getting old, and when he saw me he thought he'd buy me, and end his days with me. He said if I behave myself he'd treat me well : but, if not, he'd whip me almost to death."

Q.—" How old was he ?"

A.—" He was over forty ; I guess pretty near fifty. He was gray headed. That's the reason he was always so jealous. He never let me go out anywhere."

Q.—" Did you never go to church ?"

A.—" No, sir ; I never darken a church door from the time he bought me till after he died. I used to ask him to let me go to church. He would accuse me of some object, and said there was more rascality done there than anywhere else. He'd sometimes say, ' Go on, I guess you've made your arrangements ; go on, I'll catch up with you.' But I never dare go once."

Q.—" Had you any children while in New Orleans ?"

A.—" Yes ; I had four."

Q.—" Who was their father ?"

A.—" Mr. Williams."

Q.—" Was it known that he was living with you ?"

A.—" Every body knew I was housekeeper, but he never let on that he was the father of my children. I did all the work in his house—nobody there but me and the children."

Q.—" What children ?"

A.—" My children and his. You see he had three sons."

Q.—" How old were his children when you went there ?"

A.—" I guess the youngest was nine years old. When he had company, gentlemen folks, he took them to the hotel. He never have no gentlemen company home. Sometimes he would come and knock, if he stay out later than usual time ; and if I did not let him in in a minute, when I would be asleep, he'd come in and take the light, and look under the bed, and in the wardrobe, and all over, and then ask me why I did not let him in sooner. I did not know what it meant till I learnt his ways."

Q.—" Were your children mulattoes ?"

A.—" No, sir ! They were all white. They look just like nim. The neighbors all see that. After a while he got so disagreeable that I told him, one day, I wished he would sell me, or 'put me in his pocket'—that's the way we say—because I had no peace at all. I rather die than live in that way. Then he got awful mad, and said nothin' but death should separate

us ; and, if I run off, he'd blow my brains out. Then I thought,
if that be the way, all I could do was just to pray for him to
die."

Q.—" Where did you learn to pray ?"

A.—" I first begin to pray when I was in Georgia, about whippin'—that the Lord would make them forget it, and not whip
me : and it seems if when I pray I did not get so hard whippin'."

CHAPTER VII.

INSIDE VIEWS OF ANOTHER SOUTHERN FAMILY.

Q.—" DID you feel that you were doing right in living, as you
did, with Mr. Williams ?"

A.—" No ; when I was a little girl in Georgia the madame,
Mrs. Cook, used to read the Bible, and explain it to us.   One
night she read the commandments about stealin', and committin' adultery. They made a great impression on my mind.   I
knew what stealin' was, but I did not know what adultery was.
Then I asked her the meanin'.   She did not want to answer
for a good while.   I suppose I was so small she hated to tell
me, but I kept on askin'.   Then she said, 'You see *Lucy*,
how many children she's got ?' I told her yes.   Then she said
she did not know the father of any of them children, and said
when folks had children that way they must be married like
she (Mrs. Cook) was to her husband.   It was adultery to stay
with any one without bein' married—that was the. meanin'
of it."

Q.—" Who was this Lucy ?'

A.—" She was a seamstress in Mrs. Cook's family."

Q.—" What was her color ?"

A.—" Right white—light hair and blue eyes.   All her **children** were right white."

Q.—" And was *she* a slave ?"

A.—" Yes, sir."

Q.—" How many children had she ?"

A.—" Five or six in Georgia, and one after she went to Mobile."

Q.—" And had she no husband ?"

A.—" No, sir ; never had a husband in her life."

Q.—" Do not the slave women usually have husbands, or those they call their husbands ?"

A.—" Yes, sir ; some of them do ; but some of them do not. They can't have any husbands, because their masters have them all the time."

Q.—" How did you say it was with Lucy ?"

A.—" She sew in the house all day, and then go to her room, off, at night."

Q.—" What became of her ?"

A.—" Well, she was sold the day I was, in Mobile, and got free after a while ; and each of the white men bought his child. Mr. Moore bought his, and Mr. Hale bought his ; and then the others, that their fathers would not own, her relations bought and set free."

Q.—" Who do you mean by her relations ?"

A.—" Why Lucy's sister Judy, and Mr. ——*, who kept her. I tell you how he did : He bought Elcy, Lucy's sister, first, and lived with her till she died. He had her learn to read and write, and taught her music, and done first rate by her. Then, when Elcy died, he bought her sister, Judy, and is livin' with her yet. Then, when they heard that Lucy was sold, all her sisters and brothers unite, sent on and bought her, and set her free."

---

* We have the name, but Mrs. P. dare not have it published, as the parties are ⟩ still living, and she fears they might shoot her.

CHAPTER VIII.

OCTOROON LIFE IN NEW ORLEANS.

Q.—" WELL, now tell me about your life in New Orleans."

A.—" Well, when Mr. Williams bought me he told me where I was goin', to New Orleans, and what he bought me for. Then I thought of what Mrs. Cook told me ; and I thought, now I shall be committin' adultery, and there's no chance for me, and I'll have to die and be lost. Then I had this trouble with him and my soul the whole time."

Q.—" Did you ever say any thing to him about this trouble ?"

A.—" Yes, sir ; I told him often. Then he would dam' at it. He said *he* had all that to answer for himself. If I was only true to him, then I could get religion—that needn't hinder me from gettin' religion. But I knew better than that. I thought it was of no use to be prayin', and livin' in sin.

" I begin then to pray that he might die, so that I might get religion ; and then I promise the Lord one night, faithful, in prayer, if he would just take him out of the way, I'd get religion and be true to Him as long as I lived. If Mr. Williams only knew *that*, and get up out of his grave, he'd beat me half to death. Then it was some time before he got sick. Then, when he did get sick, he was sick nearly a year. Then he begin to get good, and talked kind to me. I could see there was a change in him. He was not all the time accusin' me of other people. Then, when I saw that he was sufferin' so, I begin to get sorry, and begin to pray that he might get religion first before he died. I felt sorry to see him die in his sins. I pray for *him* to have religion, when I did not have it myself. I thought if he got religion and then died, I knew that I could get religion.

" It seems he did get religion, because he was so much changed in his way ; but he said he wanted to see his w clearer."

Q.—" Was he rich ?"

A.—" Oh no, sir. He had to borrow some of the money of his brother to buy me."

Q.—" What kind of a house did you live in ?"

A.—" Why, it was a rented house. When he got up, one mornin', I got him up in a chair by the fire—it was cold weather—then he told me he was goin' to die, and that he could not live ; and he said that if I would promise him that I would go to New York, he would leave me and the children free. He was then writin' to a table—had a little table to the side of him. Then he told me how to conduct myself, and not to live as I had lived with him, with any person. He told me to come out this way (North), and not to let any one know who I was, or that I was colored. He said no person would know it, if I didn't tell it ; and, if I conducted myself right, some one would want to marry me, but warned me not to marry any one but a mechanic—some one who had trade, and was able to take care of me and the children."

Q.—" How many children had you then ?"

A.—" Only two. I had four, but two had died. Then I promised him to go to New York. Then he said, just as soon as he died I must go right to New York ; and he said he would leave me the things. He hadn't any thing to leave me but the things."

Q.—" What things?"

A.—" The things in the house—the beds, and tables, and such things."

CHAPTER IX.

DEATH OF HER THIRD OWNER, AND ESCAPE OF LOUISA.

" THEN, in about a month or three weeks, he died. I didn't cry nor nothin', for I was glad he was dead ; for I thought I could have some peace and happiness then. I was left *free*, and that made me so glad I could hardly believe it myself.

" Then, on Sunday, I dressed myself and went out to go to

church ; and that was the first time I had been to church in six years. I used to go to the colored church in Georgia, with my mother, in the afternoon. When I got there, to the church in New Orleans, the minister talked just as though he knew all about me, and talked about the vows I had made to the Lord about my husband. Then I said in my mind, he wan't my husband ; but then I determined to go there to church. Then I asked the people what church it was, and they said, a Methodist church. Then Mr. Williams' brother came, and told me I must go out of that house, because he would not pay the rent. Then a woman there, a friend of mine, let me come in one of her rooms. She was very kind to me, and used to give me victuals when I did not know where to get it."

Q.—" Who was this woman ?"

A.—" Her name was Helen Hopkins ; she was a colored woman that used to take in washing. I never knew how it was that she was so kind to me. I always thought it was the Lord takin' care of the widow and the fatherless.

" One day I met Mr. Williams'. brother, and he asked me what I was doin' ; and I told him, nothin'. He said that by rights I belonged to him, because his brother had not paid him the money that he borrowed to help buy me. Mr. Williams—John Williams—had said before that he would give me somethin' for the children. Then he asked me why I did not go away, as his brother told me. Then I told him it was because I had not money enough to go with, and asked him to give me some. Then he said I had better thank God for my freedom ; and that his brother had got enough from him. Then I told this friend of mine, who had given me victuals, and she advised me to get away as soon as I could.

" Then Mr. John Williams sent the things I had to a second-hand furniture store, and sold them all; and I took the money and my two children, and went to Cincinnati. I had just money enough to get there, and a little bit over."

Q.—" What made you stop at Cincinnati ?"

A.—" Because I had no money to go further ; and I met all my friends there that I knew, when I was small, in Georgia. One of them was a Mrs. Nelson. who was once a slave in Geor-

gia with my mother. Her husband had bought her, and she
was livin' with him in Cincinnati. I went right to her house.
Then, when I saw her free, and was free myself, I began to
think more about my mother."

Q.—" When had you seen your mother last ?"

A.—" At the auction, where we were all sold. It is now
most twenty years ago."

Q.—" Had you never heard from her ?"

A.—" Yes. I had one letter from her when I was in New
Orleans. Mr. Williams read the letter to me, and told me that
my mother wanted me to send her some tea and sugar. That
was just like the mornin' we parted. It grieved me so to think
that she was where she could have no sugar and tea. She
could always get it in Georgia, if she had to take in workin'
and do it at night. But I had no money, and could not send
her any thing ; and I felt bad to think my mother could not
have any of these things. Whenever I set down to eat ever
since, I always think of my mother. When Mr. Williams was
sick, before he died, he promised me, if he ever got up off from
that bed, he would buy my mother, and set us all free. But he
never did it."

Q.—" Are the two children you brought with you from New
Orleans now living ?"

A.—" No ; one of them died soon after I got to Cincinnati.
I have only one of them livin'—a daughter, about eighteen
years old."

Q.—" Is she as white as you are ?"

A.—" Oh yes ; a great deal whiter."

———

CHAPTER X.

STILL ANOTHER SOUTHERN HOUSEHOLD.

Q.—" HAVE you any other children ?"

A.—" Yes ; three others. I been in Cincinnati near twelve
years. Three years after I came there, I married Mr. Picquet,
my husband."

Q.—" Is he a white man or colored ?"

A.—" He's a mulatto. His mother is brown skin, and his father white, and that makes a mulatto, you know."

Q.—" Who was his father ?"

A.—" He was a Frenchman, in Georgia. He bought my husband's mother, and live with her public. I knew all about it there, before I left Georgia. She had four other children beside my husband."

Q.—" Were they all slaves ?"

A.—" Yes. They all belong to Mr. Picquet, but he never uses them as slaves. They are his children."

Q.—" How did they get free ?"

A.—" Why, when he got married, he sent them all to Cincinnati, the mother and five children. It would be unpleasant for them all to stay there together (*i.e.*, his wife, and concubine and her children)."

Q.—" Had your husband ever been married before ?"

A.—" Yes ; he married a slave-woman there."

Q.—" How do the slaves get married ?"

A.—" In a general way they ask the owners, and the owner says yes ; and they get married."

Q.—" Do they have a minister to marry them out on the plantations ?"

A.—" No ; not one out of three plantations. They ask the master, and then have little bit of frolic, and sometimes they don't have that."

CHAPTER XI.

DOMESTIC PURITY IN GEORGIA.

Q.—" How was it with Henry, your husband ?"

A.—" Why, he hired Eliza, and rented a house, and put her in. She was a slave-woman, and took in washin'."

Q.—" How came they to part ?"

A.—" Why, you see, she belong to heirs, and the property

was sold for the money to be divided. Then a gentleman in Macon bought Eliza for himself. Then Henry felt so bad about it that, pretty soon, he went to see her. He went there with the intention of buyin' her and her baby, which was Henry's. Mr. Picquet, Henry's father, was goin' to let him have the money. So, when he got there, he found it different from what he expected. He found he could not have her any more for his wife. You see, the gentleman had bought her for himself. So my husband writ to his father that he could not get his wife, but he could buy the child. Then his father, Mr. Picquet, sent on the money, and he bought the child, and brought it away. It was about three months old, and he raised it on a bottle, work all day, and then worry with the child all night."

Q.—" Is that child yet living ?"

A.—" Oh yes ; she is livin' with us in Cincinnati, and the smartest one we got too. She is about thirteen or fourteen."

Q.—" Is she as white as your children ?"

A.—" Oh no ; she is the darkest one in the house. But her hair is straight, only little bit wavy."

CHAPTER XII.

THE LONG-LOST MOTHER HEARD FROM.

Q.—" How came you to find out where your mother was ?"

A.—" Well, I hear she was in Texas, and I keep writin' to Texas, and supposed it was one place, but never got no answer. But I kept prayin', and always believed that I should see her or hear from her, before I died."

Q.—" You kept up praying all this time, did you ?"

A.—" Yes ; but when I came to Cincinnati, I thought more about my mother—to think I was free, and so many others that I knew in Georgia, and she was still in slavery ! It was a great weight on my mind ; and I thought if I could get relig- ion I should certainly meet her in heaven, for I knew she was a Christian woman. I had thought of it very often, and thought how often I had told the Lord I would serve him and had not done so, till I was almost afraid to make another promise. Then I made up my mind to serve the Lord. I had often been to the Methodist meeting there, when there was great excitement; but I never went up to be prayed for. I thought it was a sin if I did not go up in the right way.

"But I kept feelin' worse in my mind. Every thing I had ever done all came up before me. I felt as if I could not look up; my eyes were fixed on the ground. In the evenin'—Sunday evenin'—I went to meetin' in the Zion Baptist Church. Mr. Shelton was preachin'. After he got through, they was singin'; I felt troubled all through it. Then I went up to the altar with others. I made up my mind that I would never hold up my head again on this earth till the Lord converted me. I prayed hard enough that night. My husband was so mortified to think I prayed so loud, and made so much noise; but I told him, Henry, I have to die for myself, and it did not set me back at all. But I did not get rid of the burden I felt till near daylight that night, or next mornin'. I was prayin' nearly all night, and near mornin' I felt worse, as if I would die; and I tried to wake Henry up, but I could not wake him at all. It seemed as if I had not time. All my long prayers had gone to just the one word, 'Lord, have mercy!' and I could not say any thing but that. And the moment I believe that the Lord would relieve me, the burden went right off; and I felt as light as if I was right up in the air. And it seemed as if there was light in the room. * * * Then, the next Sunday, I joined the church, and the Sunday after was baptized. That was eight years ago, going on nine. I been in that church ever since."

Q.—" Is your husband a professor of religion?"

A.—" Yes; he belongs to the same church. He experienced religion in Georgia."

Q.—" How about the two daughters?"

A.—" Elizabeth, my daughter, belongs to the same church. My husband's daughter, Harriet, does not belong to any church."

Q.—" Does your church commune with slaveholders ?"

A.—" *No, sir;* they *will not.* The Union Baptist Church does. When white ministers come there from the South, they let them break the bread at the Communion ; but in our church, if they come there, they don't do it, unless they come with a lie in their mouth.   They ask them if they believe in slavery, or apologize for it, and if they do, then they don't preach there.   No slave-holder, or apologist for slavery, can preach in that church ; that was the foundation when they first started."

Q.—" Well, how did you find out where your mother was ?"

A.—" Well, I have made it a business for about eleven years, to inquire of every one I saw, almost, about my mother.   If any fugitives came through, I made it my business to get to see them, and inquire.   A great many fugitives come through Cincinnati.   I have had lots of them in my house.

" One time a colored woman came there, real genteel, and ask to board.   I thought she was a runaway slave, though she tried to make me believe she was free.   Her name was Mary White.   She was there two or three weeks, and I notice she never went out only on Sunday evenin's.   One afternoon she went to our church, and heard it give out by the preacher, that if any of the friends knew of a woman by the name of Mary White, to tell her to be on the look-out, for the hell-hounds were after her up to one of the hotels.   Then she spring up, and came to where I was and told me.   That night we darken up the house, and a Quaker friend came there and had her fixed up ; and next day she was on her way to Canada.   After that I got a couple of letters from her, returning thanks to us all for helpin' her on her way.   She was in a sheriff's family in Canada, and was doing well."

Q.—" Now tell me how you found your mother ?"

A.—" I used to take in washin', and one day a gentleman, Mr. B., a good friend of ours in Cincinnati, sent some shirts there to be done up, and said he was goin' to Texas.   Then my husband inquired, and found out that he knew Mr. Horton, in Texas, and told us what kind of a lookin' man he was. Then I remembered how he looked when he bought my mother in Mobile, and I knew it was the same man.   Then he told us how to send a letter, and where to mail it. [There is a kink about mailing a letter, so as to have it reach a slave, that we never before dreamed of; but Mrs. P. does not wish it published, for fear it will hinder her from getting her letters.] Then I wrote a letter [got one written], and in three weeks I had a letter from my mother."

Q.—"What became of the first letter you had from your mother, while you were in New Orleans?"

A.—"I never saw that. Mr. Williams only told me he got it, and what was in it. I only knew she was in Texas. I thought it was all Texas."

Q.—"Have you the first letter you received from your mother?"

A.—"Yes; up stairs. Shall I go and get it?"

Here the letter was brought. It is on a tough blue paper, well soiled and worn, but yet quite legible. The following chapter contains an exact copy.

———

CHAPTER XIII.

LETTER FROM A SLAVE MOTHER.

"WHARTON, March 8, 1859

" MY DEAR DAUGHTER,

"I a gane take my pen in hand to drop you a few lines.

"I have written to you twice, but I hav not yet received an answer from you I can not imagin why you do not writ I feel very much troubel I fear you hav not recived my letters or you would hav written; I sent to my little grand children a ring also a button in my first letter I want you to writ to me on recept of this letter, whether you hav ever received the letters and presents or not I said in my letter to you that Col. Horton would let you have me for 1000 dol. or a woman that could fill my place; I think you could get one cheaper where you are* that would fill my place than to pay him the money ; I am anxios to hav you to make this trade. you hav no Idea what my feelings are. I hav not spent one happy moment since I received your kind letter. it is true I was more than rejoyest to hear from you my Dear child ; but my feelings on this subject are in Expressible. no one but a mother can tell my feelings. in regard to your Brother John Col. Horton is willing for you to hav him for a fifteen years old or fifteen hundred dol I think that 1000 dollars is too much for me you must writ very kind to Col Horton and try to Get me for less money ; I think you can change his Price by writing Kindly to him aske him in a kind manner to let you hav me for less I think you can soften his heart and he will let you hav me for less than he has offered me to you for.

" you Brother John sends his love to you and 100 kisses to your little son ; Kiss my Dear little children 100 times for me particuler Elizabeth say to her that she must writ to her grand mar ofton ; I want you to hav your ambrotipe taken also your children and send them to me I would giv this world to see you and my sweet little children ; may God bless you my Dear child and protect you is my prayer.

" Your affectionate mother,

" ELIZABETH RAMSEY.

" direct your letter to Gov. A. C. Horton Wharton Wharton contey texas."

The reader will understand that the brother John, mentioned in this letter, was the " baby" sold with the mother some twenty years ago, in Mobile, whose slips were made of Louisa's pink dress bought with the half-dollars. Louisa's mother never would take the name of Randolph or Cook—the name of her owner—as other slaves do, so she still sticks to her first name of Ramsey, as when she lived in South Carolina thirty-five years ago.

---

* For particular reasons the letter was dated at St. Louis, where so many slaves are bought for Texas and Alabama ; and this letter came first to St. Louis, and was forwarded by a friend to Cincinnati. Thus all the letters come and go.

This letter is dated at Wharton. Mrs. P. says it is "in the country, where they go in the winter, and live at Matagorda in the summer." By looking upon a map of Texas it may be seen that Matagorda is at the mouth of the Colorado River, on the Gulf of Mexico; and Wharton about forty miles northwest, on the same river, both in Southern Texas.

Another friend. Mrs. Ramsey now lives with Arthur, the coachman, who was sold at the same time with her in Mobile, as her husband. The letter is, of course, written by some white person, and is printed exactly as it is written.

There is a fact worth recording in regard to the first letter that reaches Mrs. Ramsey. It is thus described by Mrs. Picquet:

"I had been tryin' hard to find out where my mother was twelve years, after I came to Cincinnati; and when I get that letter written, I just put my trust in the Lord to go with it. I had tried so long, and could not get no word at all. I prayed to the Lord to go with each seal. There was three envelopes: one to take the letter to my friend at St. Louis, to mail the letter that was in it to Matagorda for me. That letter was directed to the postmaster in Texas; and a letter to him in it, asking him, if Col. Horton was alive, to send it to him, and, if not, to send it to some of his children. And I prayed the Lord that he would work in the hearts of the man in St. Louis, and the postmaster at Matagorda, that my letter might reach my mother.

"In that letter I ask Mr. Horton if he would please to read it to my mother, to let her know that I was yet alive; and, if he did not feel disposed to read it to her, would he be so kind as to drop me a few lines, just to let me know if she was alive; and, if she was dead, how long ago, and how she died; and, if she was livin', if she was well, and how she looked—just to ease my mind, for I had been weighed down with sorrow to see her for many years. I told him I had no silver nor gold to pay him; but I trust the Lord would reward him for his kindness, if he would do that much for me. I told him I had great faith in the Lord; and I would pray that his last days might be his best. I tell him if she was livin', and he would sell her, I would try to buy her. If I thought she would die the next week, it would be a great comfort for me to have her here to bury her."

Thus it seems that the Lord did go with the letter, and that Mrs. Horton read the letter to Louisa's mother. She then wrote two letters, but they did not reach Mrs. P. One of them, the one containing the button and the ring, was afterward found in the post-office in Matagorda, by Mrs. Ramsey. It was probably either not stamped, or not properly directed.

As soon as Mrs. P. got the first letter from her mother, she wrote two letters back, one to her mother, and the other to Mr. Horton, and both dated and mailed as before. In a short time she received another from her mother, written but a few days after the first received by Mrs. P. ; and as it throws some additional light upon the question whether or not slaves have any proper affection for their offspring, we transcribe and print that also.

SECOND LETTER FROM THE SLAVE MOTHER.

"Warton, Warton County, March 13, '59.
" My Dear Daughter,

" Your very kind and affectionate letters dated at St. Louis, One in January the other in Febuary has been received and contents partickularly notist, I had them read often creating in me both Sorrow and Joy. Joy that you were living & a doing wel so far as the comforts of this world are concerned and you seem to have a bright prospect in the World to come, this the brightest of all other prospects, If a Person should gain the whole world & lose there Soul they have lost all, My Dear Daughter you say a great deal to me about instructing your Brother in his duty, I endeavor to set a good example before him it is all that I can do John is a good disposed Boy & a favorite with his Master, Arthur, Jim & Mary are all members of the Babtist Church, they are all well and a doing well, In your first letter you spoke of trying to purchase me & your Brother, the proposition was made to you to exchang Property of equal value, or to take One Thousand Dollars for me, & Fifteen Hundred for your Brother this may seem an extravagant price to you but it is not an average price for Servants, I know of nothing on this earth that would gratify me so much as to meet with My Dear & only daughter, I fear that I should not be able to retain my senses on account of the great Joy it would create in me, But time alone will develup whether this meeting will tak plase on earth or not Hope keeps the soul alive, but my Dear Daughter if this should not be our happy lot, I pray God that we may be able to hold fast to the end, & be the Happy recipients of the promise made to the faithful. There will be no parting there, but we shall live in the immediate presence and smiles of our God. It is not in our power to comply with your request in regard to the Degeurrotypes this tim, we shall move to Matagorda shortly, there I can comply with your request. Arthur, Jim, Mary and your brother desire to be very kindly remembered to you, Answer this at as early a date as convenient Direct your letter to Goven A. C. Horton, Matagorda, Texas.

" May God guide and protect you through Life, & Finally save You in Heaven is the prayer of your affectionate mother,

" ELIZABETH RAMSEY."

Before this second letter was received Mrs. P. writes to Mr. Horton, reminding him that her mother was growing old, and that it would be better for him to sell her cheaper, and buy a younger person. In answer to this letter the following was received from Mr. Horton himself.

———

CHAPTER XIV.

LETTER FROM THE OWNER OF ELIZABETH.

MATAGORDA, June 17, 1859.

" LOUISA,

" I have your favor of 16th April last, and contents duly noticed.

" You seem to think that I ask you too much for your mother.

Money would not induce me to sell her, were it not for existing circumstances. You know that she is as fine a washer, cook, and ironer as there is in the United States. It's true she is getting old, but she carries her age well, and looks as young as she did twenty years ago. I only ask you to place another of her quality and qualifications in her stead. You can not complain of this, if it's not of your power to comply with the terms. I write you to come and see her, and I pledge myself you shall not be molested either directly or indirectly, but protected to the utmost extent.

"I send you by this mail a Daguerreotype likeness of your mother and brother, which I hope you will receive. Your mother received yours in a damaged condition. Your mother and all your acquaintance are in fine health, and desire to be remembered, and would be pleased to see you.

"Respec'y yours,

"A. C. HORTON."

The Daguerreotype mentioned above was duly received, in perfect order, and is now in the hands of Mrs. Picquet. They are both taken on one plate, mother and son, and are set forth in their best possible gear, to impress us in the north with the superior condition of the slave over the free colored people.

Just here might come in a chapter more romantic and thrilling than any thing as yet narrated in this pamphlet, but, for reasons that we must not name, it must remain unprinted for the present. The time may come, and we hope soon will come, when it may be published without prejudice to any party or interest.

From the date of the last of the preceding letters, Mrs. Picquet has received letters from her mother nearly every month, but nothing further from Mr. Horton himself, though Mrs. P. has often written him, importuning him to take less for her mother. At length, in March, 1860, she wrote to Mrs. Horton, appealing to her regard for her own mother, to talk to Col. Horton, her husband, and see if he would take less than one thousand dollars for Mrs. Ramsey. Of the results of this appeal we shall learn hereafter.

CHAPTER XV.

PRIVATE EFFORTS TO BUY THE MOTHER.

MRS. PICQUET'S first plan was to draw her husband's wages two years in advance. He was in the employ of Mr. John Carlisle, of Cincinnati, and was willing to have the fruit of his labor thus taken in advance to restore his mother-in-law to freedom, and to the embrace of her daughter. But how were they to live these two years? The two years' labor would only amount to about five hundred dollars, at most; and how to get the remaining five hundred dollars, and take care of themselves and family at the same time, was the insurmountable difficulty. Mrs. P. was anxious to sell every thing she had to help buy the mother, but all she had on earth would bring but little. For one whole year Mrs. P. saved every penny she could, even denying herself many of the comforts of life; and the amount of all this rigid economy was only sixty dollars saved. By this time she began to be discouraged. She talked with friends, and they advised her to go out and solicit money for the purpose. This she was reluctant to do. She had her family of four young children to care for, as well as her husband; had never traveled, except from New Orleans to Cincinnati, and dreaded to go out for such a purpose. She knew that many were abroad soliciting money for such purposes, and feared it would be in vain for her to make the attempt. But her mother was in bondage, and she resolved to make the attempt at all hazards.

The Press of Cincinnati gave the effort their encouragement The *Daily Gazette* of Saturday, March 10, contained the following:

" TO THE BENEVOLENT OF CINCINNATI."

" Louisa Picquet, though to all appearance white, is, nevertheless, a colored woman. She was born a slave, and has a mother and brother now in slavery in Texas. She is personally known to me. She is in our midst, appealing for aid to

buy her mother out of slavery.   Let our citizens respond to her appeal.   * * *   JAMES POINDEXTER,
> " of Zion Baptist Church."

This Mr. Poindexter, it seems, was not then in active service, as pastor of the church, though still residing there.

The *Journal and Messenger* of March 16, contained the following editorial notice : "Louisa Picquet, formerly a slave, but with a complexion as white almost as that of any person, is now visiting villages in this State [Ohio], soliciting aid to purchase her mother, who is a slave in Texas.   She is a member of Zion Baptist Church, in this city, is well recommended ; and is, no doubt, worthy of public sympathy and benevolence."

Mrs. P. accordingly procured a subscription-book, pasted the above notices into the front of it, and started out in Cincinnati first.   A well-known "Friend," in Cincinnati, recommended her as follows, on a blank leaf : "The bearer of this, Louisa Picquet, I believe to be a very worthy, pious woman.   Would recommend her to the sympathy of the friends of humanity, in aiding her to redeem her mother from slavery.

> "LEVI COFFIN.

" Cincinnati, 15th 12th mo., 1860."

Similar recommendations were inserted by JOSEPH EMERY.

CHAPTER XVI.

SOLICITING HELP ABROAD TO BUY A MOTHER.

THUS fitted for her undertaking, Mrs. P. started out in Cincinnati first, and obtained subscriptions to the amount of about three hundred dollars.   Among them was one by JOHN CARLISLE, Esq. (the gentleman in whose employ Mr. Picquet has been for years), amounting to fifty dollars.   A Mr. W. Mills gave ten dollars, P. Wilson twenty dollars, and many others in Cincinnati five dollars each.

Mrs. P. then went to Lebanon, Ohio, to see Hon. Thomas
Corwin, but he had gone to Washington ; but his nephew, Mat-
thias Corwin, took her book, and wrote as follows in it :

"I hereby certify that I have known the bearer, Louisa Picquet, for the last ten years. She comes to Lebanon to ask aid
to purchase her mother, who is now a slave in Texas. I have
no doubt but the money that is given will be faithfully applied
to that purpose.   M. CORWIN.

"Lebanon, January 28, 1860."

A Mr. Suydam went one way in Lebanon with Mrs. Picquet
and the book, and Mr. Corwin another, and between them
raised a nice little sum ; but the book does not show where
that subscription ends, and the next village begins. Mr. Corwin then gave her a letter to some member of the legislature,
at Columbus, where she obtained $121. She next visited Day-
ton, Springfield, Xenia, Urbana, and Wellington, in all of
which places she obtained more or less help, though the
amounts were generally small.

CHAPTER XVII.

LOUISA IS IDENTIFIED IN OHIO BY A FELLOW-TRAVELER.

"WHILE in Ohio, going from Xenia to Springfield in the
cars," says Mrs. P., "I was expecting a letter to be left in the
cook-house, at the depot, for me. I had got my seat in the
cars, and wanted to leave a message with the cook about the
letter. A gentleman was goin' out, and I stopped him, and
asked him if he'd be kind enough to take this message to
the cook. He did so, and came back and told me what the
cook said ; and then took a seat about five or six seats back of
me, on the opposite side. As he took his seat, a lady asked
him, thinkin' he knew all about me, how that woman got along
raisin' money to buy her mother ? He asked her, what woman ? She said, that colored woman you was speakin' to just

now. He told her she was mistaken ; he was not speakin' to any colored woman. She insisted on it that he was. He told her, no ; it was that lady in front, who was givin' him some directions about a letter—and was pointin' toward me.

"Just at that time I was turnin' round to hand my book to a gentleman sittin' just behind me. The moment the first gentleman saw my face there, he asked a gentleman before him if I didn't come from Mobile, Alabama. He said he believed I did. He asked if my mother's name wan't Elizabeth ? He laughed, and said, yes, I believe that's the name.

"Then the first gentleman came to me, and, after speakin' and bowin', he asked me if I knew him ? I told him I did not know—perhaps I did—his face looked familiar to me ; thinkin' it was some one I had seen in travelin' around in askin' for money. He said, 'were you ever in Mobile ?' I told him, yes ; and he wanted to know if my mother's name was Elizabeth Ramsey ? I told him it was. Then he wanted to know if I ever lived with Mr. English, in Mobile ? I told him, yes. He then said he knew me well ; and that his name was Bolden. He is a Baptist preacher now, but was not a preacher then. He was goin' up to Springfield, to organize a church : so I heard on the cars. Then he turned to the other gentleman, and said, 'I know this lady well. I knew her when she lived at Mr. English's, in Mobile.' He told what a fine woman my mother was, and said he knew the day I was sold ; and said it had been twenty years. He even spoke to me about Lucy, and told how white she was, and her children ; and asked me what ever became of her. I told him she was sold in Mobile ; but afterward her friends bought her up, and her children."

CHAPTER XVIII.

VISIT TO OBERLIN, AND SOME OF THE " RESCUERS :" AND THENCE TO NEW YORK.

She next went to Oberlin, where she met with most cheering encouragement. Hon. Mr. Plumb (one of the " Rescuers," we

believe,) took hold of the matter with great spirit. The Wesleyan Methodist Church took a collection of $14.92 ; the Con-
gregational Church, $99.58 ; and the Episcopal Church, *ninety-
five cents !* Other private subscriptions brought the amount
collected in Oberlin up to $135 ; for which a draft was sent on
to Mr. W. T. Drake, banker, Cincinnati. She then visited
Penfield, Litchfield, Medina, and other small places, collecting
small amounts (all of which are carefully entered in the subscription-book), and finally went to Cleveland. Here she received $9.62 at the door of the Baptist Church, in the morning
on the Sabbath, and $17.14 in a collection in the First Congre-
gational Church, in the evening.

At Cleveland Mrs. P. was advised to visit Buffalo, where the
General Conference of the Methodist Episcopal Church was in
session. The Baptist minister in Cleveland wrote a letter to
another Baptist minister in Buffalo, and a Mr. Day wrote another to Rev. Mr. Hill, a delegate to the General Conference.

Mrs. Picquet then went on to Buffalo and delivered one of
her letters, but received so little encouragement, owing, doubt-
less, to the interest upon the subject of slavery then pending in
the General Conference, that she concluded to go on to New
York.

Mr. Henry R. Smith, of Cleveland, had been very active in
Mrs. P.'s behalf while she was in that city, and had given her
letters to Henry Ward Beecher and others in New York. On
reaching that city she met with excellent encouragement, so
that, in a few days, she collected $223 there ; $55.70 of this was
collected at the Anniversary of the American Anti-slavery
Society, at the Cooper Institute.

CHAPTER XIX.

AN UNEXPECTED MEETING.

WHILE in New York, Mrs. P. was going from the Brooklyn
Ferry to 29th Street, where she stopped. On her way up, between Fulton Street and the Park, she saw a man on the top

of the omnibus, with the driver. He looked at her earnestly, and she at him, and knew him in a moment. He then got off and walked along to her, and said, "You must excuse me," but asked her name, and if she did not live at English's, in Mobile. She told him she did, and who she was. Then he told her he had been in New York ever since he ran away; that no one ever thought he was colored, as he said, "I just ranked in here." Mrs. P. wanted to know who he married. He laughed, and said, "You know I would never marry any but a white girl." He told Mrs. P. he had four children, and would like her to see them; and if she would wait in the Park he would bring them down there. He did not wish to have his wife see Mrs. P., as she was there raising money, and if ——'s wife should hear of the interview, it would be natural for her to wish to know where he knew Mrs. P., and thus the fact of his being of African descent, and once a slave, might get out.

Mrs P. walked in the Park awhile, till —— went home, got three of his children, and came down in an omnibus with them, and stopped, and went into the Park. Mrs. P. says they were very pretty children. "Pretty dressed too," says Mrs. P.; "I think the mother must be very tasty woman. The two oldest were *very* white, girls. The youngest was a boy, dressed in little pants and sack, and a hat with feathers in it. He was a brunette, and I laughed, and said, 'That one has the stain on it.' He laughed, and said the family often laughed about, it, but little did they think what was the real cause of it. The family of his wife would often joke about it, and say they guessed his wife was frightened by a nigger; and he said, 'There's many a truth told in joke.'"

Here Mrs. P. added, "Now, it is astonishing, in the South, the white men run after the colored women, their own and others; but if a colored man speak to a white woman they want to shoot him." Mrs. P. promised to keep the matter secret, lest it might break up a family, or one of our white citizens in New York might be remanded back to slavery. And so they parted; but not till he had given her $5 to help purchase her mother It was put down in the book by Mr. ——, and stands here before us as we write, "Cash, $5." This is the young man who wished Louisa to run away from Mobile with him, twenty years ago.

———

CHAPTER XX.

RETURN TO BUFFALO—CALLS UPON "M."

WHILE in New York Mrs. P.'s attention was directed to the writer, who was then in Buffalo, though our whereabouts was not known by the parties directing. Neither did they know our address. They sent her, therefore, to the Colored Orphan Asylum, on 43d Street, to ascertain our address. Here she met with Mr. Wm. E. Davis, who has charge of the Asylum, and is a communicant at Union Chapel, one of the best of men, and a practical Abolitionist. He and others there gave her seven dollars for the object, and also gave her a letter to the writer, at Buffalo. This was the first we had known of the case.

On looking over the subscription list, and the certificates of deposits and drafts which Mrs. P. had in possession, obtained in New York, and elsewhere, it was evident that it was a clear case, and, after deducting her expenses in travel (an account of which she had carefully kept by the aid of a little boy), together with what would be necessary to take her to her home in Cincinnati, and to get her mother from Matagorda, Texas, it would require at least one hundred and fifty dollars more than had as yet been subscribed.

———

CHAPTER XXI.

SUSPECTED AND REPULSED BY A "FRIEND OF THE COLORED PEOPLE."

WHEN Mrs. P. first came to Buffalo, she had brought a letter to Rev. Mr. ——, a Baptist minister residing there, and also one to Rev. Mr. Hill, a delegate from the Erie Conference; but for some cause they could not then aid her, as she had hoped.

She accordingly passed on to New York; but, on her return. Mr. Hill seemed disposed to do something for her, if he could, and for this purpose introduced her to Rev. Henry Slicer, a delegate from the East Baltimore Conference, in hope of getting him to bring up the matter in the Conference. Mr. S. looked sternly at Mrs. P., and with an imperious air said, "*You* a colored woman? You're no negro. Where did you come from? If you are a negro, where are your free papers to show it?" At the same time, looking over her book of letters, he asked, "Who wrote these letters? Where is the envelope that came on them, to show the postmark? You've got no envelope here." Then he handed back the book and papers, and said he could not do any thing about it. As he went away he looked at Mr. Hill and said, "She's no negro;" and thus ended the assistance from Rev. Henry Slicer.

CHAPTER XXII.

LOUISA IS INDORSED AFRESH FROM CINCINNATI.

BEING thus repulsed, and virtually accused of being an impostor, Mrs. P. felt deeply grieved, as any sensitive and virtuous woman would; but she made no reply, except to say that she believed she had one of the envelopes at the house where she was stopping. She had not thought to keep and show them as a proof that she was not an impostor, and this was the first time they had been called for; for the reader must understand that begging was new business to her, and that she had not resorted to it till all hope of getting her mother free by any other means had fled forever.

The fact of this cold repulse and alleged suspicion becoming known H. H. Mattison, Esq., of Buffalo (a relative of the writer), told Mrs. P. to go to his house and remain till her case could be brought before the Conference. He then went to the telegraph office and telegraphed to Evans & Co., Bankers, Cincinnati, to whom Mrs. P. had referred him, to know if Mrs. P. resided there, and every thing was as she represented.*

The telegraph operator kindly sent the message (amounting to nearly three dollars) gratuitously, and the next mail brought the following letter from W. T. DRAKE, Esq., of the firm of Evans & Co., and one of the first subscribers upon Mrs Picquet's book :

JASON EVANS, }
BRIGGS SWIFT. }   EVANS & CO., BANKERS.   { H. W. HUGHES,
                                                        { W. T. DRAKE.

CINCINNATI, 22nd May, 1860.

" H. H. MATTISON, Esq., Buffalo, N. York.

" *Dear Sir*,—I am in receipt of your telegram of 21st inst., and hasten to reply.

" I *know* Mrs. Picquet has a mother in bondage in Texas, for whom she is trying to raise sufficient money to purchase her freedom.

" I know, also, Mrs. Picquet to be a truthful, and, I trust, Christian woman. You can, therefore, place the utmost confidence in her representations to you.

" I cordially commend her to your charity, in assisting her in the humane and filial endeavor of purchasing a mother from the curse of slavery.

" A mother ! Who would not brave any danger, toil, and hardship for that dear name !

" I am, very truly,

" W. T. DRAKE.

" I have just seen the husband of Mrs. Picquet. He hands me two letters from Mrs. P.'s mother, received since she has been gone. Will you please hand them to her, after reading. The master of this woman has agreed to take $100 less than is former price."

The two accompanying letters referred to will be found in the following chapter.

---

* The object of this movement on the part of Mr. Mattison was not to satisfy the writer, or himself ; but to procure fresh testimony from original sources, to either convince or silence such incredulous subjects as Rev. H. Slicer.

CHAPTER XXIII.

MORE LETTERS FROM THE MOTHER.

"APRIL 15th, '60.

"DEAR DAUGHTER,

"I have been looking for some time for a letter from you.

"I wrote to you on the business you wrote to me a bout; I have never herd if you received the letter or not.

"I received a letter from you that was written to Mrs Horton a few days since. She red it and then sent it to me. I ask her what she would do for us. She said that she was willing for him to take less

"I had a talk with Col Horton yesterday he told me that he would not take less than nine hundred dollars & no less this is hard but we can not help it so you must make your self easy & dont fret any more than you can help.

"I would help you but my Situation is such that I cant.

"You must come and see me soon your brother was well when I heard from him last kiss my little grand children for me your affectionate mother,

"ELIZABETH RAMSEY."

"MATAGORDA, April 21, 1860.

"DEAR DAUGHTER,

"I received your kind & affectionate letter, & was glad to hear that you was well, & getting along very well. I was sorry to learn that you were disappointed in raising the amount of money required to purchase me. In a conversation with my master on the subject he says he is willing to take a woman in exchange for me, of my age and capasity or he will under the circumstances take nine hundred dollars in *cash* for me he says he would not part with me except under existing circumstances. he also says that money cannot buy either Arthur or John he is a training John to take charge of one of his Plantations he has unlimited confidence in him & will not part

with him untel death parts them. I should be very happy to
see you My Dear Daughter as well as my Grandchildren. I
hope there will be a way provided for us to meet on earth once
more before we die. Cant you come and see us My Master
will give all the protection you require whilst with us. This
you may rest assured of. Your Brother John is well and desires to be very kindly remembered to you. Arthur wishes
to be kindly remembered to you.

"Farewell My Dear Daughter. May God protect you from
All evil, is the prayer of your affectionate Mother.

                                ELIZABETH RAMSEY.

This Arthur, it must be remembered, is the coachman sold
with Mrs. Ramsey in Mobile, and bought by Col. Horton
twenty years before; and John is the "baby" sold with its
mother—the brother of Mrs. Picquet. Arthur is now, and has
long been, Mrs. Ramsey's husband; and yet he is entirely willing she should go, if she can only be " free ;" and she is willing
to leave her husband and son forever, if she can only enjoy the
precious boon of freedom. Oh, how sweet is LIBERTY ! The
Daguerreotype shows John to be as white as one in a hundred
of our white fellow-citizens.

These two letters we took to Mrs. P., as directed, and read
them to her ; and the tide of emotion they created in her
bosom, we can never describe. Joy, mingled with intense sorrow—the one, to learn that her mother could be bought for
$100 less than the former price ; and sorrow, to learn, at the
same time, that *her brother could not be bought out of bondage at
any price.* These two conflicting currents seemed to sweep
over her soul in a mingled flood of joy and sorrow.

But all this only showed the importance of every proper
effort to restore the mother to freedom, even if the brother was
obliged to remain in life-long bondage.

CHAPTER XXIV.

METHODIST GENERAL CONFERENCE—CALLING UPON THE BISHOPS.

THE next evening we took Mrs. P., and went to the Bishops' rooms to see what arrangement could be made for bringing the matter up in the conference the next morning. They received us kindly, and expressed the utmost willingness to have it brought up, and the balance of the money raised. Bishop JANES gave a donation at once, and Bishops BAKER and SCOTT subsequently.

Bishop BAKER was to preside the next morning, and either he or Bishop SCOTT suggested that any one might bring up the matter as a privileged question, as soon as the audience was sufficiently large to secure the object.

We went to the conference room next morning, and spoke to one or two delegates, who seemed to have good excuses for declining. We then called upon Dr. E. O. HAVEN, editor of *Zion's Herald*, Boston, and a delegate ; and introduced him to Mrs. Picquet.

He was not quite as incredulous as Rev. H. SLICER ; but heard her brief story with deep interest and emotion, and at once consented to bring up the matter in the conference the first fitting opportunity. But the effort to do so failed, on account of the extreme sensitiveness on the slavery question, lest it should be thought the case was brought in to exert an influence upon that question, which was then pending before the conference. The only way, therefore, to do any thing was by private application. Accordingly, we took Mrs. P.'s book, and collected what we could ($68.80), and she returned home to Cincinnati.

This left still wanting, as near as we could calculate, some eighty or ninety dollars to make up the $900, and the amount necessary to purchase her mother, and bring her from Matagorda to Cincinnati.

CHAPTER XXV.

NEW DIFFICULTIES ENCOUNTERED—THE MOTHER STILL IN BONDAGE.

UPON returning to Cincinnati, Mrs. P. proceeded to collect the subscriptions made in that city, amounting to some $300, cheered by the fond hope of yet meeting her long-lost mother once more in this world. But some of the subscribers had died, others had moved away, and still others were tardy about paying what they had subscribed ; so that the last we heard of the matter (which was by letter from Mr. Coffin, mentioned on page 33, a highly respectable citizen of Cincinnati), Mrs. P. was almost in despair about ever succeeding in her filial undertaking.

We learned this fact, however, that every dollar that had thus far been given for the object was deposited with Messrs. Evans & Co., bankers, Cincinnati, and would be sacredly kept for that purpose till enough was obtained to accomplish the object. We had hoped to be able to close with a chapter entitled, " *The long-lost mother restored to her daughter,*" but are as yet denied this satisfaction.

And now, reader, you have the narrative, closed, as we are obliged to close it after all that has been done, under a cloud of disappointment and gloom. The mother and brother are yet toiling in bondage in Texas ; and the daughter weeping, and praying, and begging to obtain the amount yet needful to release the mother, at least, from her life-long oppression. Ought the object to fail for lack of about three hundred dollars ? May not this pamphlet fall into the hands of some who can sympathize with this daughter of affliction and victim of relentless oppression, and will rejoice in the opportunity of doing *something* to help alleviate her sorrow ? That there is no imposition or deception about it you must be perfectly satisfied. Mrs. P. is a child of God, a sister in Christ, as is also her mother. She loves her *mother* as you love yours, if living ; and wishes not only to see her, but to bring her from the house of bondage to a land of freedom.

Should any of our readers be willing to contribute to this object, as we hope many will, let them inclose, if it be but a single dollar, either to Evans & Co., bankers, Cincinnati, Ohio, or to Rev. H. Mattison, care of Mason Brothers, New York City, by whom all such gifts will be sacredly donated to the object for which they are contributed. And as soon as the amount is made up, and the slave-mother released, the public will be duly notified ; and all donors, whose address we have, especially informed of the happy conclusion of this hitherto sad and dark narrative.

CHAPTER XXVI.

CONCLUSION AND MORAL OF THE WHOLE STORY.

THE reader has, no doubt, been impressed with the main features of this artless and truthful story, as he has perused it ; and will need little aid in retaining in dark outline upon the pages of memory the abhorrent picture which it presents. There are a few points, however, to which we deem it important to call special attention, as we now close the narration :

I.—And first, let it be remembered that this is *no fiction.* It is a plain, unvarnished story, from the lips of one who has spent her life in the South ; has seen and known all that she asserts ; and has no motive for exaggeration or falsehood. On the other hand, the very worst things in the narrative are those which she recited with the least apparent satisfaction. And the manner in which they were referred to, in their recital, showed conclusively that they were not and could not have been inventions to serve a purpose. Of all that has ever been published respecting the actual workings of slavery in the South, nothing has ever appeared that was worthy of more implicit confidence in all its details than the preceding pages. Though unable to read or write, Mrs. P. has an excellent memory ; is decidedly intelligent ; and, more than all, is deeply pious and conscientious. All that she has said, therefore, is worthy of the most implicit belief.

II.—The darkest and most prominent feature of the whole narrative is *the deep moral corruption* which it reveals in the families concerned, resulting from the institution of slavery.

1. At the outset (p. 2), we find the mother of Mrs. P., Elizabeth, through no fault of her own, a " seamstress," or concubine, in the family of John Randolph, who becomes the father of Louisa. Then there is trouble in the family, and Elizabeth and her young babe, like Hagar of old, must leave the patriarchal mansion in South Carolina for a home among strangers in Georgia.

2. Then she has three more *quadroon* children, while Mr. Cook owned her ; but no husband, either black or white (p. 4).

3. She has another child while in Mobile (the brother now in Texas), who is as white as Louisa ; but no husband (p. 4).

4. We have the case of Lucy, the seamstress of Mr. Cook, with her " light hair and blue eyes," and her six or seven white children ; but no husband (p. 16).

5. We have the cases of Elcy and Judy, kept by Mr. —— (p. 17).

6. Next we have the very " gentlemanly" conduct of Mr. Cook, a married man, toward Louisa, while in Mobile (p. 6–11). And yet all this is tolerated even by Mrs. Bachelor, the friend of Louisa, inasmuch as the loathsome wretch was not at once driven from beneath her roof. What kind of a home would such a man find of it in a New England or Ohio family ? And yet he remains in peace, and associates with the family of Mrs. B., in Mobile, as a " gentleman," as a matter of course. Though foiled by her in his designs upon this poor slave-child, he is, nevertheless, recognized as a " gentleman," and admitted to female society, as if he were as pure as Joseph ! What, we ask, must be the moral atmosphere in which such monsters can live and breathe?

7. We have the " gentleman" in Mobile, with his " very light girl bought from Carolina for himself," which he kept " boarding out."

8. We have the " gentleman from New Orleans," who is too poor to pay his debts, but can borrow money of his brother to buy Louisa, as a concubine, at the age of fourteen ; and with

whom he lives, as slave and mistress, till she becomes the mother of six children, of whom he is the father.

9. We have the case of Mr. Picquet, the father of the husband of Louisa, who bought Elizabeth, and lived with her till she became the mother of five children—all of whom (following the condition of the mother, according to the slave laws,) were slaves.

Thus it is that we have near 300,000 mulattoes in the Slave States ; to a great extent the contributions of slaveholders and their sons to the common stock of southern chattels.

10. Finally, we see the wife of Henry, Mr. Picquet, Jr., and his babe, taken from him, a "gentleman" having "bought her for himself ;" and the bereft husband is obliged to buy his own child, and rear it alone as best he can, while his wife, as the result of a desperate act, for which few under the circumstances will blame her, ends her days upon the gallows.

And all this in the brief narrative of a single individual who has been but a few years behind the scenes. There is not a family mentioned, from first to last, that does not reek with fornication and adultery. It turns up as naturally, and is mentioned with as little specialty, as walrus beef in the narrative of the Arctic Expedition, or macaroni in a tour in Italy.

Now, if such are the glimpses of southern domestic life which a single brief narrative reveals, what must the remainder be, which is hidden from our "Abolition" eyes ? Alas for those telltale mulatto, and quadroon, and octoroon faces ! They stand out unimpeached, and still augmenting as God's testimony to the deep moral pollution of the Slave States. We may shudder at the "heathenism" of a Turkish harem, and send missionaries to convert the Mohammedans ; we may stand aghast at the idea of twenty thousand Syrian women sold to supply the harems of the Mussulmans, and pour out our money like water to relieve or release them ; but wherein is all this a whit worse than what is constantly practiced, with scarce a word of unfavorable comment, in our own "Christian" (?) land ? If there is any difference, it is certainly in favor of the Turk ; for neither his concubines nor his children by them are *slaves ;* while, in this country, our chivalrous "southern gentlemen" beget thousands of slaves ;

and hundreds of the children of our free white citizens are sold
in the southern slave markets every year.

III.—The failure of Mr. Cook, with his large cotton plantation, and the subsequent sale of his slaves by the sheriff (probably to pay some "conservative" New York merchant), illus-
trates the "happy condition" of these slaves who have such
"kind masters," but are, nevertheless, liable to be sold for debt
at the auction-block, not only upon the death of their master,
but at any time during his life ; and then, as in this case, brothers and sisters, parents and children, wives and husbands (if
there be any such), must part to meet no more in this world.

"But these," says one, " are the *evils* of slavery, to which I
am as much opposed as you are." Verily, they are the " evils,"
but they are just such " evils" as necessarily belong to the system,
and inhere in it, and without which slavery never did and
never can exist. While the tree stands it will bear just these
fruits, and no other. To sustain the system, therefore, or to
practice under or apologize for it, is virtually to abet all its
abominations. There is no escape from this conclusion.

What, then, is the duty of the American citizen who loves
his country—the Christian citizen, especially ? Ought he not
to set his face against this giant wrong in every possible way ?
Can he even hold his peace concerning it, and be innocent ?
Ought he not to use all his influence, socially, ecclesiastically,
and politically, to undermine and destroy it ? Should he not
speak and write against it, pray and protest against it, give
and vote against it, till it shall wither under the just indignation of an enlightened and humane people ? And, if a minister,
an editor, especially, is it not his solemn duty to open his mouth
for the dumb, and plead the cause of the oppressed ?

May the Lord arouse this guilty nation to a sense of its deep
and unwashed guilt, and bring us to repentance and reforma-
tion before the republic shall crumble beneath the weight of
our accumulated crimes, and He who led Israel out of Egypt,
by his sore judgments, shall arise for the sighing of the millions
whom we hold in chains, and shall pour out his fury upon us to
our utter confusion and ruin !

UNEXPECTED GOOD TIDINGS!

Since the preceding was stereotyped, the following has been sent us, marked in the *Cincinnati Daily Gazette* of October 15, 1860 :

NOTICE.—The undersigned takes this the first opportunity of expressing her thanks to those ladies and gentlemen residing in Cincinnati and elsewhere, that having accomplished through their kind aid the freedom of her mother, Elizabeth Ramsey, from slavery, by paying to her owner, Mr. A. C. Horton, of Texas, cash in hand, the sum of $900, collected by myself in small sums from different individuals, residing in this city and States of Ohio and New York.

I beg leave further to express my gratitude by thanking you all for your kindness, which will be engraved on my heart until death. My mother also desires to say that she is also most grateful to you all, and that if any of those friends who have assisted her to her freedom, feel disposed to call on her at my residence on Third Street, near Race (No. 135), she will be happy to see them, and thank them personally.

Very respectfully, yours, etc.   LOUISA PICQUET.
Cincinnati, October 13, 1860.

So the poor old mother is free at last! and the miserable wretch who bought her twenty years ago for perhaps $600, and has had her labor for twenty long years, now receives his $900 for her old and calloused flesh and bones. And yet he is probably a member of the Methodist Episcopal Church, South, and makes loud profession of piety! May Heaven save the heathen from the curse of such a Christianity!

———

CHAPTER XXVII

SLAVE-BURNING, OR THE "BARBARISM OF SLAVERY."

We often hear pathetic appeals for money to send missionaries to the heathen, who burn widows on funeral piles, or throw their children into the Ganges; but the *suttee* was long since abolished in India; and so far as we know there is but one place on earth where human beings are burned alive. That place is the Slave States of America!

The following is from the *St. Louis Democrat* of July 20, 1859; it relates to a slave-burning that had recently taken place at Marshall, Missouri :

" The negro was stripped to his waist, and barefooted. He looked the picture of despair; but there was no sympathy felt for him at the moment.

Presently, the fire began to surge up in flames around him, and its effects were soon made visible in the futile attempts of the poor wretch to move his feet. As the flames gathered about his limbs and body, he commenced the most frantic shrieks, and appeals for mercy, for death, for water. He seized his chains; they were hot, and burned the flesh off his hands. He would drop them and catch at them again and again. Then he would repeat his cries; but all to no purpose. In a few moments he was a charred mass, bones and flesh alike burned into a powder."

Read also the following description of a similar scene in Mississippi, from the *Natchez Free Trader*, 1858 :

" The victim was chained to a tree, faggots were placed around him, while he showed the greatest indifference. When the chivalry had arranged the pile, in reply to a question, if he had any thing to say, he is reported to have warned all slaves to take example by him, and asked the prayers of those around. He then asked for a drink of water, and after quaffing it said, " Now set fire, I am ready to go in peace." When the flames began to burn him, in his agony he showed gigantic strength, and actually forced the staple from the tree, and bounded from the burning mass. But he instantly fell pierced with rifle balls, and then his body was thrown into the flames and consumed, to show that no such being had ever existed. Nearly four thousand slaves from the neighboring plantations were present as at a moral lesson written in characters of hell fire. Numerous speeches were made by the magistrates and ministers of religion (facetiously so called) to the slaves, warning them that the same fate awaited them if they proved rebellious to their owners."

Read also the following, taken from the *Alton* (Ill.) *Telegraph* of April 30, 1836 ; it is part of an account of a slave-burning published in that paper under that date :

" All was silent as death when the executioners were piling wood around their victim. He said not a word, until feeling that the flames had seized upon him. He then uttered an awful howl, attempting to sing and pray, then hung his head, and suffered in silence, except in the following instance : After the flames had surrounded their prey, his eyes burned out of his head, and his mouth seemingly parched to a cinder, some one in the crowd, more compassionate than the rest, proposed to put an end to his misery by shooting him, when it was replied, ' that it would be of no use, since he was already out of pain.' ' No, no,' said the wretch, ' I am not, I am suffering as much as ever ; shoot me, shoot me.' ' No, no,' said one of the fiends who was standing about the sacrifice they were roasting, ' he shall not be shot. *I would sooner slacken the fire, if that would increase his misery ;*' and the man who said this was, as we understand, an officer of justice.

" If any one wishes evidence of other negroes being burned in the State of Missouri, I can furnish it—evidence of the burning of eight negroes within the last ten years, and innumerable instances of negroes being burned throughout the Slave States.   GILBERT J. GREENE.

" *Tarrytown, N. Y., August* 21, 1860."

———

Some time in the early part of 1860, Mr. Davis, of Mississippi, publicly denied that slaves were ever burned alive at the South. This denial led to the collection of quite an amount of testimony upon the subject, most of which was published in the *New York Tribune*. We subjoin a few of these testimonies :

The editor of *Hayneville* (Ala.), *Chronicle* very justly observes :

"It is questionable whether burning negroes by whites has any better effect than to brutalize the feeling of a community. Several have already been burned in Montgomery County, without, it seems, decreasing crime among them."

Here it is stated by an Alabama editor that "several" negroes have already been burned in Montgomery County. Several in *a single county*

———

Our next witness is a Mr. Poe, a native of Richmond, Va., and afterward a resident of Hamilton County, Ohio, where he was a highly respected ruling elder in the Presbyterian Church. In a letter written about twenty years since, upon the subject of slavery, he says : "In Goochland County, Virginia, an overseer tied a slave to a tree, flogged him again and again with great severity, then piled brush around him, set it on fire, and burned him to death. The overseer was tried and imprisoned. The whole transaction may be found on the records of the court."

———

The late John Parrish, of Philadelphia, an eminent minister of the Society of Friends, traveled through the Slave States on a religious mission, early in this century, and on his return published a pamphlet entitled "Remarks on the Slavery of the Black People." Among other instances of cruel punishment, he states that a slave "was burned to death at a stake in Charleston, surrounded by a multitude of spectators, some of whom were people of the first rank ; . . . . . . the poor object was heard to cry, as long as he could breathe, 'not guilty—not guilty!'"

———

In the year 1836, a man of color was arrested in St. Louis for some offense, but was rescued by one Mackintosh, a free man of color, a steward on board a steamboat. On his way to the jail, in order to effect his escape, he stabbed and killed one of his captors. The wife and children of the murdered man excited the rage of the people by their lamentations, the jail was surrounded, the murderer demanded, and given up. He was led into the woods, on the then outskirts of the city, but near the spot where the court-house was afterward built, brush wood and green wood was piled about him, and fire set to the heap, in presence of a concourse of two or three thousand of the citizens of St. Louis. The poor wretch was from twenty minutes to half an hour in dying, during which he was praying or singing hymns in a calm voice. When his legs were consumed, the trunk disappeared in the blazing pile. "There," said a by-stander, " it is over with him ; he does not feel any more now." " Yes, I do," answered a steady voice from out of the flames.

A correspondent of the *Cincinnati Herald*, in July, 1845, writes to that paper that, not long before, some slaves near Oakland Cottage, Mississippi, were emancipated by the will of their master. For some reason the will was not carried out, and the slaves, exasperated by the delay, and fearful of being cheated out of the property in themselves, left them by their master, set on fire the house of the overseer, and a white child was lost in the flames. The incendiaries, eight or nine in number, were seized by the neighbors, and two of them immediately hanged. The rest were confined in a log-house, and chained to the floor. A torch was then put to the building, and the miserable creatures roasted by a slow fire, while the air was rent with their cries.

" I have just received," writes a correspondent of the *N. O. Picayune*, at Jackson, Mississippi, on the 25th of December, 1855, " the particulars of a most horrid affair just transpired at Lexington, in this State. A young lady of the neighborhood was assaulted, on a lonely road, by a slave, who attempted to violate her person. She was rescued, however, before he had accomplished his purpose, and after being deposited in a place of safety, the alarm was raised, and a hunt for the negro who had fled, was instituted. He was soon found, and execution was speedy. He was taken into Lexington, chained to a stake, and burned alive.

The *Montgomery* (Ala.) *Mail* of April 3, 1856, says, "We learn that the negro who murdered Mr. Capeheart, was burned to death yesterday at Mount Meigs. He acknowledged himself guilty."

———

The *Union Springs* (Ala.) *Gazette* of the 23d of December, 1858, gives the particulars of the murder of a Mr. J. by his slave-boy Mitford. He had been whipped, and chained up from Saturday to Monday, and, when released by his master, seized an axe and killed him. The negro made no attempt to escape, and no resistance when taken. A public meeting was called on Wednesday to consider the case, and, by a unanimous vote of the assembly, it was resolved to burn him alive. "That evening," continues the *Gazette*, "at three o'clock, in the presence of five hundred persons, he was chained to a tree and burned."

———

They closed their pleasant Christmas holidays of 1858 in the same way in Troy, Ky. On the first day of last year, 1859, at the annual negro sales at Troy, Mr. James Calaway, the brother-in-law of one Simon B. Thornhill, who, it seems, had been murdered by a slave in revenge for some punishment, mounted a box in the street, and exhorted the people to do speedy justice upon the murderer, and closed by saying, "All that feel as I do, will follow me." Eight hundred or a thousand followed him. They went to the jail, took out the prisoner, and in the jail-yard itself, drove down a stake, to which they chained him hand and feet. Fine split wood was piled around him, and he was miserably burned to death. "He gave," says a correspondent of the *Maysville* (Ky.) *Eagle*, "some of the most hideous screams I ever heard come from any human being."

———

The *Vicksburg Sun* of Saturday, March 31, 1860, says that a negro man belonging to Mr. Woodfolk, on Deer Creek, was recently burned at the stake for the murder of a negro woman. All the negroes on that and the adjoining plantations witnessed the burning. "His fate was decreed by a council of *highly respectable gentlemen*."

In 1856, Dr. Parsons, of Boston, a gentleman of unquestionable character, published a little work of travels at the South. He copies from the *Sumter* (Ala.) *Whig* an account of a recent burning of a slave in that county. "Dave," the slave, belonged to James D. Thornton, was accused of having murdered a daughter of his mistress, and, after his arrest, confessed his guilt. Thornton and his friends took him from the jail by a stratagem, and bore him off in triumph. "They left in high glee," says the *Whig*, and carried their prisoner to the appointed place of sacrifice. Here he was "tied to a stake, with fat light wood piled around him, and the torch was applied in the presence of two thousand persons, who had met there to witness the novel scene." There were, it seems, some rumors afloat, that "Dave" was tortured, but these, the *Whig* declares, were "entirely untrue." So, burning men alive is *not* torture in Alabama. An inquiring mind, which is not sensitive, might seek to know what is.

———

Dr. Parsons gives another instance which occurred not long before his visit in Georgia, the particulars of which he received from eye-witnesses. A slave had received from his mistress some punishment of great severity, when he seized a hatchet, and, as he supposed, killed her, though she afterward recovered. On committing the deed, he ran at once to the court-house and surrendered himself to justice. Justice in civilized countries would have been hanging. In Georgia, it was this : The slave was given to the mob, who first gave him fifty lashes a day for five days to prepare him for what was to follow. On the following Sunday, he was taken from the jail, and suspended, naked, by his two hands, from the limp of a large oak-tree near the court-house. A fire made of hard-pine shavings was kindled beneath him, and "then the clear bright flames quickly ascended, curling about the limbs, encircling the body, scorching the nerves, crushing the fibers, charring the flesh—and, in mortal anguish, he was (in the words of an eye-witness) 'sweating as it were, great drops of blood.'" But before life was entirely extinguished, the lungs, the heart, the liver, were cut and torn from the body, with knives fastened upon poles, and with these quivering organs elevated above the crowd, the executioners shouted, "So shall it be done to the slave that murders his mistress!"

On the 7th of January, 1857, three years ago, Mr. John Kingsley, of Portsmouth, Ohio, wrote to the *Antislavery Standard* of this city that he was the week before in Carter County, Ky., where he saw a negro tied to a stake, a pile of dry wood heaped about him, and set on fire. The man belonged to one Wm. McMinnis, of that county, and was suspected of planning an insurrection. He was first whipped, 200 lashes, but denied his guilt. Fire was then tried, and, though not burned to death, he died next day. Mr. Kingsley, unable to remain and witness the sufferings of the agonized creature, rode away and attempted to excite the neighbors to a rescue; he was told to mind his own business.

BIG RAPIDS, Mecosta Co., Mich., March 28, 1860.
* * * * In the township of Extra, in Ashley County, Arkansas, the discovery was made, that a widow named Hill, and a slave woman, belonging to J. L. M——, Esq., who lived with her, had been murdered, and the house burned to conceal the deed. The alarm soon spread, and an investigation was instituted by Mr. M——, in connection with many of the leading citizens. Suspicion fell upon a slave named Ike, belonging to a man named Perdue. Ike was whipped nearly to death, in order to extort from him a confession, but he persisted in denying any knowledge of the affair. Mr. M—— then poured upon his bleeding back *spirits of turpentine*, and set it on fire! Ike then confessed that he and a negro named Jack, belonging to J. F. Norrell, were hired by one Miller to assist in performing the deed. One fact, however, greatly invalidated this testimony, and that was, that Mr. M—— and Mr. Norrell were deadly enemies, and Ike must have known that nothing could have pleased Mr. M—— more than to convict Jack, thus subjecting his most bitter enemy to a loss of a favorite slave, worth twelve or fifteen hundred dollars. Jack was, however, immediately arrested and brought before the regulators, and certain circum-

stances seeming in some degree to corroborate Ike's statement, stakes were driven into the ground, and the two slaves chained to them. A large quantity of *fat pine* was piled around them, and J. L. M—— set it on *fire !* In a few minutes, nothing but charred and blackened corpses remained. A subscription was circulated to indemnify the owners for their losses.

Mr. Norrell told me that when the flames were rising ten feet above Jack's head, he said to the dying slave, "I have raised you, Jack, and I never caught you in a lie. You are going to die! nothing can save you; and now, tell me truly, as you hope for heaven, are you guilty ?" Jack answered from the flames, "Master, I don't know any more about it than you do." Mr. Norrell and all his family believed Jack to have been innocent, and shed tears as they spoke of him.

The act of burning turpentine upon the lacerated back, I had from the lips of Mr. M—— himself, who rather boasted of his ingenuity in thus eliciting testimony when ordinary means had failed.

I have given true names and can give the names of more than one hundred men in the vicinity, and I am ready at any time to make affidavit to what I have stated. CORYDON E. FULLER.

————

Such is the barbarism of slavery. And let no man say that these " evils" of slavery are no part of the system, and not justly chargeable to it. As well may we expect drunkenness without broils and litigation, and idleness and destitution, as to expect to hold men and women in slavery without scourgings, and thumb-screws, and murder, and almost every species of torture.

God never made a man to be a slave, and no measure of cruelty can reduce an immortal spirit, made in the image of God, to entire submission to life-long bondage. Hence, while slavery exists, chains, and thumb-screws, and slave-maiming, and slave-burnings must exist, as the *only* means by which one race can be kept in a state of even partial submission to another. And even with all these terrors before them, the wonder is that the slaves do not arise, and assert their freedom at all hazards.

The Narrative of Bethany Veney

A SLAVE WOMAN.

The Narrative of Bethany Veney

A SLAVE WOMAN.

With Introduction by REV. BISHOP MALLALIEU,

AND

Commendatory Notices from REV. V. A. COOPER, Superintendent of Home
for Little Wanderers, Boston, Mass.,

AND

REV. ERASTUS SPAULDING, Millbury, Mass.

WORCESTER, MASS.
1889.

Press of Geo. H. Ellis, 141 Franklin Street, Boston.

INTRODUCTORY LETTER FROM BISHOP MALLALIEU.

THERE have been many histories written, but they do not tell a thousandth part of what has been done in the ages past. The unwritten histories would fill the world. It is so with biographies: many have been written, but unnumbered millions have found no record outside of throbbing hearts. If we could know perfectly the inner life of almost any person; if we could only know the hopes and fears and loves and heartaches; if we could only know the conflicts, the defeats, the victories of the soul,— we should see that the humblest and most uneventful life is more thrillingly wonderful than any romance that was ever written. All this is emphatically true of thousands upon thousands born and reared in slavery.

It was the lot of the subject of this brief biography to have been born in the same State as Washington the savior of his country, as Jefferson the author of the Declaration of Independence, and as Patrick Henry the sublime orator of freedom; and yet she was born a slave. She was born in a commonwealth that was nominally Christian, and yet she was born a slave. She was born in a land of Bibles and sanctuaries and Sabbaths, and yet she was born a slave. Let all the people everywhere in all our borders thank God that the shame and sin and curse of slavery have been done away. Betty Veney may have been born a slave, but the pure soul that looked out of her flashing eyes was never in bondage to any miserable being calling himself her master. Redeemed from the galling yoke her body was compelled for years to wear, she has lived a pure and spotless life. Though poor and unknown among men, the angels of God have camped around her for, lo! these many years; and she has been able, by the abounding grace of God, to walk the rough and dusty paths of a toilsome life with garments spotless and wrinkleless.

The day is coming when slaveholders and their descendants will no more think of boasting of the fact, or even mentioning it, than the grandchildren of the slave-stealers and pirates of Newport, and other Northern seaports, now think of priding themselves on the unspeakable villany of their ancestors. In the mean time, the biographies of saintly, enduring spirits like that of Betty Veney will be read, and will serve to inspire the discouraged and down-trodden to put their trust in the almighty arm of Jehovah, who alone works deliverance and salvation to all those who put their trust in him.

W. F. MALLALIEU.

NEW ORLEANS, LA., Jan. 30, 1889.

PREFACE.

THIS little book, now offered to the many kind friends of Bethany Veney, contains the simple story of one of the five millions of human beings who, less than thirty years ago, were bought and sold like beasts of burden, in fifteen out of thirty-two, States of our American Republic.

Already, this fact in our national history is largely overlooked, and to the generation now coming upon the stage of action is almost unknown.

Compared with the lives of many of her class, Betty's was uneventful. Yet in it was much of tragic adventure and tender pathos. Her endurance under hardship, her fidelity to trust, and, withal, her religious faith, commend her as a fit subject, not only to impress the lesson of slavery in the past, but to inspire and deepen a sense of responsibility toward the wronged and perse-cuted race which she represents.

Beyond these considerations is this: her days have already far outrun the allotted threescore years and ten, and her natural strength is much abated. If sold, these pages may help to render her declining years easier and freer from care.

It is greatly to be regretted that the language and personal characteristics of Bethany cannot be transcribed. The little par-ticulars that give coloring and point, tone and expression, are largely lost. Only the outline can be given. As it is, possessing only the merit of a "plain, unvarnished tale," it asks for generous consideration and extended sale.

M. W. G.

EAST GREENWICH, R.I., 1889.

AUNT BETTY'S STORY.

CHAPTER I.

CHILDHOOD — FIRST LESSONS IN MORALITY — FIRST LESSON
IN THE ART OF ENTERTAINING.

I HAVE but little recollection of my very early life. My mother and her five children were owned by one James Fletcher, Pass Run, town of Luray, Page County, Virginia. Of my father I know nothing.

The first thing I remember with any distinctness was when, about seven years old, I was, with other children, knocking apples from a tree, when we were surprised by my young mistress, Miss Nasenath Fletcher, calling to us, in a loud and threatening tone, demanding what we were doing. Without waiting for reply, she told us to follow her; and, as she led the way down to a blackberry pasture not far off, she endeavored, in a very solemn manner, to impress us with the importance of always telling the truth. "If asked a question," she said, "we must answer directly, yes or no." I asked her "what we must say if asked something which we did not know." She answered, "Why, you must say you don't know, of course." I said, "I shall say, 'Maybe 'tis, and maybe 'tain't.'" I remember well how the children laughed at this; and then Miss Nasenath went on to tell us that *some time* all this world that we saw would be burned up,

—that the moon would be turned into blood, the stars would fall out of the sky, and everything would melt away with a great heat, and that everybody, *every little child* that had told a lie, would be cast into a lake of fire and brimstone, and would burn there for ever and ever, and, what was more, though they should burn for ever and ever, they would never be burned up.

I was dreadfully frightened; and, as soon as I could get away, I ran to my mammy, and, repeating what mistress had said, begged to know if it could be true. To my great sorrow, she confirmed it all, but added what Miss Nasenath had failed to do; namely, that those who told the truth and were good would always have everything they should want. It seemed to me then there was nothing so good as molasses and sugar; and I eagerly asked, "Shall I have all the molasses and sugar I want, if I tell the truth?" "Yes," she replied, "*if you are good;* but remember, if you tell lies, you will be burned in the lake that burns for ever and ever."

This made a very strong impression upon me. I can never forget my mammy's manner at the time. I believed every word she said, and from that day to this I have never doubted its truth.

Though my conception of what constituted the truth was very dim, my fear of what should befall me, if I were to tell a lie, was very great. Still, I was only a young child, and could not, long at a time, be very unhappy.

My old master, who at times was inclined to be jolly, had a way of entertaining his friends by my singing and dancing. Supper over, he would call me into his room, and, giving me to understand what he wanted of me, I would, with all manner of grotesque grimaces, gestures, and positions, dance and sing:—

" Where are you going, Jim ?
　Where are you going, Sam ?
　To get a proper larning,
　To jump Jim Crow."

　　　　or

" David the king was grievit and worrit,
　He went to his chamber —
　His chamber and weppit;
　And, as he went, he weppit and said,
' O my son, O my son!
　Would to God I had died
　For thee, O Absalom,
　My son, my son,' "—

and many other similar songs, of the meaning of which I had of course no idea, and I have since thought neither he nor his friends could have had any more than I.

CHAPTER II.

BEREAVEMENT — CHANGE OF MASTER AND HOME — UNJUST DEMANDS — PUNISHMENT ESCAPED.

THE next thing I recall as being of any particular importance to me was the death of my mother, and, soon after, that of Master Fletcher. I must have been about nine years old at that time.

Master's children consisted of five daughters and two sons. As usual in such cases, an inventory was taken of his property (all of which nearly was in slaves), and, being apportioned in shares, lots were drawn, and, as might chance, we fell to our several masters and mistresses.

My sister Matilda and myself were drawn by the eldest daughter, Miss Lucy. My grandmother had begged hard to be reckoned with me, but she and Uncle Peter fell to Miss Nasenath; but as after a time she married David Kibbler, and Miss Lucy went to live with them, taking her human property with her, to wait on her, and also to work for Mr. Kibbler, we were brought together again. In the mean time, I was put out with an old woman, who gave me my food and clothes for whatever work I could do for her. She was kind to me, as I then counted kindness, never whipping me or starving me; but it was not what a free-born white child would have found comforting or needful.

Going into the family of David Kibbler as I did with my mistress, I was really under his direction and subject to his control, almost as much as if he and not Miss Lucy had owned me.

Master Kibbler was a Dutchman,— a man of most violent temper, ready to fight anything or anybody who resisted his authority or in any way crossed his path. His one redeeming quality was his love for his horses and dogs. These must be fed before his servants, and their comfort and health always considered. He was a blacksmith by trade, and would have me hold his irons while he worked them. I was awkward one day, and he struck me with a nail-rod, making me so lame my mistress noticed it, and asked Matilda what was the matter with me; and, when she was told, she was greatly troubled, and as I suppose spoke to Kibbler about it, for he called me to him, and bade me go a long way off into a field, and, as he said, *cut some sprouts there*. But he very soon followed me, and, cutting a rod, beat me severely, and then told me to "go again and tell my mistress that he had hit me with a nail-rod, if I wanted to."

Poor Miss Lucy! She was kind and tender-hearted. She often said she hated slavery, and wanted nothing to do with it; but she could see no way out of it.

It will give a clearer idea of the kind of a man Kibbler was, and the way I grew to manage with him, if I tell here a circumstance that happened after I had grown much older and stronger. I had been in the field a good ways from the house, helping him to haul logs. Our work was done, and he had mounted the team to go home, and the bars were let down for him to pass out, when a drove of hogs ran in to get the clover that was growing in a part of the field. He called to me to drive out the hogs. I clapped my hands together, and shouted, "Shoo! shoo!" This frightened the horses, and Kibbler was unable to control them;

and, rushing through the gateway, the team hit the side post, tearing it up from its place. Of course, all this made him very angry; and, of course, I was to blame for it all. As soon as he could hold the horses, he turned, and shouted to me to drive out the hogs, set the post into the ground, and get back to the house by the time he did, or he would whip me so I would remember it.

A big boy who had been hauling the logs with us now helped me drive out the hogs and plant the post. We hurried with all our might, and then tried to run home; but, by the time we got out of the woods, we saw master so far ahead of us I knew it was no use to try, and I said I would risk the whipping and not run any longer. So, when we came up to the house, master was sitting in his chair by the window; and, as I passed into the room near him, he handed me his jack-knife, and said, "Now, girl, go cut me a good hickory,—a good one, mind you; for, if I have to cut it myself, I'll get a hard one, you may be sure." I took the knife, passed through the kitchen to the back door, just beside which was a little shelf where the pails of water just filled from the spring were standing. I laid the knife on the shelf, and passed out the door, and ran for the woods and the mountain. By the time I reached the woods, it began to rain, and poured fearfully all the night. I crowded my head under the alder bushes, while my shoulders and body were dripping wet. All night I crouched in this way; and, when morning came, I was afraid to show myself, and all day kept concealed by the trees and bushes as best I could. As night came on, I was very hungry, having eaten nothing for more than thirty-six hours; and so I decided to go down the mountain where old Kibbler, my master's father, lived, knowing that he would give me something to satisfy my hunger. As I drew nigh the house, the dogs barked; and I was afraid to encounter them, and so laid out all night on the side of the hill. In the morning,— it was Sunday,— I ventured near the house; and the old man, seeing me, came out and gave me "How-dye," and asked how the home folks were. I told him I had not seen them since Friday, and added the reason for my running away, to which he listened, and then said, "Well, what are you going to do about it?" I said, "Won't you, Masser Kibbler, go home with me, and tell Masser David he mustn't whip me?"

I don't know how I dared to say this, for to his own slaves he was a hard, ugly man; but he gave me something to eat, then went home with me, and, after repeating my story to Master David, asked him if that was true, and added, "Then you have no right to whip her." And that was the end of it.

I must go back here to my mistress and her wish not to hold slaves. A gentleman from Ohio was visiting in the neighborhood; and Miss Lucy, knowing he was from a free State, asked him if he would not take me North with him. He very readily consented, promising to do the best he could for me; but, when Master David and others heard about it, they said it was a foolish thing to do, for this man would very likely sell me before he left the South, and put the money into his own pocket, and I should find myself worse off than ever. It was true that many Northern men came South very bitter in their opposition to slavery, and after a little while came to be the hardest and most cruel slaveholders.

I have sometimes tried to picture what my life might have been could I have been set free at that age; and I have imagined myself with a young girl's ambition, working hard and carefully saving my earnings, then getting a little home with garden, where I could plant the kind of things I had known in the South, then bringing my sisters and brothers to share with me these blessings of freedom. But I had yet to know far deeper sorrows before I could have any of this glad experience.

Miss Lucy now told me, if I would be contented and stay quietly where I was, and not be married, she would, when her nephew Noe came to be of age, give me my freedom. Instead of this, however, I was told soon after that she had made her will, bequeathing me already to this nephew. I was never sure this was true. Her kindness to me and my love for her made it always seem impossible.

CHAPTER III.

I COME now to a phase in my experience which aroused the impressions made upon me so long before in the blackberry pasture.

At Powell's Fort, not far from where I now lived, was the Mount Asa school-house, where the different religious denominations held their meetings. My master's brother, Jerry Kibbler, and his sister Sally had been to a camp-meeting, and got "religion." They came home determined their religion should help others; and, through their influence, this little school-house had been fitted up with pulpit and seats, and now there was to be a series of revival meetings held there. I had never been to any kind of a meeting since I was a little girl, and then my mistress had sometimes taken me along for company.

At this time, Miss Ellen Mills was spinning wool at Mr. Jonathan Grandstaff's; and one night, as it was growing dusk, she came down to master's, to see if some of the family would go to meeting with her. No one cared to go; and Miss Lucy, turning to me, said: "There is Betty. Take Betty. She will be company for you." So I went. The minister was preaching when we entered; and I have no recollection of anything he said in his sermon, but, when he took his seat, he sang the hymn,—

> "Then let this feeble body fail,
>   Or let it faint or die,
> My soul shall quit this mournful vale,
>   And soar to worlds on high,
> Shall join those distant saints,
>   And find its long-sought rest."

It was a hymn of many verses (I afterwards got an old woman to teach them to me); and there was such tender-ness in his voice and such solemnity in his manner that I was greatly affected. When the singing was over, he moved about among the congregation; and, coming close to me, he said, "Girl, don't you want religion? don't you want to be happy when you die?" Then he asked me to promise him that, when I got home, I would go upon my knees and ask God to give me the witness that I was his. I made him no answer; but, as soon as I reached home and was alone, I knelt down, and in my feeble and ignorant way begged to be saved. From that day to this, I have been praying and trying to do as I thought my heavenly Master has required of me; and I think I have had the witness of the Spirit.

So, night after night, I went to the little school-house, and had many precious seasons. Master Jerry and Miss Sally were very kind to me, and tried to show me the way to be a Christian.

But there came a time when Master David said he was not going to have me running to meeting all the time any longer. He had decided to send me up to old Mr. Levers, two miles away, there to stay until I should get over my "religious fever," as he called it. Accordingly, I went as directed; but, when it came night, I asked if I might go down to Mount Asa school-house for meeting. The old

man said: "Yes.   You can go; and, as it is so far away, you
need not come back here till morning.   But go home, and
stay with the children, as you always do, and have the care
of them."   I couldn't understand it, but I went; and, when
in the morning Kibbler saw me, he scolded, and sent me off
to Levers again.   Every night, old Mr. Levers would tell me
I could go; and I did, till, in the middle of the meeting one
night, Master Kibbler came up to me, and, taking me by the
arm, carried me out, scolding and fuming, declaring that old
Webster (the minister) was a liar, and that for himself he
didn't want such a "whoopin' and hollerin' religion," and, if
that was the way to heaven, he didn't "want to go there."
After this, my conscience troubled me very much about
going.   Mr. Levers would tell me to go; but I knew that
Master David had forbidden me to do so.   One night, I
started out, and, as I came to a persimmon-tree, I felt moved
to go down on my knees and ask the Lord to help me, and
make Master David willing.   In a few minutes, I felt very
happy.   I wanted to remain on my knees, and wished I could
walk on them till I could come before Master David.   I tried
to do so, and was almost surprised to find I could get along
so well.   At last, I reached the piazza, and was able to enter
the room, where I saw him sitting; and, as I did so, I said,
"O Master, *may* I go to meeting?"   He saw my position;
and, as if "rent by the Spirit," he cried out: "Well, I'll go to
the devil if you ain't *my match!*   Yes: go to meeting, and
stay there."

After this, I had no trouble from this cause.   When I was
to be taken into the church, I asked him if he was willing,
and he said: "I don't care.   If that's your way of getting
to heaven, I don't care.   I only wish you were all there."
So I was baptized, and have been trying, in my poor way
ever since to serve the Lord.

CHAPTER IV.

COURTSHIP AND MARRIAGE — A SLAVEHOLDER'S IDEA OF ITS
REQUIREMENTS — SEPARATION.

YEAR after year rolled on. Master Jonas Mannyfield
lived seven miles from us, on the other side of the Blue
Ridge ; and he owned a likely young fellow called Jerry.
We had always known each other, and now he wanted to
marry me. Our masters were both willing ; and there was
nothing to hinder, except that there was no minister about
there to marry us. "No matter for that," Kibbler said to
Jerry. "If you want Bett, and she wants you, that's the
whole of it." But I didn't think so. I said, "No : neve
till somebody comes along who can marry us." So it hap
pened, one day, there was a colored man — a pedler, wit'
his cart — on the road, and Jerry brought him in, and said h
was ready to be minister for us. He asked us a few que:
tions, which we answered in a satisfactory manner, and the
he declared us husband and wife. I did not want him t
make us promise that we would always be true to each othe
forsaking all others, as the white people do in their marriage
service, because I knew that at any time our masters coul
compel us to break such a promise ; and I had never fo
gotten the lesson learned, so many years before, in tl
blackberry pasture.

So Jerry and I were happy as, under all the circumstance
we could well be. When he asked his master's consent 1
our marriage, he told him he had had thoughts of removin

to Missouri, in which case he should take him with him, and we would have to be separated; but, if he chose to run the risk, he had nothing to say. Jerry did not think there was any danger, and we were not dissuaded; for hearts that love are much the same in bond or free, in white or black.

Eight or ten months passed on, when one night my brother Stephen, who lived on the Blue Ridge, near Master Mannyfield, came to see me, and, as we talked of many things, he spoke of Jerry in a way that instantly roused my suspicion. I said: "Tell me what is the matter? I know there is something. Is Jerry dead? Is he sold? Tell me what it is." I saw he dreaded to speak, and that frightened me the more.

At last, he said: "'Tis no use, Betty. You have got to know it. Old Look-a-here's people are all in jail for debt." "Old Look-a-here" was the nickname by which Manny-field was known by the colored people far and near, because he had a way of saying, when he was about to whip one of his slaves, "Now look-a-here, you black rascal," or "you black wench."

The next day was Saturday, and I hurried to complete my task in the corn-field, and then asked my master if I could go to see Jerry. He objected at first, but at last gave me a pass to see my brother, and be gone until Monday morning.

The sun might have been two hours high when I started; but, before I was half over the mountain, night had closed round me its deepest gloom. The vivid flashes of lightning made the carriage path plain at times, and then I could not see a step before me; and the rolling thunder added to my fear and dread. I was dripping wet when, about nine o'clock, I reached the house. It had been my plan to get Stephen to go on with me to Jerry's mother's, and stay the

night there; but his mistress, who was sister to my Miss
Lucy, declared we must not go on in the storm, and, giving
me supper, brought bedding, that I might lie on the kitchen
floor and rest me there. In the morning, after a good
breakfast, she started us off, with a bag of biscuits to eat by
the way. Jerry's mother was glad to go with us; and we
hurried along to Jerry, in jail at Little Washington, where
he with his fellow-slaves was confined, like sheep or oxen,
shut up in stalls, to be sold to pay their owner's debts.

Jerry saw us, as we came along the road, through the prison
bars; and the jailer allowed us to talk together there, not,
however, without a witness to all we might say. We had
committed no offence against God or man. Jerry had not;
and yet, like base criminals, we were denied even the con-
solation of privacy. This was a necessary part of the system
of American slavery. Neither wife nor mother could inter-
vene to soften its rigors one jot.

Several months passed, and Mannyfield was still unable to
redeem his property; and they were at last put up at auction,
and sold to the highest bidder. Frank White, a slave-trader,
bought the entire lot, and proceeded at once to make up a
gang for the Southern market.

Arrangements were made to start Friday morning; and
on Thursday afternoon, chained together, the gang were
taken across the stream, and encamped on its banks. White
then went to Jerry, and, taking the handcuffs from his
wrists, told him to go and stay the night with his wife, and
see if he could persuade her to go with him. If he could, he
would buy her, and so they need not be separated. He
would pass that way in the morning, and see. Of course,
Jerry was only too glad to come; and, at first, I thought I
would go with him. Then came the consciousness that this

inducement was only a sham, and that, once exposed for
sale in a Southern market, the bidder with the largest sum
of money would be our purchaser singly quite as surely as
together ; and, if separated, what would I do in a strange
land ? No : I would not go. It was far better for me to stay
where, for miles and miles, I knew every one, and every one
knew me. Then came the wish to secrete ourselves together
in the mountains, or elsewhere, till White should be gone ;
but, to do this, detection was sure. Then we remembered
that White had trusted us, in letting him come to me, and
we felt ashamed, for a moment, as if we had tried to cheat ;
but what *right* had White to carry him away, or even to
own him at all ? Our poor, ignorant reasoning found it hard
to understand his rights or our own ; and we at last decided
that, as soon as it was light, Jerry should take to the mountains, and, when White was surely gone, either I would join
him there, and we would make for the North together, or he
would come back, go to White's mother, who lived a few
miles distant, and tell her he would work for her and obey
her, but he would never go South to be worked to death in
the rice-swamps or cotton-fields.

We talked late into the night ; and at last, in the silence
and dread, worn out with sorrow and fear, my head on his
shoulder, we both dropped asleep.

Daylight was upon us when we waked. The sad consciousness of our condition, and our utter helplessness, over-
powered us. I opened the door, and there was my mistress,
with pail in hand, going to the spring for water. "Oh,
what shall I do ? Where shall I go ?" cried Jerry, as he saw
her. "Have no fear," I said. "Go right along. I know
mistress will never betray you." And, with a bound, he
was over the fence, into the fields, and off to the mountains.

In a very short time, White and his poor, doomed company came along, and called for Jerry. I had taken my pail to milk the cows; and, seeing me, he sung out, "Woman, where is Jerry, I say?" "I don't know where Jerry is," I answered. Then, turning to Kibbler, who, hearing the outcry, now came out, he said, "You told me that woman wouldn't lie; and you know well enough she is lying now, when she says she don't know where that —— rascal is." Kibbler answered very slowly and thoughtfully, "I never knowed her to lie; but may be this time,— may be this time." White then turned to me, and said, "I took off his handcuffs, and let him go to you, and you had no business to serve me so."

It was true I did not know where Jerry was at that time. We had agreed that we would meet that night near the blacksmith's old shop, on the other side of the run; and that was all I knew of his whereabouts, though he had not been gone long enough to be far away. It was true he had trusted us, and I felt very badly; but what else *could* we have done? Kind reader, *what* think you?

I then told him that Jerry had said he was willing to work, and would go to his mother's and serve her, but *never*, if he could help it, would he be carried South.

Then White tried to bargain with Kibbler for my purchase, saying he would give any price he should name for me, because he knew I would then find Jerry. But it was no use. Kibbler had a kind spot in his heart, and would not consent to let me go. So the slave-trader moved on with his human cattle.

Five miles on the road lived David McCoy, another slave-trader. When White reached his house, it was agreed by them that, if McCoy could find Jerry within two days, he should bring him on, and they would meet at Stanton, Va.

CHAPTER V.

THE place where I was to meet Jerry was, as I have said, across the run, in a corn-field, near the blacksmith's shop, the time Friday night.

It had rained hard all day, and the stream was swollen, and pouring and rushing at a fearful rate. I waited till everybody was in bed and asleep, when I lighted my pine knot, and started for the Pass. It was still raining, and the night was very dark. Only by my torch could I see a step before me; and, when I attempted to wade in, as I did in many different places, I found it was no use. I should surely be drowned if I persisted. So, disappointed and grieved, I gave up and went home. The next morning I was able to get over on horseback to milk the cows, but I neither heard nor saw anything of Jerry.

Saturday night came. I knew well that, if not caught by White, Jerry would be round. At last, every one was in bed, and all was still. I waited and listened. I listened and waited. Then I heard his step at the door. I hurriedly opened it, and he came in. His clothes were still damp and stiff from the rain of yesterday. He was frightened and uneasy. He had been hiding around in different places, constantly fearing detection. He had seen me from behind the old blacksmith's shop when I had tried the night before, with my pine knot, to ford the stream; and he was glad, he said, when he saw me go back, for he knew I should be car-

ried down by the current and be drowned, if I had persisted.
I went to my mistress's bedroom, and asked her if I might
go to the cellar.   She knew at once what I meant, and whispered softly, "Betty, has Jerry come?" then, without waiting for reply, added, "get him some milk and light bread
and butter."   I was not long in doing so; and the poor fellow ate like one famishing.   Then he wanted to know all
that had happened, and what White had said when he found
he was gone.   We talked a long time, and tried to devise
some plans for our mutual safety and possible escape from
slavery altogether; but, every way we looked, the path was
beset with danger and exposure.   We were both utterly dis-
heartened.   But sleep came at last and, for the time being,
relieved us of our fears.

In the morning, which was Sunday, we had our breakfast
together, and, as the hours passed, began to feel a little comforted.   After dinner, we walked out to the field and strolled
about for some time; and, when ready to go back to the
house, we each took an armful of fodder along for the horses.
As we laid it down and turned to go into the house, David
McCoy rode up on horseback.   He saw Jerry at once, and
called him to come to the fence.   The excitement of the last
days — the fasting and the fear — had completely cowed and
broken whatever of manhood, or even of brute courage, a
slave might by any possibility be presumed at any time to
be possessed of, and the last remains of these qualities in
poor Jerry were gone.   He mutely obeyed; and when, with
an oath, McCoy commanded him to mount the horse behind
him, he mutely seated himself there.   McCoy then called to
me to go to the house and bring Jerry's clothes.   "Never,"
— I screamed back to him,— "never, not to save your miserable life."   But Jerry said: "O Betty, 'tis no use.   We

can't help it." I knew this was so. I stifled my anger and my grief, brought his little bundle, into which I tucked a testament and catechism some one had given me, and shook hands "good-by" with him. So we *parted forever*, in this world.

CHAPTER VI.

SEVERAL months passed, and I became a mother.

My dear white lady, in your pleasant home made joyous by the tender love of husband and children all your own, you can never understand the slave mother's emotions as she clasps her new-born child, and knows that a master's word can at any moment take it from her embrace; and when, as was mine, that child is a girl, and from her own experience she sees its almost certain doom is to minister to the unbridled lust of the slave-owner, and feels that the law holds over her no protecting arm, it is not strange that, rude and uncultured as I was, I felt all this, and would have been glad if we could have died together there and then.

Master Kibbler was still hard and cruel, and I was in constant trouble. Miss Lucy was kind as ever, and it grieved her to see me unhappy. At last, she told me that perhaps, if I should have some other home and some other master, I should not be so wretched, and, if I chose, I might look about and see what I could do. I soon heard that John Prince, at Luray, was wanting to buy a woman. Miss Lucy told me, if it was agreeable to me, I might go to him and work for a fortnight, and if at the end of that time he wanted me, and I chose to stay, she would arrange terms with him; but, if I did not want to stay, not to believe anything that any one might tell me, but come back at once to her.

At the end of two weeks, Master John said he was going over to have a talk with Miss Lucy; and did I think, if he should conclude to buy me, that I should steal from him? I answered that, if I worked for him, I ought to expect him to give me enough to eat, and then I should have no need to steal. "You wouldn't want me to go over yonder, into the garden of another man, and steal his chickens, when I am working for you, would you, Master John? I expect, of course, you will give me enough to eat and to wear, and then I shall have no reason to steal from anybody." He seemed satisfied and pleased, and bargained with Miss Lucy, both for me and my little girl. Both master and Mrs. Prince were kind and pleasant to me, and my little Charlotte played with the little Princes, and had a good time. I worked very hard, but I was strong and well, and willing to work; and for several years there was little to interrupt this state of things.

At last, I can't say how long, I was told that John O'Neile, the jailer, had bought me; and he soon took me to his home, which was in one part of the jail. He, however, was not the real purchaser. This was David McCoy, the same who had grabbed Jerry on that fatal morning; and he had bought me with the idea of taking me to Richmond, thinking he could make a speculation on me. I was well known in all the parts around as a faithful, hard-working woman, when well treated, but ugly and wilful, if abused beyond a certain point. McCoy had bought me away from my child; and now, he thought, he could sell me, if carried to Richmond, at a good advantage. I did not think so; and I determined, if possible, to disappoint him.

The night after being taken in charge by John O'Neile, as soon as I was sure everybody was asleep, I got up and crawled out of the house, and went to my old Methodist friend, Jerry Kibbler. I knew the way into his back door; and, though I presumed he would be asleep, I was sure he would willingly get up and hear what I had to say. I was not mistaken. He heard my voice inquiring for him, and in a very few minutes dressed himself, and came out, and in his pleasant, kind manner said: "Aunt Betty, what is the matter? What can I do for you?" I told him McCoy had bought me, away from my child, and was going to send me to Richmond. I *couldn't* go there. *Wouldn't* he buy me? I saw he felt very badly; but *what*, he said, could *he* do with me? He didn't believe in buying slaves,— and, finally, he hadn't "money enough to do it." I begged so hard that he said he would see what he could do, and I went back to the jail. Mrs. O'Neile had discovered my absence, and was on the watch for me. The next day, she told me I was to start for Richmond the day after, and it was no use for me to make a fuss, so I might as well bring my mind to it first as last.

The day was almost gone, and I had had no word from Mr. Jerry. As it was growing dark, I saw a colored man whom I knew, and I managed to make him see, through the jail windows, that I wanted to speak with him. I induced him to find Master Jerry; but he came back with word from him that he had seen both O'Neile and McCoy, and could make no kind of an arrangement with them. He had not come to me, because he felt so sorry for me, and had waited, in the hope that some one else would tell me. So there seemed nothing else before me; and when, on the next morning, Mrs. O'Neile told me to make myself ready for the journey, I tried to be submissive, and dressed myself in a new calico dress that Miss Lucy had given me long before.

I had never in my life felt so sad and so completely for-
saken. I thought my heart was really breaking. Mr.
O'Neile called me; and, as I passed out of the door, I heard
Jackoline, the jailer's daughter, singing in a loud, clear
voice,—

> "When through the deep waters I call thee to go,
> The rivers of woe shall not thee overflow;
> For I will be with thee, and cause thee to stand,
> Upheld by my righteous, omnipotent hand."

I can never forget the impression these *words* and the
music and the tones of Jackoline's voice made upon me. It
seemed to me as if they all came directly out of heaven. It
was my Saviour speaking directly to me. Was not *I* passing
the deep waters? What rivers of woe could be sorer than
these through which I was passing? Would not this righteous, omnipotent hand uphold me and help me? Yes, here
was His word for it. I would trust it; and I was comforted.

We mounted the stage, and were off for Charlotteville,
where we stopped over night, and took the cars next morning for Richmond.

Arrived in Richmond, we were again shut up in jail, all
around which was a very high fence, so high that no communication with the outside world was possible. I say we,
for there was a young slave girl whom McCoy had taken
with me to the Richmond market. The next day, as the
hour for the auction drew near, Jailer O'Neile came to us,
with a man, whom he told to take us along to the dressmaker
and to charge her to "fix us up fine." This dressmaker was
a most disagreeable woman, whose business it was to array
such poor creatures as we in the gaudiest and most striking
attire conceivable, that, when placed upon the auction stand,
we should attract the attention of all present, if not in one

way, why, in another. She put a white muslin apron on me, and a large cape, with great pink bows on each shoulder, and a similar rig also on Eliza. Thus equipped, we were led through a crowd of rude men and boys to the place of sale, which was a large open space on a prominent square, under cover.

I had been told by an old negro woman certain tricks that I could resort to, when placed upon the stand, that would be likely to hinder my sale; and when the doctor, who was employed to examine the slaves on such occasions, told me to let him see my tongue, he found it coated and feverish, and, turning from me with a shiver of disgust, said he was obliged to admit that at that moment I was in a very bilious condition. One after another of the crowd felt of my limbs, asked me all manner of questions, to which I replied in the ugliest manner I dared; and when the auctioneer raised his hammer, and cried, " How much do I hear for this woman ? " the bids were so low I was ordered down from the stand, and Eliza was called up in my place. Poor thing! there were many eager bids for her; for, for such as she, the demands of slavery were insatiable.

CHAPTER VII.

RETURN — IMPROVED CONDITION — COMFORTABLE HOME.

I was now taken back to Luray; and, though McCoy was greatly disappointed at the result of his Richmond venture, he was wise enough to make the best of it. Mrs. McCoy took a fancy to keep me; and, as she had not work enough to employ all my time, I found I could earn in the neighborhood enough money to carry home a large interest on my cost. After a while, McCoy agreed that, if I should bring him one dollar and a half every Saturday night, he would be satisfied, and I could do what I pleased with myself.

I washed blankets and bed-quilts, as well as weekly washings. I cleaned house, and worked in the fields, getting a job whenever I could find it and whatever it might be. I was near my child, where I could see her often; and I was comparatively happy.

After a time, master took a job of work on the pike, designing to work it with free negroes, whom he could hire for a small sum, and board them. He took me out there to cook for them. It gratified me to know that he placed confidence enough in me to do this; and I did my best to deserve it. The negroes were a rude set, as might be expected; for at that time they were the one class despised by everybody. They were despised by the master-class, because they could not subject them to their will quite in the same way as if they were slaves, and despised by the slave-class, because envied as possessing a nominal freedom, which they were denied. Thus are contempt and envy closely allied.

Sometimes, one or another of these men would be insulting to me, and impose upon me; but there was always one of their number who at such times would come to my rescue. He would often bring water from the spring for me, and in many kind ways caused me to regard him with a different feeling from any one I had met since I had lost my poor Jerry. This man was Frank Veney, afterwards my second husband.

I remember telling Master McCoy that, with such a hungry set of fellows to feed, I couldn't see how he could make any money out of that job, so much bread and meat must cost so much. He laughed very heartily, and, as I could see, very approvingly, and said, "Oh, yes, Betty, I know it costs a heap; but I have reckoned that all up, and I know how it is coming out." It pleased him well to see that I thought of his interest; and I think he saw in it, too, that I might have some business tact myself. When the work on this pike was finished, my master took other similar jobs elsewhere, and I had many changes during three or four years. At last, we got back to Luray, and master agreed with me that I should pay him thirty dollars per year for my time, and whatever I earned above that should be my own.

I rented of John Prince a little house at Dry Run, just at the foot of the mountain, and with my little boy Joe, now about two years old, lived very contentedly.

CHAPTER VIII.

ANOTHER CHANGE — NEW HOPES AND OLD FEARS — VICISSI-
TUDES POSSIBLE IN SLAVE LIFE — FREEDOM ATTAINED.

THE spur of the Blue Ridge, against which my little
house leaned, was called " Stony Man "; and it was supposed
to be full of copper. Some time ago, some Northern advent-
urers had set up an engine, in order to mine the copper and
test its quality. But, for reasons which I had never understood, the project was abandoned and the men went home.
They had built a small shanty on the ground, and I had lived
with them to do their work. It had been a dreary experience
to me, and I was thankful when it was over. It was not,
therefore, a pleasant circumstance to me when Lorenze
Prince called at my door, and told me he had come to see if
I would go up Stony Man again, to keep house for two
Northern gentlemen, who had just arrived in Luray, and
were going to start up the old engine, and see what they
could make of the copper. I answered him hastily that he
needn't ask me, for I wouldn't go to that lonesome place
again for love or money. Lorenze thought I was very
foolish, for he had seen them, and knew they were nice
gentlemen ; and, besides, they would pay me a dollar and a
half a week, sure pay. I at last agreed he might tell them
that I would be up there the next morning, and would get

their dinner for them, and then I would decide about staying longer.

My little home seemed pleasanter to me than ever that night, when I thought of leaving it. I was enjoying a good degree of freedom there. I could go out and come in as I pleased; and for a good distance about the country, with Master McCoy's pass in my bosom, I was safe to a certain extent. It never once occurred to me that this change might lead up to the end I had so long desired; namely, a life where I should need no pass written by a human hand to insure my safety as I went from place to place, but where the stamp of my humanity, imprinted by the Infinite Father of all, should be an all-sufficient guarantee in every emergency. I have repeated to myself many times since, when I have thought over those times,

> " God moves in a mysterious way
>   His wonders to perform."

And it is with deep and loving gratitude I refer every blessing to him.

Mr. G. J. Adams and Mr. J. Butterworth were the two gentlemen from Providence, R.I. The next morning, as I neared the engine-house, Mr. Butterworth saw me, and came forward to speak with me. His manner of speaking was gentle and kind. He told me to go to the house; and Mr. Adams, who was now at the village, would be back soon, and would arrange with me.

It did not seem lonesome, as I had imagined; and I set myself to work at once, pulling up the weeds that had overgrown everything and everywhere.

It was not long before Mr. Adams came, and we were soon acquainted; and I felt contented and at home there

My boy was happy, as was I.   Several months passed, I do not remember how many, when it became necessary for both Mr. Adams and Mr. Butterworth to go home for a time ; and they paid me in advance to remain where I was while they should be gone.   At last they returned, and things went on as before until one night I was down at the village, in old Mr. Aulman's store, and he asked me "how many niggers that could work had Master McCoy?"   The question was like a sword cutting me in two, or like a sudden flash of lightning striking me to the ground.   I knew well there was trouble ahead, and that, for McCoy's debts, I might at any moment be sold away from my boy, as I had been before from my girl.   I determined this should never be.   I would take my child and hide in the mountains.   I would do *anything* sooner than I would be sold.

A few days passed, and my worst fears were confirmed by Isaac Prince, who told me that all McCoy's property was posted to be sold.   The next day, as I was planning how I could get off, I saw a white horse, and a man standing at the smelting-mill.   The man was busily talking with Mr. Adams, and both seemed very earnest.   At last, the man mounted the horse and rode away, while Mr. Adams came into the house.   He said it was true that McCoy's property had been attached, to pay his debts, incurred by gambling, and everything would go under the auctioneer's hammer. "*I* won't be sold.   He shall never find *me*, to sell me again," I angrily cried.   Mr. Adams looked at me, and I saw the great pity in his eyes.   He said, "Betty, I have given my word in writing to this man, whom you saw, that, provided he will leave you here with us, instead of taking you to the jail, he shall find you here whenever he shall come for you." I felt the floor giving way under me.   It was with difficulty

I kept from falling. A few moments of deep agony passed, and then I was able to say to him that, since he had pledged his word in black and white, he should not be obliged to break it. He need not fear for me, for I would stay just as he had promised; but "I was, oh! so sorry he had promised."

I cannot tell now in what way it was first suggested that Mr. Adams should buy me and take me North with him. I think, when he was home, he had talked with his wife and her sister, Miss Sarah Brown, about such a possibility, and Miss Sarah had offered to advance a part of the price for which I might be purchased.

However that might have been, Mr. Adams now saw Mr. McCoy, and found he was greatly pressed for money, and would sell me as readily to him as to any one; and, not to spend too much time over what was really a very simple business transaction, a bill of sale was at once made out to Mr. Adams, which reads as follows: —

Received of G. J. Adams seven hundred and seventy-five dollars ($775), it being the purchase of my negro woman Berthena and her child Joe. The right and title to the said negro woman I warrant and defend against any person or persons whatsoever.

Given under my hand and seal the 27th day of December, 1858.

[SEAL.]   DAVID McCOY.

BENJ. F. GRAYSON.

Not long afterward,— I forget how long,— Messrs. Adams and Butterworth suspended operations at the mine, and, taking me and my boy, turned their faces homeward. They at that time expected to return, after a few months, and promised me I should go with them, so I did not feel so badly at parting with all the old faces and places as I should other-

wise have done. However, before their business arrangements for going were matured, John Brown had made his
invasion into Virginia; and the excitement that followed
made it unsafe for any one who sympathized with or defended him to be seen in any Southern State.

Then followed the War of the Rebellion; and it was not
till a much later date, and in a different way from what I had
anticipated when I left, that I saw again the old fields where
I had toiled and suffered, and grasped again the hands that
before had beaten and bruised me.

CHAPTER IX.

NEW EXPERIENCES — HOME IN THE NORTH.

The feelings with which I entered my Northern home, 22 Chares-Field Street, Providence, R.I., on a bright pleasant morning in August, 1858, can be more easily fancied than described. A new life had come to me. I was in a land where, by its laws, I had the same right to myself that any other woman had. No jailer could take me to prison, and sell me at auction to the highest bidder. My boy was my own, and no one could take him from me. But I had left behind me every one I had ever known. I did not forget the dreadful hardships I had endured, and yet somehow I did not think of them with half the bitterness with which I had endured them. I was a stranger in a strange land; and it was no wonder, perhaps, that a dreadful loneliness and homesickness came over me.

The family were just rising when Mr. Adams, with his night-key, opened the door, and showed me the way to the sitting-room, and then went to find his wife. I had only a moment to look about me, when the girl from the kitchen came in, and in a very friendly manner asked me to go there with her. Then, in a few minutes more, Mrs. Adams came, and, in her smiling, motherly way, held out her hand to me, saying, " Good-morning, Betty." She met me as if I

were an old acquaintance. At any rate, she made me feel
that I was with friends.

It was not easy at first to accommodate myself to the new
surroundings. In the Southern kitchen, under slave rule,
there was little thought of convenience or economy. Here
I found all sorts of Yankee inventions and improvements to
make work easy and pleasant. There were dishes and pans
of every description, clean and distinct cloths for all purposes, brushes and brooms for different uses. I couldn't
help feeling bewildered sometimes at the difference in so
many ways, and for a moment wished myself back in "old
Virginny," with my own people; and I very, very often
longed to see the old familiar faces and hear the old sounds,
but never could I forget to be grateful for my escape from
a system under which I had suffered so much.

CHAPTER X.

For a while after my coming North, I was able to hear occasionally from the old home; but, after the trouble over John Brown, followed as it was by the war for Secession, all communication was at an end.

In the mean time, I made acquaintance among both white and colored people, who were interested in my history and glad to help me.

I had been here only about three months, when my little Joe sickened and died; and this was a great affliction to me.

After this, Mr. Adams removed his family to Worcester, Mass.; and I went with them. From business considerations, his stay there was shortened; and he returned to Providence. I liked the friends I had made in Worcester, and decided to cast in my lot with them. I had joined the Park Street Methodist Church, and was treated with such kind consideration by the brothers and sisters there that I was at home with them; and, as I could find all the work I was able to do, I was very comfortable in many ways.

When at last the war was over, my wish to go back revived.

I had saved some money; and, as soon as it was deemed safe by my friends, I undertook the journey. I purchased my

tickets, taking me to Culpepper Court House, *via* railroad;
and all passed off well. Arriving there, I found the stage
would not leave for Luray for four hours. I really did not
see how I could wait so long. I, however, went over to the
stable, and, seeing a colored man there grooming the horses,
I asked him how things were getting on down there. He
saw I was a stranger; and, as one in haste to impart good
news, he quickly answered: "Oh, all's free here now. De
colored peoples has free times 'bout here now, de war's ober."
His face and eyes fairly shone with delight. I turned into a
store near by, and bought a large watermelon, and asked him
to come and eat it with me, by way of celebrating "de free
times." As we ate, we saw an old colored man and woman
coming along the road; and, when they reached us, I said:
"O aunty, you look happy. How are the times going with
you?" She repeated: "How's times? Why, de ole man an'
me just dun got married las' night, an' we're takin' our
weddin' journey." They ate watermelon with us, and we all
laughed together over the new times, that made it possible
for this woman, whose many children had enriched her
master's treasury, lo! these many years, now to realize in
any degree the sanctity of a marriage relation and a wedding
journey.

I did not wait for the stage to take me on my journey, for
I was too eager to reach the end. I engaged a colored boy
to take my satchel, to whom I was proud to pay one dollar in
advance; and we started on foot for the top of the mountain,
over which my course lay. Remaining there over night, I
pursued my way on the next day, reaching Luray before
night. The country everywhere had been laid waste by
the soldiers of both armies; but, as there had been no battle
fought in the immediate neighborhood, things were not so

much changed as I had expected. I found my daughter Charlotte grown to womanhood, married, and had one child. My old masters, Kibbler, Prince, and McCoy, expressed pleasure at seeing me, and had many questions to ask of people and things at the North. My dear, kind old mistress, Miss Lucy, had been paralyzed; and her face was drawn on one side, which greatly changed her. She was delighted with a pair of cloth shoes that I carried to her.

After visiting about for six or seven weeks, I turned my face again to the North, my daughter, her husband and child, coming with me.

Three times since I have made the same journey, bringing back with me, from time to time, in all sixteen of my relatives, and have encountered many interesting incidents. I have always found some one — sometimes a policeman, and sometimes a simple woman or boy — ready and willing to help me in every emergency, when I had need. I have great reason to speak well of my fellow-men, and to be most thankful to the overruling Providence that brought me up out of the " house of bondage."

I forget the exact date, but one day I was busy with my work at home, when a message came to me from Mrs. Warner, asking me to come to her. I went at once; and, on being shown into her presence, I found her engaged in conversation with my old master, David McCoy,— he who had taken Jerry away from me, and afterwards had sent me to Richmond to be sold. But all was changed now. He was not even Master McCoy. He was Mr. McKay. He put out his hand, and said, " How d'ye ? " not exactly, perhaps, as a reconstructed man, but as one who had at least learned something from the " logic of events " of the difference in our relations to each other. After a friendly interchange of inquiry, he invited me to call on him at the Waverly House, where he was stopping. Accordingly, the next day I inquired at the Waverly House office for Mr. McKay, of Virginia, and a servant showed me to his room. He welcomed me very cordially this time; and after a long talk, and I arose to come away, I asked him to dine with me the next day. He expressed much satisfaction, and at the appointed hour made his appearance. I prepared such a dinner as I thought he would enjoy, and was glad to find I had not been mistaken in my selections.

On rising to go, he turned to me, and said : "Aunt Betty, when you came down South, you wore a nice pair of kid gloves, with fur round their wrists. Can you tell me where you bought them, and what they cost?" I told him I would gladly go with him and try to find such; but, as Dr. Warner gave mine to me, I did not know their price. So together we looked through the different stores, and at last succeeded in finding a pair that suited him; and I had the pleasure of paying for them, and then presenting them to him, as a remembrance of his visit to the North, as well as of me. I never saw him again, for it was not long after that he died. My old master, David Kibbler, died also. Jerry Kibbler, my good Methodist friend and class-leader, came to Worcester, and spent several days, boarding with my friend, Mrs. Stearns, during the time, because I could not then make him comfortable in my own home. I took him to Providence to see Mr. Adams, who showed him much attention; and he returned home with a very warm appreciation of New England hospitality, as well as of Northern thrift and energy, and regretted that the South had been so long blind to her own interests.

My life in the North, as in the South, has been full of experiences, both sad and joyful.

Sixteen years ago this winter, I was sent for to the dying bed of Mrs. Adams. A twelvemonth is scarcely passed since I was again called to assist in the care of Mr. Adams, as he lingered week after week, only half-conscious of life, and then passed away. His recognition of my poor service gladdens me now, for I can never express the satisfaction it gave me to minister to his wants. For I was a stranger, and he took me in : I had fallen amongst thieves, and he had rescued me.

I have spoken of the kindness of my Methodist brothers and sisters. To tell the half of it would be impossible. One thing, however, I must not omit. It is this : on going to Sterling, last summer, to camp-meeting, I found on the spot where I had been accustomed to pitch my tent a nice wooden building, waiting for my occupation. The surprise was so great to me, I am afraid I did not express the gratitude I really felt ; and this is only one of the many ways in which I have tasted the loving-kindness of my friends, and found it, like that of the infinite Father, " oh, how free ! "

I am now, at seventy-four years of age, the owner and occupant of a small house at 21 Tufts Street, Worcester, Mass. My daughter and family are near me, in an adjoining house, also owned by me. I have three grandchildren living.

My back is not so straight nor so strong, my sight is not so clear, nor my limbs so nimble as they once were ; but I am still ready and glad to do whatsoever my hand findeth to do, waiting only for the call to " come up higher."

BETHANY VENEY.

WORCESTER, MASS., 1889.

LETTER FROM REV. V. A. COOPER,

SUPERINTENDENT OF HOME FOR LITTLE WANDERERS, BOSTON, MASS.

Two hundred years of human bondage! From generation to generation the vast system of tyranny, oppressing every faculty of mind and capability of moral nature, transmitting its baneful influence from parent to child, and then, by its injustice, dishonesty, and utter disregard of all the most sacred relationships of life, stifling the earliest instincts and smothering the first breathings of the innate personality which distinguishes the race created in God's image, the wonder of wonders is that there was anything left of the nobility of a true manhood and womanhood in a single member of the oppressed and ravished race at the end of two hundred years. Whatever happened at the Fall of Adam and Eve, the strength of brain and heart that could withstand such treatment and retain in itself the fibre and life of noble aspirations, strength to stand for justice, truth, virtue, and courage of conviction, must have had something left in it both God-like and sublime. Such characters there were all through the South.

Betty Veney was one of them. The story of her life speaks nobly for herself, sublimely for human nature, grandly for her race. Amid dishonesty she was honest, amid injustice she had the soul of honor, amid corruption she was pure, amid persecutions dauntless and patient. I see her industrious, beautiful, heroically suffering life, against the white man's lecherous greed, against slavery's oppression, as a natural development amid rank and noxious weeds fed and watered by the grace of God, as lilies are which lie in virgin purity on the bosom of fetid waters in dank swamps.

We can never undo the past wrong; but wherever a colored hand, worn out with honest labor, which has never been requited, is stretched out palm up in the midst of Christian plenty, its silent appeal is more pathetic than any language. It seems to come from the body of the race, to bear in its lines the sad story, not of one person, but of the millions buried and forgotten in their unmarked graves. It would be the simplest act of justice to pension all the remaining slaves. The cotton-fields and rice-swamps of the South would seem then to be yielding the peaceable fruits of righteousness. It would then appear to all mankind that our religion had awakened our seared Christian conscience to the sense of the wrongs done this people.

Dear Aunt Betty! Her race is nearly run. Her sun goes down the sky. How broad the chart from horizon to horizon! Long years of trouble, toil, self-sacrifice, and suffering! May thy sunset be the sun-rising of a cloudless day, where justice shall compensate thee and thine, and thy independent free spirit, equal to the angels', enjoy forever the freedom of the sons of God!

Your former pastor and wife,

V. A. AND ELIZABETH COOPER.

LETTER FROM REV. ERASTUS SPAULDING.

For twenty-five years, I have been acquainted with the subject of the foregoing pages. I know her to be a woman of strict integrity of character, good judgment, full of sympathy, and ever ready to do all in her power to relieve the sick and suffering. Born in slavery, and freed from her master by the kindness of a friend, she has yet more whereof to glory in that she has been freed from the bondage of sin, and made an heir of God and a joint-heir with Christ. If I am ever so happy as to get to heaven, I shall feel myself honored if I can have a seat so near the throne as Betty Veney.

REV. ERASTUS SPAULDING.

Millbury, Feb. 5, 1889.

REMINISCENCES OF
MY LIFE IN CAMP

Susie King Taylor.

REMINISCENCES OF
MY LIFE IN CAMP

WITH THE 33D UNITED STATES
COLORED TROOPS LATE 1ST
S. C. VOLUNTEERS

BY

SUSIE KING TAYLOR

WITH ILLUSTRATIONS

BOSTON
PUBLISHED BY THE AUTHOR
1902

PREFACE

I HAVE been asked many times by my friends, and also by members of the Grand Army of the Republic and Women's Relief Corps, to write a book of my army life, during the war of 1861–65, with the regiment of the 1st South Carolina Colored Troops, later called 33d United States Colored Infantry.

At first I did not think I would, but as the years rolled on and my friends were still urging me to start with it, I wrote to Colonel C. T. Trowbridge (who had command of this regiment), asking his opinion and advice on the matter. His answer to me was, "Go ahead! write it; that is just what I should do, were I in your place, and I will give you all the assistance you may need, whenever you require it." This inspired me very much.

In 1900 I received a letter from a gentleman, sent from the Executive Mansion at St. Paul, Minn., saying Colonel Trowbridge had told him I was about to write a book, and when it was published he wanted one of the first copies. This, coming from a total stranger, gave me more confidence, so I now present these reminiscences to you, hoping they may prove of some interest, and show how much service and good we can do to each other, and what sacrifices we can make for our liberty and rights, and that there were "loyal women," as well as men, in those days, who did not fear shell or shot, who cared for the sick and dying; women who camped and fared as the boys did, and who are still caring for the comrades in their declining years.

So, with the hope that the following pages will accomplish some good and instruction for its readers, I shall proceed with my narrative.

SUSIE KING TAYLOR.

BOSTON, 1902.

CONTENTS

LIST OF ILLUSTRATIONS

INTRODUCTION

ACTUAL military life is rarely described by a woman, and this is especially true of a woman whose place was in the ranks, as the wife of a soldier and herself a regimental laundress. No such description has ever been given, I am sure, by one thus connected with a colored regiment; so that the nearly 200,000 black soldiers (178,-975) of our Civil War have never before been delineated from the woman's point of view. All this gives peculiar interest to this little volume, relating wholly to the career of the very earliest of these regiments, — the one described by myself, from a wholly different point of view, in my volume " Army Life in a Black Regiment," long since translated into French by the Comtesse de Gasparin under the title " Vie Militaire dans un Régiment Noir."

The writer of the present book was very exceptional among the colored laundresses, in that she could read and write and had taught children to do the same ; and her whole life and career were most estimable, both during the war and in the later period during which she has lived in Boston and has made many friends. I may add that I did not see the book until the sheets were in print, and have left it wholly untouched, except as to a few errors in proper names. I commend the narrative to those who love the plain record of simple lives, led in stormy periods.

THOMAS WENTWORTH HIGGINSON,

Former Colonel 1st S. C. Volunteers

(afterwards 33d U. S. Colored Infantry)

CAMBRIDGE, MASS.,
    November 3, 1902.

LETTER FROM COL. C. T. TROWBRIDGE

St. Paul, Minn., April 7, 1902.

Mrs. Susan King Taylor:

Dear Madam, — The manuscript of the story of your army life reached me to-day. I have read it with much care and interest, and I most willingly and cordially indorse it as a truthful account of your unselfish devotion and service through more than three long years of war in which the 33d Regiment bore a conspicuous part in the great conflict for human liberty and the restoration of the Union. I most sincerely regret that through a technicality you are debarred from having your name placed on the roll of pensioners, as an Army Nurse; for among all the number of heroic women whom the government is now rewarding, I know of no one more deserving than yourself.

Yours in F. C. & L.,

C. T. TROWBRIDGE,
Late Lt.-Col. 33d U. S. C. T.

REMINISCENCES

I

My great-great-grandmother was 120 years old when she died. She had seven children, and five of her boys were in the Revolutionary War. She was from Virginia, and was half Indian. She was so old she had to be held in the sun to help restore or prolong her vitality.

My great-grandmother, one of her daughters, named Susanna, was married to Peter Simons, and was one hundred years old when she died, from a stroke of paralysis in Savannah. She was the mother of twenty-four children, twenty-three being girls. She was one of the noted mid-wives of her day. In 1820 my grandmother was born, and named after her grandmother, Dolly, and in 1833 she married Fortune Lambert Reed. Two children blessed their union, James and Hagar Ann. James died at the age of twelve years.

My mother was born in 1834. She married Raymond Baker in 1847. Nine children were born to them, three dying in infancy. I was the first born. I was born on the Grest Farm (which was on an island known as Isle of Wight), Liberty County, about thirty-five miles from Savannah, Ga., on August 6, 1848, my mother being waitress for the Grest family. I have often been told by mother of the care Mrs. Grest took of me. She was very fond of me, and I remember when my brother and I were small children, and Mr. Grest would go away on business, Mrs. Grest would place us at the foot of her bed to sleep and keep her company. Sometimes he would return home earlier than he had expected to ; then she would put us on the floor.

When I was about seven years old, Mr. Grest allowed my grandmother to take my brother and me to live with her in Savannah. There were no railroad connections in those days between this place and Savannah ; all travel was by stage-coaches. I remember, as if it were yesterday, the coach which ran in from Savannah, with its driver, whose beard nearly reached his knees. His name was Shakespeare, and often I would go to the stable where he kept his horses, on Barnard Street in front of the old Arsenal, just to look at his wonderful beard.

My grandmother went every three months to see my mother. She would hire a wagon to carry bacon, tobacco, flour, molasses, and sugar. These she would trade with people in the neighboring places, for eggs, chickens, or cash, if they had it. These, in turn, she carried back to the city market, where she had a customer who sold them for her. The profit from these, together with laundry work and care of some bachelors' rooms, made a good living for her.

The hardest blow to her was the failure of the Freedmen's Savings Bank in Savannah, for in that bank she had placed her savings, about three thousand dollars, the result of her hard labor and self-denial before the war, and which, by dint of shrewdness and care, she kept together all through the war. She felt it more keenly, coming as it did in her old age, when her life was too far spent to begin anew; but she took a practical view of the matter, for she said, " I will leave it all in God's hand. If the Yankees did take all our money, they freed my race; God will take care of us."

In 1888 she wrote me here (Boston), asking me to visit her, as she was getting very feeble and wanted to see me once before she passed away. I made up my mind to leave at once, but about the time I planned to go, in March, a fearful blizzard swept our country, and travel was at a standstill for nearly two weeks; but March 15 I left on the first through steamer from New York, en route for the South, where I again saw my grandmother, and we felt thankful that we were spared to meet each other once more.   This was the last time I saw her, for in May, 1889, she died.

II

MY CHILDHOOD

I was born under the slave law in Georgia, in 1848, and was brought up by my grandmother in Savannah. There were three of us with her, my younger sister and brother. My brother and I being the two eldest, we were sent to a friend of my grandmother, Mrs. Woodhouse, a widow, to learn to read and write. She was a free woman and lived on Bay Lane, between Habersham and Price streets, about half a mile from my house. We went every day about nine o'clock, with our books wrapped in paper to prevent the police or white persons from seeing them. We went in, one at a time, through the gate, into the yard to the L kitchen, which was the schoolroom. She had twenty-five or thirty children whom she taught, assisted by her daughter, Mary Jane. The neighbors would see us going in sometimes, but they supposed we were there learning trades, as it was the custom to give children a trade of some kind. After school we left the same way we entered, one by one, when we would go to a square, about a block from the school, and wait for each other. We would gather laurel leaves

and pop them on our hands, on our way home.
I remained at her school for two years or more,
when I was sent to a Mrs. Mary Beasley, where
I continued until May, 1860, when she told my
grandmother she had taught me all she knew,
and grandmother had better get some one else
who could teach me more, so I stopped my studies
for a while.

I had a white playmate about this time, named
Katie O'Connor, who lived on the next corner
of the street from my house, and who attended
a convent. One day she told me, if I would promise not to tell her father, she would give me
some lessons. On my promise not to do so, and
getting her mother's consent, she gave me lessons
about four months, every evening. At the end
of this time she was put into the convent per-
manently, and I have never seen her since.

A month after this, James Blouis, our land-
lord's son, was attending the High School, and
was very fond of grandmother, so she asked him
to give me a few lessons, which he did until the
middle of 1861, when the Savannah Volunteer
Guards, to which he and his brother belonged,
were ordered to the front under General Barton.
In the first battle of Manassas, his brother
Eugene was killed, and James deserted over to
the Union side, and at the close of the war went
to Washington, D. C., where he has since resided.

I often wrote passes for my grandmother, for all colored persons, free or slaves, were compelled to have a pass; free colored people having a guardian in place of a master. These passes were good until 10 or 10.30 P. M. for one night or every night for one month. The pass read as follows: —

SAVANNAH, GA., March 1st, 1860.

Pass the bearer ———— from 9 to 10.30. P. M.
VALENTINE GREST.

Every person had to have this pass, for at nine o'clock each night a bell was rung, and any colored persons found on the street after this hour were arrested by the watchman, and put in the guard-house until next morning, when their owners would pay their fines and release them. I knew a number of persons who went out at any time at night and were never arrested, as the watchman knew them so well he never stopped them, and seldom asked to see their passes, only stopping them long enough, sometimes, to say "Howdy," and then telling them to go along.

About this time I had been reading so much about the "Yankees" I was very anxious to see them. The whites would tell their colored people not to go to the Yankees, for they would harness them to carts and make them pull the carts around, in place of horses. I asked grandmother, one day, if this was true. She replied, "Cer-

tainly not!" that the white people did not want
slaves to go over to the Yankees, and told them
these things to frighten them. "Don't you see
those signs pasted about the streets? one reading,
'I am a rattlesnake; if you touch me I will
strike!' Another reads, 'I am a wild-cat! Be-
ware,' etc. These are warnings to the North; so
don't mind what the white people say." I wanted
to see these wonderful "Yankees" so much, as I
heard my parents say the Yankee was going to
set all the slaves free. Oh, how those people
prayed for freedom! I remember, one night,
my grandmother went out into the suburbs of the
city to a church meeting, and they were fervently
singing this old hymn, —

> "Yes, we all shall be free,
>   Yes, we all shall be free,
>   Yes, we all shall be free,
>   When the Lord shall appear," —

when the police came in and arrested all who were
there, saying they were planning freedom, and
sang "the Lord," in place of "Yankee," to blind
any one who might be listening. Grandmother
never forgot that night, although she did not stay
in the guard-house, as she sent to her guardian,
who came at once for her; but this was the last
meeting she ever attended out of the city proper.

On April 1, 1862, about the time the Union
soldiers were firing on Fort Pulaski, I was sent
out into the country to my mother. I remember

what a roar and din the guns made. They jarred
the earth for miles. The fort was at last taken
by them. Two days after the taking of Fort
Pulaski, my uncle took his family of seven and
myself to St. Catherine Island. We landed under
the protection of the Union fleet, and remained
there two weeks, when about thirty of us were
taken aboard the gunboat P———, to be transferred to St. Simon's Island; and at last, to my
unbounded joy, I saw the "Yankee."

After we were all settled aboard and started on
our journey, Captain Whitmore, commanding the
boat, asked me where I was from. I told him
Savannah, Ga. He asked if I could read; I said,
"Yes!" "Can you write?" he next asked. "Yes,
I can do that also," I replied, and as if he had
some doubts of my answers he handed me a book
and a pencil and told me to write my name and
where I was from. I did this; when he wanted
to know if I could sew. On hearing I could, he
asked me to hem some napkins for him. He was
surprised at my accomplishments (for they were
such in those days), for he said he did not know
there were any negroes in the South able to read
or write. He said, "You seem to be so different
from the other colored people who came from the
same place you did." "No!" I replied, "the
only difference is, they were reared in the country and I in the city, as was a man from Darien,
Ga., named Edward King." That seemed to

satisfy him, and we had no further conversation
that day on the subject.

In the afternoon the captain spied a boat in
the distance, and as it drew nearer he noticed it
had a white flag hoisted, but before it had reached
the Putumoka he ordered all passengers between
decks, so we could not be seen, for he thought
they might be spies. The boat finally drew along-
side of our boat, and had Mr. Edward Donegall
on board, who wanted his two servants, Nick and
Judith. He wanted these, as they were his own
children. Our captain told him he knew nothing
of them, which was true, for at the time they
were on St. Simon's, and not, as their father
supposed, on our boat. After the boat left, we
were allowed to come up on deck again.

III

1862

NEXT morning we arrived at St. Simon's, and the captain told Commodore Goldsborough about this affair, and his reply was, "Captain Whitmore, you should not have allowed them to return; you should have kept them." After I had been on St. Simon's about three days, Commodore Goldsborough heard of me, and came to Gaston Bluff to see me. I found him very cordial. He said Captain Whitmore had spoken to him of me, and that he was pleased to hear of my being so capable, etc., and wished me to take charge of a school for the children on the island. I told him I would gladly do so, if I could have some books. He said I should have them, and in a week or two I received two large boxes of books and testaments from the North. I had about forty children to teach, beside a number of adults who came to me nights, all of them so eager to learn to read, to read above anything else. Chaplain French, of Boston, would come to the school, sometimes, and lecture to the pupils on Boston and the North.

About the first of June we were told that there

was going to be a settlement of the war. Those who were on the Union side would remain free, and those in bondage were to work three days for their masters and three for themselves. It was a gloomy time for us all, and we were to be sent to Liberia. Chaplain French asked me would I rather go back to Savannah or go to Liberia. I told him the latter place by all means. We did not know when this would be, but we were prepared in case this settlement should be reached. However, the Confederates would not agree to the arrangement, or else it was one of the many rumors flying about at the time, as we heard nothing further of the matter. There were a number of settlements on this island of St. Simon's, just like little villages, and we would go from one to the other on business, to call, or only for a walk.

One Sunday, two men, Adam Miller and Daniel Spaulding, were chased by some rebels as they were coming from Hope Place (which was between the Beach and Gaston Bluff), but the latter were unable to catch them. When they reached the Beach and told this, all the men on the place, about ninety, armed themselves, and next day (Monday), with Charles O'Neal as their leader, skirmished the island for the "rebs." In a short while they discovered them in the woods, hidden behind a large log, among the thick underbrush. Charles O'Neal was the first to see them, and he was killed; also John Brown, and their bodies were never found.   Charles O'Neal was an uncle of Edward King, who later was my husband and a sergeant in Co. E., U. S. I.   Another man was shot, but not found for three days.   On Tuesday, the second day, Captain Trowbridge and some soldiers landed, and assisted the skirmishers. Word having been sent by the mail-boat Uncas to Hilton Head, later in the day Commodore Goldsborough, who was in command of the naval station, landed about three hundred marines, and joined the others to oust the rebels.   On Wednesday, John Baker, the man shot on Monday, was found in a terrible condition by Henry Batchlott, who carried him to the Beach, where he was attended by the surgeon.   He told us how, after being shot, he lay quiet for a day.   On the second day he managed to reach some wild grapes growing near him.   These he ate, to satisfy his hunger and intense thirst, then he crawled slowly, every movement causing agony, until he got to the side of the road.   He lived only three months after they found him.

On the second day of the skirmish the troops captured a boat which they knew the Confederates had used to land in, and having this in their possession, the " rebs " could not return; so pickets were stationed all around the island.   There was an old man, Henry Capers, who had been left on one of the places by his old master, Mr. Hazzard, as he was too old to carry away. These rebels went to his house in the night, and he hid them up in the loft. On Tuesday all hands went to this man's house with a determination to burn it down, but Henry Batchlott pleaded with the men to spare it. The rebels were in hiding, still, waiting a chance to get off the island. They searched his house, but neglected to go up into the loft, and in so doing missed the rebels concealed there. Late in the night Henry Capers gave them his boat to escape in, and they got off all right. This old man was allowed by the men in charge of the island to cut grass for his horse, and to have a boat to carry this grass to his home, and so they were not detected, our men thinking it was Capers using the boat. After Commodore Goldsborough left the island, Commodore Judon sent the old man over to the mainland and would not allow him to remain on the island.

There were about six hundred men, women, and children on St. Simon's, the women and children being in the majority, and we were afraid to go very far from our own quarters in the daytime, and at night even to go out of the house for a long time, although the men were on the watch all the time ; for there were not any soldiers on the island, only the marines who were on the gunboats along the coast. The rebels, knowing this, could steal by them under cover of the night, and getting on the island would capture any per-

sons venturing out alone and carry them to the
mainland.   Several of the men disappeared, and
as they were never heard from we came to the
conclusion they had been carried off in this
way.

The latter part of August, 1862, Captain C. T.
Trowbridge, with his brother John and Lieutenant Walker, came to St. Simon's Island from
Hilton Head, by order of General Hunter, to get
all the men possible to finish filling his regiment
which he had organized in March, 1862.   He had
heard of the skirmish on this island, and was very
much pleased at the bravery shown by these men.
He found me at Gaston Bluff teaching my little
school, and was much interested in it.   When I
knew him better I found him to be a thorough
gentleman and a staunch friend to my race.

Captain Trowbridge remained with us until
October, when the order was received to evacuate,
and so we boarded the Ben-De-Ford, a transport,
for Beaufort, S. C.   When we arrived in Beaufort, Captain Trowbridge and the men he had
enlisted went to camp at Old Fort, which they
named " Camp Saxton."   I was enrolled as laundress.

The first suits worn by the boys were red
coats and pants, which they disliked very much,
for, they said, " The rebels see us, miles away."

The first colored troops did not receive any
pay for eighteen months, and the men had to de-

pend wholly on what they received from the commissary, established by General Saxton. A great many of these men had large families, and as they had no money to give them, their wives were obliged to support themselves and children by washing for the officers of the gunboats and the soldiers, and making cakes and pies which they sold to the boys in camp. Finally, in 1863, the government decided to give them half pay, but the men would not accept this. They wanted "full pay" or nothing. They preferred rather to give their services to the state, which they did until 1864, when the government granted them full pay, with all the back pay due.

I remember hearing Captain Heasley telling his company, one day, "Boys, stand up for your full pay! I am with you, and so are all the officers." This captain was from Pennsylvania, and was a very good man; all the men liked him. N. G. Parker, our first lieutenant, was from Massachusetts. H. A. Beach was from New York. He was very delicate, and had to resign in 1864 on account of ill health.

I had a number of relatives in this regiment, — several uncles, some cousins, and a husband in Company E, and a number of cousins in other companies. Major Strong, of this regiment, started home on a furlough, but the vessel he was aboard was lost, and he never reached his home. He was one of the best officers we had. After-

CAPT. A. W. HEASLEY

CAPT. WALKER   CAPT. W. W. SAMPSON

CAPT. CHARLES E. PARKER

his death, Captain C. T. Trowbridge was promoted
major, August, 1863, and filled Major Strong's
place until December, 1864, when he was promoted lieutenant-colonel, which he remained until he was mustered out, February 6, 1866.

In February, 1863, several cases of varioloid
broke out among the boys, which caused some
anxiety in camp. Edward Davis, of Company E
(the company I was with), had it very badly. He
was put into a tent apart from the rest of the
men, and only the doctor and camp steward, James
Cummings, were allowed to see or attend him;
but I went to see this man every day and nursed
him. The last thing at night, I always went in
to see that he was comfortable, but in spite of
the good care and attention he received, he
succumbed to the disease.

I was not in the least afraid of the small-pox.
I had been vaccinated, and I drank sassafras tea
constantly, which kept my blood purged and pre-
vented me from contracting this dread scourge,
and no one need fear getting it if they will only
keep their blood in good condition with this sassafras tea, and take it before going where the patient
is.

IV

CAMP SAXTON — PROCLAMATION AND BARBECUE

1863

ON the first of January, 1863, we held services for the purpose of listening to the reading of President Lincoln's proclamation by Dr. W. H. Brisbane, and the presentation of two beautiful stands of colors, one from a lady in Connecticut, and the other from Rev. Mr. Cheever. The presentation speech was made by Chaplain French. It was a glorious day for us all, and we enjoyed every minute of it, and as a fitting close and the crowning event of this occasion we had a grand barbecue. A number of oxen were roasted whole, and we had a fine feast. Although not served as tastily or correctly as it would have been at home, yet it was enjoyed with keen appetites and relish. The soldiers had a good time. They sang or shouted "Hurrah!" all through the camp, and seemed overflowing with fun and frolic until taps were sounded, when many, no doubt, dreamt of this memorable day.

I had rather an amusing experience; that is, it seems amusing now, as I look back, but at the time it occurred it was a most serious one to me.

When our regiment left Beaufort for Seabrooke, I left some of my things with a neighbor who lived outside of the camp. After I had been at Seabrooke about a week, I decided to return to Camp Saxton and get them. So one morning, with Mary Shaw, a friend who was in the company at that time, I started off. There was no way for us to get to Beaufort other than to walk, except we rode on the commissary wagon. This we did, and reached Beaufort about one o'clock. We then had more than two miles to walk before reaching our old camp, and expected to be able to accomplish this and return in time to meet the wagon again by three o'clock that afternoon, and so be taken back. We failed to do this, however, for when we got to Beaufort the wagon was gone. We did not know what to do. I did not wish to remain overnight, neither did my friend, although we might easily have stayed, as both had relatives in the town.

It was in the springtime, and the days were long, and as the sun looked so bright, we concluded to walk back, thinking we should reach camp before dark. So off we started on our ten-mile tramp. We had not gone many miles, however, before we were all tired out and began to regret our undertaking. The sun was getting low, and we grew more frightened, fearful of meeting some animal or of treading on a snake on our way. We did not meet a person, and we were frightened almost to death. Our feet were so sore we could hardly walk. Finally we took off our shoes and tried walking in our stocking feet, but this made them worse. We had gone about six miles when night overtook us. There we were, nothing around us but dense woods, and as there was no house or any place to stop at, there was nothing for us to do but continue on. We were afraid to speak to each other.

. Meantime at the camp, seeing no signs of us by dusk, they concluded we had decided to remain over until next day, and so had no idea of our plight. Imagine their surprise when we reached camp about eleven P. M. The guard challenged us, "Who comes there?" My answer was, "A friend without a countersign." He approached and saw who it was, reported, and we were admitted into the lines. They had the joke on us that night, and for a long time after would tease us ; and sometimes some of the men who were on guard that night would call us deserters. They used to laugh at us, but we joined with them too, especially when we would tell them our experience on our way to camp. I did not undertake that trip again, as there was no way of getting in or out except one took the provision wagon, and there was not much dependence to be put in that returning to camp. Perhaps the driver would say one hour and he might be there earlier or later. Of course it was not his fault, as it depended when the order was filled at the Commissary Department; therefore I did not go any more until the regiment was ordered to our new camp, which was named after our hero, Colonel Shaw, who at that time was at Beaufort with his regiment, the 54th Massachusetts.

I taught a great many of the comrades in Company E to read and write, when they were off duty. Nearly all were anxious to learn. My husband taught some also when it was convenient for him. I was very happy to know my efforts were successful in camp, and also felt grateful for the appreciation of my services. I gave my services willingly for four years and three months without receiving a dollar. I was glad, however, to be allowed to go with the regiment, to care for the sick and afflicted comrades.

V

MILITARY EXPEDITIONS, AND LIFE IN CAMP

In the latter part of 1862 the regiment made an expedition into Darien, Georgia, and up the Ridge, and on January 23, 1863, another up St. Mary's River, capturing a number of stores for the government ; then on to Fernandina, Florida. They were gone ten or twelve days, at the end of which time they returned to camp.

March 10, 1863, we were ordered to Jacksonville, Florida. Leaving Camp Saxton between four and five o'clock, we arrived at Jacksonville about eight o'clock next morning, accompanied by three or four gunboats. When the rebels saw these boats, they ran out of the city, leaving the women behind, and we found out afterwards that they thought we had a much larger fleet than we really had. Our regiment was kept out of sight until we made fast at the wharf where it landed, and while the gunboats were shelling up the river and as far inland as possible, the regiment landed and marched up the street, where they spied the rebels who had fled from the city. They were hiding behind a house about a mile or so away, their faces blackened to disguise themselves as negroes, and our boys, as they advanced toward them, halted a second, saying, "They are black men! Let them come to us, or we will make them know who we are." With this, the firing was opened and several of our men were wounded and killed. The rebels had a number wounded and killed. It was through this way the discovery was made that they were white men. Our men drove them some distance in retreat and then threw out their pickets.

While the fighting was on, a friend, Lizzie Lancaster, and I stopped at several of the rebel homes, and after talking with some of the women and children we asked them if they had any food. They claimed to have only some hard-tack, and evidently did not care to give us anything to eat, but this was not surprising. They were bitterly against our people and had no mercy or sympathy for us.

The second day, our boys were reinforced by a regiment of white soldiers, a Maine regiment, and by cavalry, and had quite a fight. On the third day, Edward Herron, who was a fine gunner on the steamer John Adams, came on shore, bringing a small cannon, which the men pulled along for more than five miles. This cannon was the only piece for shelling. On coming upon the enemy, all secured their places, and they had a lively fight, which lasted several hours, and our boys were nearly captured by the Confederates; but the Union boys carried out all their plans that day, and succeeded in driving the enemy back. After this skirmish, every afternoon between four and five o'clock the Confederate General Finegan would send a flag of truce to Colonel Higginson, warning him to send all women and children out of the city, and threatening to bombard it if this was not done. Our colonel allowed all to go who wished, at first, but as General Finegan grew more hostile and kept sending these communications for nearly a week, Colonel Higginson thought it not best or necessary to send any more out of the city, and so informed General Finegan. This angered the general, for that night the rebels shelled directly toward Colonel Higginson's headquarters. The shelling was so heavy that the colonel told my captain to have me taken up into the town to a hotel, which was used as a hospital. As my quarters were just in the rear of the colonel's, he was compelled to leave his also before the night was over. I expected every moment to be killed by a shell, but on arriving at the hospital I knew I was safe, for the shells could not reach us there. It was plainly to be seen now, the ruse of the flag of truce coming so often to us. The bearer was evidently a spy getting the location of the headquarters, etc., for the shells were sent too accurately to be at random.

Next morning Colonel Higginson took the cav-

THOMAS WENTWORTH HIGGINSON
COLONEL FIRST SOUTH CAROLINA VOLUNTEERS
Afterwards 33d U. S. C. T.

alry and a regiment on another tramp after the rebels. They were gone several days and had the hardest fight they had had, for they wanted to go as far as a station which was some distance from the city. The gunboats were of little assistance to them, yet notwithstanding this drawback our boys returned with only a few killed and wounded, and after this we were not troubled with General Finegan.

We remained here a few weeks longer, when, about April first, the regiment was ordered back to Camp Saxton, where it stayed a week, when the order came to go to Port Royal Ferry on picket duty. It was a gay day for the boys. By seven o'clock all tents were down, and each company, with a commissary wagon, marched up the shell road, which is a beautiful avenue ten or twelve miles out of Beaufort. We arrived at Seabrooke at about four o'clock, where our tents were pitched and the men put on duty. We were here a few weeks, when Company E was ordered to Barnwell plantation for picket duty.

Some mornings I would go along the picket line, and I could see the rebels on the opposite side of the river. Sometimes as they were changing pickets they would call over to our men and ask for something to eat, or for tobacco, and our men would tell them to come over. Sometimes one or two would desert to us, saying, they " had no negroes to fight for." Others would shoot across at our picket, but as the river was so wide there was never any damage done, and the Confederates never attempted to shell us while we were there.

I learned to handle a musket very well while in the regiment, and could shoot straight and often hit the target. I assisted in cleaning the guns and used to fire them off, to see if the cartridges were dry, before cleaning and reloading, each day. I thought this great fun. I was also able to take a gun all apart, and put it together again.

Between Barnwell and the mainland was Hall Island. I went over there several times with Sergeant King and other comrades. One night there was a stir in camp when it was found that the rebels were trying to cross, and next morning Lieutenant Parker told me he thought they were on Hall Island ; so after that I did not go over again.

While planning for the expedition up the Edisto River, Colonel Higginson was a whole night in the water, trying to locate the rebels and where their picket lines were situated. About July the boys went up the Edisto to destroy a bridge on the Charleston and Savannah road. This expedition was twenty or more miles into the mainland. Colonel Higginson was wounded in this fight and the regiment nearly captured. The steamboat John Adams always assisted us, carrying soldiers, provisions, etc. She carried several guns and a good gunner, Edward Herron. Henry Batchlott, a relative of mine, was a steward on this boat. There were two smaller boats, Governor Milton and the Enoch Dean, in the fleet, as these could go up the river better than the larger ones could. I often went aboard the John Adams. It went with us into Jacksonville, to Cole and Folly Island, and Gunner Herron was always ready to send a shell at the enemy.

One night, Companies K and E, on their way to Pocotaligo to destroy a battery that was situated down the river, captured several prisoners. The rebels nearly captured Sergeant King, who, as he sprang and caught a "reb," fell over an embankment. In falling he did not release his hold on his prisoner. Although his hip was severely injured, he held fast until some of his comrades came to his aid and pulled them up. These expeditions were very dangerous. Sometimes the men had to go five or ten miles during the night over on the rebel side and capture or destroy whatever they could find.

While at Camp Shaw, there was a deserter who came into Beaufort. He was allowed his freedom about the city and was not molested. He remained about the place a little while and returned to the rebels again. On his return to Beaufort a second time, he was held as a spy, tried, and sentenced to death, for he was a traitor. The day he was shot, he was placed on a hearse with his coffin inside, a guard was placed either side of the hearse, and he was driven through the town. All the soldiers and people in town were out, as this was to be a warning to the soldiers. Our regiment was in line on dress parade. They drove with him to the rear of our camp, where he was shot. I shall never forget this scene.

While at Camp Shaw, Chaplain Fowler, Robert Defoe, and several of our boys were captured while tapping some telegraph wires. Robert Defoe was confined in the jail at Walterborough, S. C., for about twenty months. When Sherman's army reached Pocotaligo he made his escape and joined his company (Company G). He had not been paid, as he had refused the reduced pay offered by the government. Before we got to camp, where the pay-rolls could be made out, he sickened and died of small-pox, and was buried at Savannah, never having been paid one cent for nearly three years of service. He left no heirs and his account was never settled.

In winter, when it was very cold, I would take a mess-pan, put a little earth in the bottom, and go to the cook-shed and fill it nearly full of coals, carry it back to my tent and put another pan over it; so when the provost guard went through camp after taps, they would not see the light, as it was against the rules to have a light after taps. In this way I was heated and kept very warm.

A mess-pan is made of sheet iron, something

MAJOR H. A. WHITNEY   LIEUT. J. B. WEST
HENRY BATCHLOTT
STEWARD OF THE JOHN ADAMS

like our roasting pans, only they are nearly as large round as a peck measure, but not so deep. We had fresh beef once in a while, and we would have soup, and the vegetables they put in this soup were dried and pressed. They looked like hops. Salt beef was our stand-by. Sometimes the men would have what we called slap-jacks. This was flour, made into bread and spread thin on the bottom of the mess-pan to cook. Each man had one of them, with a pint of tea, for his supper, or a pint of tea and five or six hard-tack. I often got my own meals, and would fix some dishes for the non-commissioned officers also.

Mrs. Chamberlain, our quartermaster's wife, was with us here. She was a beautiful woman; I can see her pleasant face before me now, as she, with Captain Trowbridge, would sit and converse with me in my tent two or three hours at a time. She was also with me on Cole Island, and I think we were the only women with the regiment while there. I remember well how, when she first came into camp, Captain Trowbridge brought her to my tent and introduced her to me. I found her then, as she remained ever after, a lovely person, and I always admired her cordial and friendly ways.

Our boys would say to me sometimes, " Mrs. King, why is it you are so kind to us ? you treat us just as you do the boys in your own company." I replied, " Well, you know, all the boys in other companies are the same to me as those in my Company E; you are all doing the same duty, and I will do just the same for you." " Yes," they would say, " we know that, because you were the first woman we saw when we came into camp, and you took an interest in us boys ever since we have been here, and we are very grateful for all you do for us."

When at Camp Shaw, I visited the hospital in Beaufort, where I met Clara Barton. There were a number of sick and wounded soldiers there, and I went often to see the comrades. Miss Barton was always very cordial toward me, and I honored her for her devotion and care of those men.

There was a man, John Johnson, who with his family was taken by our regiment at Edisto. This man afterwards worked in the hospital and was well known to Miss Barton. I have been told since that when she went South, in 1883, she tried to look this man up, but learned he was dead. His son is living in Edisto, Rev. J. J. Johnson, and is the president of an industrial school on that island and a very intelligent man. He was a small child when his father and family were captured by our regiment at Edisto.

VI

FORT WAGNER being only a mile from our camp, I went there two or three times a week, and would go up on the ramparts to watch the gunners send their shells into Charleston (which they did every fifteen minutes), and had a full view of the city from that point. Outside of the fort were many skulls lying about; I have often moved them one side out of the path. The comrades and I would have quite a debate as to which side the men fought on. Some thought they were the skulls of our boys; others thought they were the enemy's; but as there was no definite way to know, it was never decided which could lay claim to them. They were a gruesome sight, those fleshless heads and grinning jaws, but by this time I had become accustomed to worse things and did not feel as I might have earlier in my camp life.

It seems strange how our aversion to seeing suffering is overcome in war, — how we are able to see the most sickening sights, such as men with their limbs blown off and mangled by the deadly shells, without a shudder; and instead of turning away, how we hurry to assist in alleviating their pain, bind up their wounds, and press the cool water to their parched lips, with feelings only of sympathy and pity.

About the first of June, 1864, the regiment was ordered to Folly Island, staying there until the latter part of the month, when it was ordered to Morris Island. We landed on Morris Island between June and July, 1864. This island was a narrow strip of sandy soil, nothing growing on it but a few bushes and shrubs. The camp was one mile from the boat landing, called Pawnell Landing, and the landing one mile from Fort Wagner.

Colonel Higginson had left us in May of this year, on account of wounds received at Edisto. All the men were sorry to lose him. They did not want him to go, they loved him so. He was kind and devoted to his men, thoughtful for their comfort, and we missed his genial presence from the camp.

The regiment under Colonel Trowbridge did garrison duty, but they had troublesome times from Fort Gregg, on James Island, for the rebels would throw a shell over on our island every now and then. Finally orders were received for the boys to prepare to take Fort Gregg, each man to take 150 rounds of cartridges, canteens of water, hard-tack, and salt beef. This order was sent three days prior to starting, to allow them to be in readiness. I helped as many as I could to pack haversacks and cartridge boxes.

The fourth day, about five o'clock in the afternoon, the call was sounded, and I heard the first sergeant say, "Fall in, boys, fall in," and they were not long obeying the command. Each company marched out of its street, in front of their colonel's headquarters, where they rested for half an hour, as it was not dark enough, and they did not want the enemy to have a chance to spy their movements. At the end of this time the line was formed with the 103d New York (white) in the rear, and off they started, eager to get to work. It was quite dark by the time they reached Pawnell Landing. I have never forgotten the good-bys of that day, as they left camp. Colonel Trowbridge said to me as he left, "Good-by, Mrs. King, take care of yourself if you don't see us again." I went with them as far as the landing, and watched them until they got out of sight, and then I returned to the camp. There was no one at camp but those left on picket and a few disabled soldiers, and one woman, a friend of mine, Mary Shaw, and it was lonesome and sad, now that the boys were gone, some never to return.

Mary Shaw shared my tent that night, and we went to bed, but not to sleep, for the fleas nearly ate us alive. We caught a few, but it did seem, now that the men were gone, that every flea in camp had located my tent, and caused us to vacate. Sleep being out of the question, we sat up the remainder of the night.

About four o'clock, July 2, the charge was made. The firing could be plainly heard in camp. I hastened down to the landing and remained there until eight o'clock that morning. When the wounded arrived, or rather began to arrive, the first one brought in was Samuel Anderson of our company. He was badly wounded. Then others of our boys, some with their legs off, arm gone, foot off, and wounds of all kinds imaginable. They had to wade through creeks and marshes, as they were discovered by the enemy and shelled very badly. A number of the men were lost, some got fastened in the mud and had to cut off the legs of their pants, to free themselves. The 103d New York suffered the most, as their men were very badly wounded.

My work now began. I gave my assistance to try to alleviate their sufferings. I asked the doctor at the hospital what I could get for them to eat. They wanted soup, but that I could not get; but I had a few cans of condensed milk and some turtle eggs, so I thought I would try to make some custard. I had doubts as to my success, for cooking with turtle eggs was something new to me, but the adage has it, " Nothing ventured, nothing done," so I made a venture and the result was a very delicious custard. This I carried to the men, who enjoyed it very much. My services were given at all times for the comfort of these men. I was on hand to assist whenever needed. I was enrolled as company laundress, but I did very little of it, because I was always busy doing other things through camp, and was employed all the time doing something for the officers and comrades.

After this fight, the regiment did not return to the camp for one month. They were ordered to Cole Island in September, where they remained until October. About November 1, 1864, six companies were detailed to go to Gregg Landing, Port Royal Ferry, and the rebels in some way found out some of our forces had been removed and gave our boys in camp a hard time of it, for several nights. In fact, one night it was thought the boys would have to retreat. The colonel told me to go down to the landing, and if they were obliged to retreat, I could go aboard one of our gunboats. One of the gunboats got in the rear, and began to shell General Beauregard's force, which helped our boys retain their possession.

About November 15, I received a letter from Sergeant King, saying the boys were still lying three miles from Gregg Landing and had not had a fight yet; that the rebels were waiting on them and they on the rebels, and each were holding their own; also that General Sherman had taken Fort McAllister, eight miles from Savannah. After receiving this letter I wanted to get to Beaufort, so I could be near to them and so be able to get news from my husband. November

23 I got a pass for Beaufort. I arrived at Hilton Head about three o'clock next day, but there had been a battle, and a steamer arrived with a number of wounded men; so I could not get a transfer to Beaufort. The doctor wished me to remain over until Monday. I did not want to stay. I was anxious to get off, as I knew no one at Hilton Head.

I must mention a pet pig we had on Cole Island. Colonel Trowbridge brought into camp, one day, a poor, thin little pig, which a German soldier brought back with him on his return from a furlough. His regiment, the 74th Pennsylvania, was just embarking for the North, where it was ordered to join the 10th corps, and he could not take the pig back with him, so he gave it to our colonel. That pig grew to be the pet of the camp, and was the special care of the drummer boys, who taught him many tricks; and so well did they train him that every day at practice and dress parade, his pigship would march out with them, keeping perfect time with their music. The drummers would often disturb the devotions by riding this pig into the midst of evening praise meeting, and many were the complaints made to the colonel, but he was always very lenient towards the boys, for he knew they only did this for mischief. I shall never forget the fun we had in camp with " Piggie."

LIEUT. JOHN A. TROWBRIDGE

LIEUT. ELI C. MERRIAM   LIEUT. JAMES M. THOMPSON

LIEUT. JEROME T. FURMAN

VII

THERE was a yacht that carried passengers from Hilton Head to Beaufort. There were also five small boats which carried people over. The only people here, beside the soldiers, were Mrs. Lizzie Brown, who came over on a permit to see her husband, who was at this place, and was very ill (he died while she was there), Corporal Walker's wife, with her two years old child, and Mrs. Seabrooke. As soon as we could get the yacht, these persons I have mentioned, together with a comrade just discharged, an officer's boy, and myself, took passage on it for Beaufort. It was nearly dark before we had gone any distance, and about eight o'clock we were cast away and were only saved through the mercy of God. I remember going down twice. As I rose the second time, I caught hold of the sail and managed to hold fast. Mrs. Walker held on to her child with one hand, while with the other she managed to hold fast to some part of the boat, and we drifted and shouted as loud as we could, trying to attract the attention of some of the government boats which were going up and down the river. But it was in vain, we could not make ourselves heard, and just when we gave up all hope, and in the last moment (as we thought) gave one more despairing cry, we were heard at Ladies' Island. Two boats were put off and a search was made, to locate our distressed boat. They found us at last, nearly dead from exposure. In fact, the poor little baby was dead, although her mother still held her by her clothing, with her teeth. The soldier was drowned, having been caught under the sail and pinned down. The rest of us were saved. I had to be carried bodily, as I was thoroughly exhausted. We were given the best attention that we could get at this place where we were picked up. The men who saved us were surprised when they found me among the passengers, as one of them, William Geary, of Darien, Georgia, was a friend of my husband. His mother lived about two miles from where we were picked up, and she told me she had heard cries for a long time that night, and was very uneasy about it. Finally, she said to her son, " I think some poor souls are cast away." " I don't think so, mother," he replied ; " I saw some people going down the river to-day. You know this is Christmas, and they are having a good time." But she still persisted that these were cries of distress, and not of joy, and begged him to go out and see. So to satisfy her, he went outside and listened, and then he heard them also, and

hastened to get the boats off to find us. We
were capsized about 8.15 P. M. and it was near
midnight when they found us. Next day, they
kept a sharp lookout on the beach for anything
that might be washed in from the yacht, and got
a trunk and several other things. Had the tide
been going out, we should have been carried to
sea and lost.

I was very ill and under the doctor's care for
some time, in Beaufort. The doctor said I ought
to have been rolled, as I had swallowed so much
water. In January, 1865, I went back to Cole
Island, where I could be attended by my doctor,
Dr. Miner, who did all in his power to alleviate
my suffering, for I was swollen very much. This
he reduced and I recovered, but had a severe
cough for a long time afterward.

VIII

A FLAG OF TRUCE

In October, 1864, six companies of the regiment were ordered to Gregg Landing, S. C. Captain L. W. Metcalf, of Co. G, was appointed on General Saxton's staff as provost captain, Lieutenant James B. West acting as assistant general. As in some way our mail had been sent over to the Confederate side and their mail to us, Captain Metcalf and Lieutenant West were detailed to exchange these letters under a flag of truce. So, with an escort of six men of the companies at Port Royal Ferry, the flag was unfurled and the message shouted across the river to the Confederates. Captain Metcalf asked them to come over to our side under the protection of our flag of truce. This the Confederates refused to do, having for their excuse that their boat was too far up the river and so they had no way to cross the river to us. They asked Metcalf to cross to them. He at once ordered his men to "stack arms," the Confederates following suit, and his boys in blue rowed him over, and he delivered the message, after having introduced himself to the rebel officers. One of these officers

CAPT. L. W. METCALF
CAPT. MIRON W. SAXTON   CAPT. A. W. JACKSON
CORPORAL PETER WAGGALL

was Major Jones, of Alabama, the other Lieutenant Scott, of South Carolina. Major Jones was very cordial to our captain, but Lieutenant Scott would not extend his hand, and stood aside, in sullen silence, looking as if he would like to take revenge then and there. Major Jones said to Captain Metcalf, " We have no one to fight for. Should I meet you again, I shall not forget we have met before." With this he extended his hand to Metcalf and bade him good-by, but Lieutenant Scott stood by and looked as cross as he possibly could. The letters were exchanged, but it seemed a mystery just how those letters got missent to the opposite sides. Captain Metcalf said he did not feel a mite comfortable while he was on the Confederate soil; as for his men, you can imagine their thoughts. I asked them how they felt on the other side, and they said, " We would have felt much better if we had had our guns with us." It was a little risky, for sometimes the flag of truce is not regarded, but even among the enemy there are some good and loyal persons.

Captain Metcalf is still living in Medford. He is 71 years old, and just as loyal to the old flag and the G. A. R. as he was from 1861 to 1866, when he was mustered out. He was a brave captain, a good officer, and was honored and beloved by all in the regiment.

CAPTURE OF CHARLESTON

ON February 28, 1865, the remainder of the
regiment were ordered to Charleston, as there
were signs of the rebels evacuating that city.
Leaving Cole Island, we arrived in Charleston
between nine and ten o'clock in the morning, and
found the " rebs " had set fire to the city and fled,
leaving women and children behind to suffer and
perish in the flames. The fire had been burning
fiercely for a day and night. When we landed,
under a flag of truce, our regiment went to work
assisting the citizens in subduing the flames. It
was a terrible scene. For three or four days the
men fought the fire, saving the property and
effects of the people, yet these white men and
women could not tolerate our black Union soldiers, for many of them had formerly been their
slaves ; and although these brave men risked life
and limb to assist them in their distress, men
and even women would sneer and molest them
whenever they met them.

I had quarters assigned me at a residence on
South Battery Street, one of the most aristocratic
parts of the city, where I assisted in caring for

the sick and injured comrades. After getting the fire under control, the regiment marched out to the race track, where they camped until March 12, when we were ordered to Savannah, Ga. We arrived there on the 13th, about eight o'clock in the evening, and marched out to Fairlong, near the A. & G. R. R., where we remained about ten days, when we were ordered to Augusta, Ga., where Captain Alexander Heasley, of Co. E, was shot and killed by a Confederate. After his death Lieutenant Parker was made captain of the company, and was with us until the regiment was mustered out. He often told me about Massachusetts, but I had no thought at that time that I should ever see that State, and stand in the " Cradle of Liberty."

The regiment remained in Augusta for thirty days, when it was ordered to Hamburg, S. C., and then on to Charleston. It was while on their march through the country, to the latter city, that they came in contact with the bushwhackers (as the rebels were called), who hid in the bushes and would shoot the Union boys every chance they got. Other times they would conceal themselves in the cars used to transfer our soldiers, and when our boys, worn out and tired, would fall asleep, these men would come out from their hiding places and cut their throats. Several of our men were killed in this way, but it could not be found out who was committing these murders until one night one of the rebels was caught in the act, trying to cut the throat of a sleeping soldier. He was put under guard, court-martialed, and shot at Wall Hollow.

First Lieutenant Jerome T. Furman and a number of soldiers were killed by these South Carolina bushwhackers at Wall Hollow. After this man was shot, however, the regiment marched through unmolested to Charleston.

X

MUSTERED OUT

THE regiment, under Colonel Trowbridge, reached Charleston in November, 1865, and camped on the race track until January, when they returned to Morris Island, and on February 9, 1866, the following " General Orders " were received and the regiment mustered out.

They were delighted to go home, but oh ! how they hated to part from their commanding chief, Colonel C. T. Trowbridge. He was the very first officer to take charge of black soldiers. We thought there was no one like him, for he was a " man " among his soldiers. All in the regiment knew him personally, and many were the jokes he used to tell them. I shall never forget his friendship and kindness toward me, from the first time I met him to the end of the war. There was never any one from the North who came into our camp but he would bring them to see me.

While on a visit South in 1888, I met a comrade of the regiment, who often said to me, " You up North, Mrs. King, do you ever see Colonel Trowbridge ? How I should like to see him ! I don't see why he does not come South sometime.

Why, I would take a day off and look up all the
' boys ' I could find, if I knew he was coming."
I knew this man meant what he said, for the men
of the regiment knew Colonel Trowbridge first of
all the other officers.   He was with them on St.
Simon and at Camp Saxton.   I remember when
the company was being formed, we wished Captain C. T. was our captain, because most of the
men in Co. E were the men he brought with him
from St. Simon, and they were attached to him.
He was always jolly and pleasing with all.   I remember, when going into Savannah in 1865, he
said that he had been there before the war, and
told me many things I did not know about the
river.   Although this was my home, I had never
been on it before.   No officer in the army was
more beloved than our late lieutenant-colonel, C.
T. Trowbridge.

[*Copy of General Orders.*]

" GENERAL ORDERS.

" HEADQUARTERS 33D U. S. C. T.,
" LATE 1ST So. CAROLINA VOLUNTEERS,
" MORRIS ISLAND, S. C., Feb. 9, 1866.

" *General Order,* }
   " *No.* 1.   }

" COMRADES : The hour is at hand when we
must separate forever, and nothing can take from
us the pride we feel, when we look upon the history of the ' First South Carolina Volunteers,'

C. T. TROWBRIDGE
LIEUT. COL. 33D U. S. C. T.

the first black regiment that ever bore arms in defense of freedom on the continent of America.

" On the 9th day of May, 1862, at which time there were nearly four millions of your race in bondage, sanctioned by the laws of the land and protected by our flag, — on that day, in the face of the floods of prejudice that well-nigh deluged every avenue to manhood and true liberty, you came forth to do battle for your country and kindred.

" For long and weary months, without pay or even the privilege of being recognized as soldiers, you labored on, only to be disbanded and sent to your homes without even a hope of reward, and when our country, necessitated by the deadly struggle with armed traitors, finally granted you the opportunity again to come forth in defense of the nation's life, the alacrity with which you responded to the call gave abundant evidence of your readiness to strike a manly blow for the liberty of your race. And from that little band of hopeful, trusting, and brave men who gathered at Camp Saxton, on Port Royal Island, in the fall of '62, amidst the terrible prejudices that surrounded us, has grown an army of a hundred and forty thousand black soldiers, whose valor and heroism has won for your race a name which will live as long as the undying pages of history shall endure; and by whose efforts, united with those of the white man, armed rebellion has been

conquered, the millions of bondsmen have been
emancipated, and the fundamental law of the land
has been so altered as to remove forever the possibility of human slavery being established within
the borders of redeemed America. The flag of
our fathers, restored to its rightful significance,
now floats over every foot of our territory, from
Maine to California, and beholds only free men !
The prejudices which formerly existed against
you are well-nigh rooted out.

"Soldiers, you have done your duty and ac-
quitted yourselves like men who, actuated by such
ennobling motives, could not fail; and as the result of your fidelity and obedience you have won
your freedom, and oh, how great the reward !
It seems fitting to me that the last hours of our
existence as a regiment should be passed amidst
the unmarked graves of your comrades, at Fort
Wagner. Near you rest the bones of Colonel
Shaw, buried by an enemy's hand in the same
grave with his black soldiers who fell at his side;
where in the future your children's children will
come on pilgrimages to do homage to the ashes of
those who fell in this glorious struggle.

"The flag which was presented to us by the Rev.
George B. Cheever and his congregation, of New
York city, on the 1st of January, 1863, — the day
when Lincoln's immortal proclamation of freedom
was given to the world, — and which you have
borne so nobly through the war, is now to be

rolled up forever and deposited in our nation's capital. And while there it shall rest, with the battles in which you have participated inscribed upon its folds, it will be a source of pride to us all to remember that it has never been disgraced by a cowardly faltering in the hour of danger, or polluted by a traitor's touch.

"Now that you are to lay aside your arms, I adjure you, by the associations and history of the past, and the love you bear for your liberties, to harbor no feelings of hatred toward your former masters, but to seek in the paths of honesty, virtue, sobriety, and industry, and by a willing obedience to the laws of the land, to grow up to the full stature of American citizens. The church, the school-house, and the right forever to be free are now secured to you, and every prospect before you is full of hope and encouragement. The nation guarantees to you full protection and justice, and will require from you in return that respect for the laws and orderly deportment which will prove to every one your right to all the privileges of freemen. To the officers of the regiment I would say, your toils are ended, your mission is fulfilled, and we separate forever. The fidelity, patience, and patriotism with which you have discharged your duties to your men and to your country entitle you to a far higher tribute than any words of thankfulness which I can give you from the bottom of my heart. You will find your reward in the proud conviction that the cause for which you have battled so nobly has been crowned with abundant success.

"Officers and soldiers of the 33d U. S. Colored Troops, once the First So. Carolina Volunteers, I bid you all farewell!

"By order of

"Lt. Colonel C. T. Trowbridge,

"*Commanding regiment.*

"E. W. Hyde,

"1st Lieut. 33d U. S. C. T. and acting adjutant."

I have one of the original copies of these orders still in my possession.

My dear friends! do we understand the meaning of war? Do we know or think of that war of '61? No, we do not, only those brave soldiers, and those who had occasion to be in it, can realize what it was. I can and shall never forget that terrible war until my eyes close in death. The scenes are just as fresh in my mind to-day as in '61. I see now each scene, — the roll-call, the drum tap, "lights out," the call at night when there was danger from the enemy, the double force of pickets, the cold and rain. How anxious I would be, not knowing what would happen before morning! Many times I would dress, not sure but all would be captured. Other times I would stand at my tent door and try to see what was going on, because night was the time the rebels would try to get into our lines and capture some of the boys. It was mostly at night that our men went out for their scouts, and often had a hand to hand fight with the rebels, and although our men came out sometimes with a few killed or wounded, none of them ever were captured.

We do not, as the black race, properly appreciate the old veterans, white or black, as we ought to. I know what they went through, especially those black men, for the Confederates had no mercy on them; neither did they show any toward the white Union soldiers. I have seen the terrors of that war. I was the wife of one of those men who did not get a penny for eighteen months for their services, only their rations and clothing.

I cannot praise General David Hunter too highly, for he was the first man to arm the black man, in the beginning of 1862. He had a hard struggle to hold all the southern division, with so few men, so he applied to Congress; but the answer to him was, "Do not bother us," which was very discouraging. As the general needed more men to protect the islands and do garrison duty, he organized two companies.

I look around now and see the comforts that our younger generation enjoy, and think of the blood that was shed to make these comforts possible for them, and see how little some of them appreciate the old soldiers. My heart burns within me, at this want of appreciation. There are only a few of them left now, so let us all, as the ranks close, take a deeper interest in them. Let the younger generation take an interest also, and remember that it was through the efforts of these veterans that they and we older ones enjoy our liberty to-day.

XI

AFTER THE WAR

In 1866, the steamers which ran from Savannah to Darien would not take colored people unless they stayed in a certain part of the boat, away from the white people; so some of the colored citizens and ex-soldiers decided to form a syndicate and buy a steamer of their own. They finally bought a large one of a New York company. It arrived in fine shape, apparently, and made its first trip to Darien. The next trip was to Beaufort. I went on this trip, as the pilot, James Cook, was a friend of my family, and I thought I would enjoy the trip; and I did, getting back in safety. The next trip was to go to Florida, but it never reached there, for on the way down the boat ran upon St. John bar and went entirely to pieces. They found out afterwards that they had been swindled, as the boat was a condemned one, and the company took advantage of them; and as they carried no insurance on the boat they lost all the money they had invested in it. The best people of the city expressed great sympathy for them in their loss, as it promised to prove a great investment at first.

At the close of the war, my husband and I returned to Savannah, a number of the comrades returning at the same time. A new life was before us now, all the old life left behind. After getting settled, I opened a school at my home on South Broad Street, now called Oglethorpe Avenue, as there was not any public school for negro children. I had twenty children at my school, and received one dollar a month for each pupil. I also had a few older ones who came at night. There were several other private schools besides mine. Mrs. Lucinda Jackson had one on the same street I lived on.

I taught almost a year, when the Beach Institute opened, which took a number of my scholars, as this was a free school. On September 16, 1866, my husband, Sergeant King, died, leaving me soon to welcome a little stranger alone. He was a boss carpenter, but being just mustered out of the army, and the prejudice against his race being still too strong to insure him much work at his trade, he took contracts for unloading vessels, and hired a number of men to assist him. He was much respected by the citizens, and was a general favorite with his associates.

In December, 1866, I was obliged to give up teaching, but in April, 1867, I opened a school in Liberty County, Georgia, and taught there one year ; but country life did not agree with me, so I returned to the city, and Mrs. Susie Carrier took charge of my school.

MY SCHOOLHOUSE IN SAVANNAH

On my return to Savannah, I found that the free school had taken all my former pupils, so I opened a night school, where I taught a number of adults. This, together with other things I could get to do and the assistance of my brother-in-law, supported me. I taught this school until the fall of 1868, when a free night school opened at the Beach Institute, and again my scholars left me to attend this free school. So I had to close my school. I put my baby with my mother and entered in the employ of a family, where I lived quite a while, but had to leave, as the work was too hard.

In 1872 I put in a claim for my husband's bounty and received one hundred dollars, some of which I put in the Freedmen's Savings Bank. In the fall of 1872 I went to work for a very wealthy lady, Mrs. Charles Green, as laundress. In the spring of 1873, Mr. and Mrs. Green came North to Rye Beach for the summer, and as their cook did not care to go so far from home, I went with them in her place. While there, I won a prize for excellent cooking at a fair which the ladies who were summering there had held to raise funds to build an Episcopal Church, and Mrs. Green was one of the energetic workers to make this fair a success; and it was a success in every respect and a tidy sum was netted.

I returned South with Mrs. Green, and soon after, she went to Europe. I returned to Boston again in 1874, through the kindness of Mrs. Barnard, a daughter of ex-Mayor Otis of Boston. She was accompanied by her husband, Mr. James Barnard (who was an agent for the line of steamers), her six children, the nurse, and myself. We left Savannah on the steamship Seminole, under Captain Matthews, and when we had passed Hatteras some distance, she broke her shaft. The captain had the sails hoisted and we drifted along, there being a stiff breeze, which was greatly in our favor. Captain Matthews said the nearest point he could make was Cape Henry Light. About noon, Mr. Barnard spied the light and told the captain if he would give him a boat and some of the crew, he would row to the light for help. This was done, the boat was manned and they put off. They made the light, then they made for Norfolk, which was eight miles from the light, and did not reach the city until eight o'clock that night.

Next morning he returned with a tug, to tow us into Norfolk for repairs; but the tug was too small to move the steamer, so it went back for more help, but before it returned, a Norfolk steamer, on its way to Boston, stopped to see what was the matter with our steamer. Our trouble was explained to them, and almost all the passengers were transferred to this steamer. Mr. Barnard remained on the steamer, and Mrs. Barnard deciding to remain with him, I went aboard this other steamer with the rest of the passengers. We left them at anchor, waiting for the tugs to return.

This accident brought back very vividly the time previous to this, when I was in that other wreck in 1864, and I wondered if they would reach port safe, for it is a terrible thing to be cast away; but on arriving in Boston, about two days later, I was delighted to hear of the arrival of their steamer at T Wharf, with all on board safe.

Soon after I got to Boston, I entered the service of Mr. Thomas Smith's family, on Walnut Avenue, Boston Highlands, where I remained until the death of Mrs. Smith. I next lived with Mrs. Gorham Gray, Beacon Street, where I remained until I was married, in 1879, to Russell L. Taylor.

In 1880 I had another experience in steamer accidents. Mr. Taylor and I started for New York on the steamer Stonington. We were in bed when, sometime in the night, the Narragansett collided with our boat. I was awakened by the crash. I was in the ladies' cabin. There were about thirty-five or forty others in the cabin. I sprang out of my berth, dressed as quickly as I could, and tried to reach the deck, but we found the cabin door locked, and two men stood outside and would not let us out. About twenty minutes after, they opened the doors and we went up on deck, and a terrible scene was before us. The

Narragansett was on fire, in a bright blaze; the water was lighted as far as one could see, the passengers shrieking, groaning, running about, leaping into the water, panic-stricken. A steamer came to our assistance; they put the life-rafts off and saved a great many from the burning steamer, and picked a number up from the water. A colored man saved his wife and child by giving each a chair and having them jump overboard. These chairs kept them afloat until they were taken aboard by the life-raft. The steamer was burned to the water's edge. The passengers on board our steamer were transferred to another one and got to New York at 9.30 the next morning. A number of lives were lost in this accident, and the bow of the Stonington was badly damaged. I was thankful for my escape, for I had been in two similar experiences and got off safely, and I have come to the conclusion I shall never have a watery grave.

XII

THE WOMEN'S RELIEF CORPS

ALL this time my interest in the boys in blue had not abated. I was still loyal and true, whether they were black or white. My hands have never left undone anything they could do towards their aid and comfort in the twilight of their lives. In 1886 I helped to organize Corps 67, Women's Relief Corps, auxiliary to the G. A. R., and it is a very flourishing corps to-day. I have been Guard, Secretary, Treasurer for three years, and in 1893 I was made President of this corps, Mrs. Emily Clark being Department President this year. In 1896, in response to an order sent out by the Department W. R. C. to take a census to secure a complete roster of the Union Veterans of the war of the Rebellion now residing in Massachusetts, I was allotted the West End district, which (with the assistance of Mrs. Lizzie L. Johnson, a member of Corps 67, and widow of a soldier of the 54th Mass. Volunteers) I canvassed with splendid success, and found a great many comrades who were not attached to any post in the city or State.

In 1898 the Department of Mass. W. R. C.

gave a grand fair at Music Hall. I made a large quilt of red, white, and blue ribbon that made quite a sensation. The quilt was voted for and was awarded to the Department President, Mrs. E. L. W. Waterman, of Boston.

XIII

THOUGHTS ON PRESENT CONDITIONS

LIVING here in Boston where the black man is given equal justice, I must say a word on the general treatment of my race, both in the North and South, in this twentieth century. I wonder if our white fellow men realize the true sense or meaning of brotherhood? For two hundred years we had toiled for them; the war of 1861 came and was ended, and we thought our race was forever freed from bondage, and that the two races could live in unity with each other, but when we read almost every day of what is being done to my race by some whites in the South, I sometimes ask, "Was the war in vain? Has it brought freedom, in the full sense of the word, or has it not made our condition more hopeless?"

In this "land of the free" we are burned, tortured, and denied a fair trial, murdered for any imaginary wrong conceived in the brain of the negro-hating white man. There is no redress for us from a government which promised to protect all under its flag. It seems a mystery to me. They say, "One flag, one nation, one country indivisible." Is this true? Can we say this truthfully, when one race is allowed to burn, hang, and inflict the most horrible torture weekly, monthly, on another? No, we cannot sing, " My country, 't is of thee, Sweet land of Liberty"! It is hollow mockery. The Southland laws are all on the side of the white, and they do just as they like to the negro, whether in the right or not.

I do not uphold my race when they do wrong. They ought to be punished, but the innocent are made to suffer as well as the guilty, and I hope the time will hasten when it will be stopped forever. Let us remember God says, " He that sheds blood, his blood shall be required again." I may not live to see it, but the time is approaching when the South will again have cause to repent for the blood it has shed of innocent black men, for their blood cries out for vengeance. For the South still cherishes a hatred toward the blacks, although there are some true Southern gentlemen left who abhor the stigma brought upon them, and feel it very keenly, and I hope the day is not far distant when the two races will reside in peace in the Southland, and we will sing with sincere and truthful hearts, " My country, 't is of thee, Sweet land of Liberty, of thee I sing."

I have been in many States and cities, and in each I have looked for liberty and justice, equal for the black as for the white; but it was not until I was within the borders of New England, and reached old Massachusetts, that I found it.

Here is found liberty in the full sense of the word, liberty for the stranger within her gates, irrespective of race or creed, liberty and justice for all.

We have before us still another problem to solve. With the close of the Spanish war, and on the entrance of the Americans into Cuba, the same conditions confront us as the war of 1861 left. The Cubans are free, but it is a limited freedom, for prejudice, deep-rooted, has been brought to them and a separation made between the white and black Cubans, a thing that had never existed between them before; but to-day there is the same intense hatred toward the negro in Cuba that there is in some parts of this country.

I helped to furnish and pack boxes to be sent to the soldiers and hospitals during the first part of the Spanish war; there were black soldiers there too. At the battle of San Juan Hill, they were in the front, just as brave, loyal, and true as those other black men who fought for freedom and the right; and yet their bravery and faithfulness were reluctantly acknowledged, and praise grudgingly given. All we ask for is "equal justice," the same that is accorded to all other races who come to this country, of their free will (not forced to, as we were), and are allowed to enjoy every privilege, unrestricted, while we are denied what is rightfully our own in a country which the labor of our forefathers helped to make what it is.

One thing I have noticed among my people in the South : they have accumulated a large amount of real estate, far surpassing the colored owners in the North, who seem to let their opportunity slip by them. Nearly all of Brownsville (a suburb of Savannah) is owned by colored people, and so it is in a great many other places throughout the State, and all that is needed is the protection of the law as citizens.

In 1867, soon after the death of my father, who had served on a gunboat during the war, my mother opened a grocery store, where she kept general merchandise always on hand. These she traded for cash or would exchange for crops of cotton, corn, or rice, which she would ship once a month, to F. Lloyd & Co., or Johnson & Jackson, in Savannah. These were colored merchants, doing business on Bay Street in that city. Mother bought her first property, which contained ten acres. She next purchased fifty acres of land. Then she had a chance to get a place with seven hundred acres of land, and she bought this.

In 1870, Colonel Hamilton and Major Devendorft, of Oswego, N. Y., came to the town and bought up a tract of land at a place called Doctortown, and started a mill. Mrs. Devendorft heard of my mother and went to see her, and persuaded her to come to live with her, assuring her she would be as one of the family. Mother went with her, but after a few months she went to Doctortown, where she has been since, and now owns the largest settlement there. All trains going to Florida pass her place, just across the Altamaha River. She is well known by both white and black; the people are fond of her, and will not allow any one to harm her.

Mr. Devendorft sold out his place in 1880 and went back to New York, where later he died.

I read an article, which said the ex-Confederate Daughters had sent a petition to the managers of the local theatres in Tennessee to prohibit the performance of "Uncle Tom's Cabin," claiming it was exaggerated (that is, the treatment of the slaves), and would have a very bad effect on the children who might see the drama. I paused and thought back a few years of the heart-rending scenes I have witnessed; I have seen many times, when I was a mere girl, thirty or forty men, handcuffed, and as many women and children, come every first Tuesday of each month from Mr. Wiley's trade office to the auction blocks, one of them being situated on Drayton Street and Court Lane, the other on Bryant Street, near the Pulaski House. The route was down our principal street, Bull Street, to the court-house, which was only a block from where I resided.

All people in those days got all their water

from the city pumps, which stood about a block apart throughout the city. The one we used to get water from was opposite the court-house, on Bull Street. I remember, as if it were yesterday, seeing droves of negroes going to be sold, and I often went to look at them, and I could hear the auctioneer very plainly from my house, auctioning these poor people off.

Do these Confederate Daughters ever send petitions to prohibit the atrocious lynchings and wholesale murdering and torture of the negro? Do you ever hear of them fearing this would have a bad effect on the children? Which of these two, the drama or the present state of affairs, makes a degrading impression upon the minds of our young generation? In my opinion it is not "Uncle Tom's Cabin," but it should be the one that has caused the world to cry "Shame!" It does not seem as if our land is yet civilized. It is like times long past, when rulers and high officers had to flee for their lives, and the negro has been dealt with in the same way since the war by those he lived with and toiled for two hundred years or more. I do not condemn all the Caucasian race because the negro is badly treated by a few of the race. No! for had it not been for the true whites, assisted by God and the prayers of our forefathers, I should not be here to-day.

There are still good friends to the negro.

Why, there are still thousands that have not bowed to Baal. So it is with us. Man thinks two hundred years is a long time, and it is, too; but it is only as a week to God, and in his own time — I know I shall not live to see the day, but it will come — the South will be like the North, and when it comes it will be prized higher than we prize the North to-day. God is just; when he created man he made him in his image, and never intended one should misuse the other. All men are born free and equal in his sight.

I am pleased to know at this writing that the officers and comrades of my regiment stand ready to render me assistance whenever required. It seems like " bread cast upon the water," and it has returned after many days, when it is most needed. I have received letters from some of the comrades, since we parted in 1866, with expressions of gratitude and thanks to me for teaching them their first letters. One of them, Peter Waggall, is a minister in Jacksonville, Fla. Another is in the government service at Washington, D. C. Others are in Darien and Savannah, Ga., and all are doing well.

There are many people who do not know what some of the colored women did during the war. There were hundreds of them who assisted the Union soldiers by hiding them and helping them to escape. Many were punished for taking food to the prison stockades for the prisoners. When I

went into Savannah, in 1865, I was told of one of
these stockades which was in the suburbs of the
city, and they said it was an awful place. The
Union soldiers were in it, worse than pigs, without
any shelter from sun or storm, and the colored
women would take food there at night and pass it
to them, through the holes in the fence. The soldiers were starving, and these women did all they
could towards relieving those men, although they
knew the penalty, should they be caught giving
them aid. Others assisted in various ways the
Union army. These things should be kept in
history before the people. There has never been
a greater war in the United States than the one
of 1861, where so many lives were lost, — not men
alone but noble women as well.

Let us not forget that terrible war, or our
brave soldiers who were thrown into Anderson-
ville and Libby prisons, the awful agony they
went through, and the most brutal treatment they
received in those loathsome dens, the worst ever
given human beings; and if the white soldiers
were subjected to such treatment, what must have
been the horrors inflicted on the negro soldiers
in their prison pens? Can we forget those cruel-
ties? No, though we try to forgive and say,
"No North, no South," and hope to see it in reality before the last comrade passes away.

XIV

A VISIT TO LOUISIANA

THE inevitable always happens. On February 3, 1898, I was called to Shreveport, La., to the bedside of my son, who was very ill. He was traveling with Nickens and Company, with "The Lion's Bride," when he fell ill, and had been ill two weeks when they sent to me. I tried to have him brought home to Boston, but they could not send him, as he was not able to sit and ride this long distance; so on the sixth of February I left Boston to go to him. I reached Cincinnati on the eighth, where I took the train for the south. I asked a white man standing near (before I got my train) what car I should take. "Take that one," he said, pointing to one. "But that is a smoking car!" "Well," he replied, "that is the car for colored people." I went to this car, and on entering it all my courage failed me. I have ridden in many coaches, but I was never in such as these. I wanted to return home again, but when I thought of my sick boy I said, "Well, others ride in these cars and I must do likewise," and tried to be resigned, for I wanted to reach my boy, as I did not know whether I should find him alive. I arrived in Chattanooga at eight o'clock in the evening, where the porter took my baggage to the train which was to leave for Marion, Miss. Soon after I was seated, just before the train pulled out, two tall men with slouch hats on walked through the car, and on through the train. Finally they came back to our car and stopping at my seat said, "Where are those men who were with you?" I did not know to whom they were speaking, as there was another woman in the car, so I made no reply. Again they asked me, standing directly in front of my seat, "Where are those men who came in with you?" "Are you speaking to me?" I said. "Yes!" they said. "I have not seen any men," I replied. They looked at me a moment, and one of them asked where I was from. I told him Boston; he hesitated a minute and walked out of our car to the other car.

When the conductor came around I told him what these men had said, and asked him if they allowed persons to enter the car and insult passengers. He only smiled. Later, when the porter came in, I mentioned it to him. He said, "Lady, I see you do not belong here; where are you from?" I told him. He said, "I have often heard of Massachusetts. I want to see that place." "Yes!" I said, "you can ride there on the cars, and no person would be allowed to speak to you as those men did to me." He explained that those men were constables, who were in search of a man who had eloped with another man's wife. "That is the way they do here. Each morning you can hear of some negro being lynched;" and on seeing my surprise, he said, "Oh, that is nothing; it is done all the time. We have no rights here. I have been on this road for fifteen years and have seen some terrible things." He wanted to know what I was doing down there, and I told him it was only the illness of my son that brought me there.

I was a little surprised at the way the poor whites were made to ride on this road. They put them all together by themselves in a car, between the colored people's coach and the first-class coach, and it looked like the "laborers' car" used in Boston to carry the different day laborers to and from their work.

I got to Marion, Miss., at two o'clock in the morning, arrived at Vicksburg at noon, and at Shreveport about eight o'clock in the evening, and found my son just recovering from a severe hemorrhage. He was very anxious to come home, and I tried to secure a berth for him on a sleeper, but they would not sell me one, and he was not strong enough to travel otherwise. If I could only have gotten him to Cincinnati, I might have brought him home, but as I could not I was forced to let him remain where he was. It seemed very hard, when his father fought to protect the Union and our flag, and yet his boy was denied, under this same flag, a berth to carry him home to die, because he was a negro.

Shreveport is a little town, made up largely of Jews and Germans and a few Southerners, the negroes being in the majority. Its sidewalks are sand except on the main street. Almost all the stores are kept either by the Jews or Germans. They know a stranger in a minute, as the town is small and the citizens know each other; if not personally, their faces are familiar.

I went into a jewelry store one day to have a crystal put in my watch, and the attendant remarked, "You are a stranger." I asked him how he knew that. He said he had watched me for a week or so. I told him yes, I was a stranger and from Boston. "Oh! I have heard of Boston," he said. "You will not find this place like it is there. How do you like this town?" "Not very well," I replied.

I found that the people who had lived in Massachusetts and were settled in Shreveport were very cordial to me and glad to see me. There was a man murdered in cold blood for nothing. He was a colored man and a " porter " in a store in this town. A clerk had left his umbrella at home. It had begun to rain when he started for home, and on looking for the umbrella he could not, of course, find it. He asked the porter if he had seen it. He said no, he had not. " You answer very saucy," said the clerk, and drawing his revolver, he shot the colored man dead. He was taken up the street to an office where he was placed under one thousand dollars bond for his appearance and released, and that was the end of the case. I was surprised at this, but I was told by several white and colored persons that this was a common occurrence, and the persons were never punished if they were white, but no mercy was shown to negroes.

I met several comrades, white and colored, there, and noticed that the colored comrades did not wear their buttons. I asked one of them why this was, and was told, should they wear it, they could not get work. Still some would wear their buttons in spite of the feeling against it. I met a newsman from New York on the train. He was a veteran, and said that Sherman ought to come back and go into that part of the country.

Shreveport is a horrid place when it rains. The earth is red and sticks to your shoes, and it is impossible to keep rubbers on, for the mud pulls them off. Going across the Mississippi River, I was amazed to see how the houses were built, so close to the shore, or else on low land; and when the river rises, it flows into these houses and must make it very disagreeable and unhealthy for the inmates.

After the death of my son, while on my way back to Boston, I came to Clarksdale, one of the stations on the road from Vicksburg. In this town a Mr. Hancock, of New York, had a large cotton plantation, and the Chinese intermarry with the blacks.

At Clarksdale, I saw a man hanged. It was a terrible sight, and I felt alarmed for my own safety down there. When I reached Memphis I found conditions of travel much better. The people were mostly Western and Northern here; the cars were nice, but separate for colored persons until we reached the Ohio River, when the door was opened and the porter passed through, saying, "The Ohio River! change to the other car." I thought, "What does he mean? We have been riding all this distance in separate cars, and now we are all to sit together." It certainly seemed a peculiar arrangement. Why not let the negroes, if their appearance and respectability warrant it, be allowed to ride as they do in the North, East, or West?

There are others beside the blacks, in the South and North, that should be put in separate cars while traveling, just as they put my race. Many black people in the South do not wish to be thrown into a car because all are colored, as there are many of their race very objectionable to them, being of an entirely different class; but they have to adapt themselves to the circumstances and ride with them, because they are all negroes. There is no such division with the whites. Except in one place I saw, the workingman and the millionaire ride in the same coaches together. Why not allow the respectable, law-abiding classes of the blacks the same privilege? We hope for better conditions in the future, and feel sure they will come in time, surely if slowly.

While in Shreveport, I visited ex-Senator Harper's house. He is a colored man and owns a large business block, besides a fine residence on Cado Street and several good building lots. Another family, the Pages, living on the same street, were quite wealthy, and a large number of colored families owned their homes, and were industrious, refined people; and if they were only allowed justice, the South would be the only place for our people to live.

We are similar to the children of Israel, who, after many weary years in bondage, were led into that land of promise, there to thrive and be forever free from persecution; and I don't despair, for the Book which is our guide through life declares, "Ethiopia shall stretch forth her hand."

What a wonderful revolution! In 1861 the Southern papers were full of advertisements for "slaves," but now, despite all the hindrances and "race problems," my people are striving to attain the full standard of all other races born free in the sight of God, and in a number of instances have succeeded. Justice we ask, — to be citizens of these United States, where so many of our people have shed their blood with their white comrades, that the stars and stripes should never be polluted.

APPENDIX

APPENDIX

ROSTER OF SURVIVORS OF THIRTY–THIRD UNITED STATES COLORED TROOPS

THE following are the names of officers and men as near as I have been able to reach.

Colonel T. W. Higginson.
Lieut.-Col. C. T. Trowbridge.

COMPANY A.

Capt. Charles E. Parker,
Lieut. John A. Trowbridge,
Lieut. J. B. West,
O.-Sergt. Joseph Holden,
1st Sergt. —— Hattent,
2d Sergt. Wm. Jackson,
Thomas Smith,
George Green,
Manly Gater,
Paul Jones,
Sancho Jenkins,
London Bailey,
Edmund Mack,
Andrew Perry,
Morris Williams,
James Dorsen,
Abel Haywood.

COMPANY B.

Capt. Wm. James,

O.-Sergt. Bob Bowling,
2d Sergt. Nathan Hagans,
3d Sergt. Cato Wright,
4th Sergt. Frederick Parker,
5th Sergt. Wm. Simmons,
Corp. Monday Stewart,
Corp. Allick Seymore,
Corp. Lazarus Fields,
Corp. Boson Green,
Corp. Steven Wright,
Corp. Carolina Hagans,
Corp. Richard Robinson,
David Hall,
Edward Houston,
Smart Givins,
John Mills,
Jacob Riley,
Frederick Procter,
Benj. Gordon,
Benj. Mason,
Sabe Natteal,

Joseph Noyels,
Benj. Mackwell,
Thos. Hernandes,
Israel Choen,
Steplight Gordon,
Chas. Talbert,
Isaac Jenkins,
Morris Polite,
Robert Freeman,
Jacob Watson,
Benj. Managualt,
Richard Adams,
Mingo Singleton,
Toney Chapman,
Jos. Knowell,
Benj. Gardner.

COMPANY C.

Capt. A. W. Jackson,
2d Sergt. Billy Milton,
Corp. Peter Waggall,
Corp. Henry Abrams,
Martin Dickson, Drummer,
Roddrick Langs, Fifer,
Joseph Smith,
Solomon Major,
John Brown,
Bram Strowbridge,
Robert Trewell,
Jerry Fields,
Paul Fields,
William Johnson,
Bram Stoved,
Robert Mack,
Samuel Mack,
Jack Mack,

Simon Gatson,
Bob Bolden,
James Long,
O.-S. Frederick Brown.

COMPANY D.

Sergt. Isaiah Brown,
Luke Wright,
Dick Haywood,
Stephen Murrel,
Jos. Halsley,
Nathan Hazeby,
O.-Sergt. Robert Godwen,
Peter Johnson,
Cæsar Johnson,
Sampson Cuthbert.

COMPANY E.

Capt. N. G. Parker,
Corp. Jack Sallens,
Quaker Green,
Abram Fuller,
Levan Watkins,
Peter Chisholm,
Scipio Haywood,
Paul King,
Richard Howard,
Esau Kellison,
Chas. Armstrong,
Washington Demry,
Benj. King,
Luke Harris,
William Cummings.

COMPANY F.

Capt. John Thompson,
Sergt. Robert Vandross,

Sergt. Cæsar Alston,
2d Sergt. Moses Green,
Corp. Samuel Mack,
Edmund Washington,
Isaac Jenkins,
Chas. Seymore,
Frank Grayson,
Bristow Eddy,
Abram Fields,
Joseph Richardson,
James Brown,
Frederick Tripp,
Frost Coleman,
Paul Coleman,
Robert Edward,
Milton Edward.

COMPANY G.

Capt. L. W. Metcalf,
Sergt. T. W. Long,
Corp. Prince Logan,
Corp. Mark Clark,
Corp. James Ash,
Corp. Henry Hamilton,
Roddrick Long,
Benjamin Turner,
David Wanton,
Benjamin Martin,
John Ryals,
Charles Williams,
Hogarth Williams,
Benjamin Wright,
Henry Harker.

COMPANY H.

Capt. W. W. Sampson,
1st Sergt. Jacob Jones,

2d Sergt. Thomas Fields,
Corp. A. Brown,
Corp. Emmanuel Washington,
Jackson Danner,
Joseph Wright,
Phillips Brown,
Luke Harris,
Lazarus Aikens,
Jonah Aikens,
Jacob Jones,
Thomas Howard,
William Williams,
Jack Parker,
Jack Ladson,
Poll McKee,
Lucius Baker.

COMPANY I.

2d Sergt. Daniel Spaulding,
Corp. Uandickpe,
Corp. Floward,
Corp. Thompson.

COMPANY K.

O.-Sergt. Harry Williams,
2d Sergt. Billy Coleman,
3d Sergt. Cæsar Oston,
Jacob Lance,
Jack Burns,
Wm. McLean,
Geo. Washington,
David Wright,
Jerry Mitchell,
Jackson Green,
David Putnam,

B. Lance, | Leon Simmons,
Ward McKen, | Prince White,
Edmond Cloud, | Stephen Jenkins.
Chance Mitchel, |

Quarter-Master Harry West.
Quarter-Master's Sergt., Edward Colvin.

A LIST OF THE BATTLES FOUGHT BY THE THIRTY-THIRD U. S. COLORED TROOPS, FORMERLY FIRST S. C. VOLUNTEERS.

Darien, Ga., and Ridge	1862
St. Mary's River and Hundred Pines . .	1862
Pocotaligo Bridge [1]	1862
Jacksonville, Fla.	1863
Township	1863
Mill Town Bluff [2]	1863
Hall Island	1863
Johns Island	1863
Coosaw River	1863
Combahee and Edisto [3]	1863
James Island [4]	1864
Honey Hill	1864

[1] Many prisoners and stores captured.
[2] Four prisoners captured.
[3] 300 prisoners captured.
[4] Fort Gregg captured.

DATE DUE
